INTRODUCTION TO RHETORICAL THEORY

Ars project in 344.

1. select text

2. main claim / key sub claim (consider
   using stock topics)

3. explore how claims supported —
   Toulmin / Perelman

For Jay and Kirsten

INTRODUCTION TO RHETORICAL THEORY

Gerard A. Hauser
The Pennsylvania State University

WAVELAND
PRESS, INC.
Prospect Heights, Illinois

Credits:
p. 77: Adapted from Edward D. Steele and W. Charles Redding, "The American Value System: Premises for Persuasion," *Western Speech,* 26 (Winter 1962), 83–91. pp. 77–78: Advertisement appearing in the *New York Times Magazine,* May 27, 1984, copyright © 1984 by R. J. Reynolds Tobacco Co. p. 86: Adapted from Gresham M. Sykes and David Matza, "Techniques of Neutralization: A Theory of Delinquency," *American Sociological Review,* 22 (1957), 664–670. p. 87: Adapted from Marvin B. Scott and Stanford M. Lyman, "Accounts," *American Sociological Review,* 33 (1968), 46–62. p. 88: Jackson Toby, "Some Variables in Role Conflict Analysis," *Social Forces,* 30 (March 1952), 323–327. p. 103: "Don't Cry for Me Argentina," lyrics by Tim Rice, music by Andrew Lloyd Webber. Copyright © 1976, 1977 by Evita Music Ltd., London, England. Sole selling agent Leeds Music Corporation (MCA), New York, NY. Used by permission. All rights reserved. pp. 162–163: Summarized with permission of the University of South Carolina Press from *Symbolic Inducement and Knowing: A Study in the Foundations of Rhetoric* by Richard B. Gregg. p. 180: Alan Alda, an address to the graduating class, Columbia University College of Physicians and Surgeons, May 1979. pp. 183–185: Adapted from Chaim Perelman and L. Olbrechts-Tyteca, *The New Rhetoric: A Treatise on Argumentation,* trans. John Wilkinson and Purcell Weaver (Notre Dame, Ind.: University of Notre Dame Press, 1969). p. 187: From "My Speech to the Graduates," copyright © 1980 by Woody Allen. Reprinted from *Side Effects,* by Woody Allen, by permission of Random House, Inc.

For information about this book, write or call:

Waveland Press, Inc.
P.O. Box 400
Prospect Heights, Illinois 60070
(708) 634-0081

Contents

Preface

The study of rhetoric is currently enjoying a renaissance. The rhetorical uses of language are widely recognized as a means for achieving social cooperation and fulfilling human potential. Scholars in a variety of fields and university and college courses in several curricula have fastened on the importance of language as an instrument of expression and influence. In addition to courses on spoken and written composition, there has been a rise in the study of rhetorical analysis and criticism and the rhetorical foundations of communication. Yet today's student interested in learning about rhetoric will not find the basic theory readily available in systematic, easy-to-understand exposition.

This book is written to make a rhetorical approach to human communication accessible to readers. It sets forth a humanistic account of what transpires when people communicate for some purpose. It discusses ancient and contemporary thinking about influential uses of language and the value of symbolic inducements for social cooperation. This, then, is a book about fundamental rhetorical precepts and their implications for shaping human realities.

I have attempted to organize the text so as to provide readers with an overview of the subject and to work progressively through the more subtle and demanding aspects of rhetoric. For this reason, the book begins with four chapters on the nature of rhetoric that are intended to introduce broad themes and issues essential for a rhetorical approach to communication.

Chapter 1 defines rhetoric, setting it apart from communication in general, and indicates its essential character as a mode of action. Chapter 2 addresses the common concern that rhetorical communication is deceptive. The issue of trustworthy speech is discussed in terms of the values of narrative, dialectic, and rhetoric, and the importance of rhetoric in making sound social decisions is considered. Chapter 3 takes up the *rhetorical situation,* in which speaking and writing are called into existence. Chapter 4 is devoted to the risk involved in communicating rhetorically, so that decisions to resolve problems through communication have profound implications for self-understanding and for social relations.

The next four chapters are devoted to the content of rhetoric; namely, methods of invention and the three ancient modes of argument: logos, ethos, and pathos. Chapter 5 explains the theory of invention by relating it to creativity as symbolic expression. It describes the theory of topical analysis (topoi) as the method of inventive reasoning peculiar to rhetoric. Chapter 6 discusses good reasons for persuasion (logos). Though emphasis is placed on modes of arguments (enthymemes and examples) and adapting good reasons to issues (stasis), the concept of good reasons is applied to everyday life in terms of account giving in our interpersonal relations. Chapter 7 introduces the persuasive role of character (ethos). Chapter 8 concludes this part of the book with a discussion of the passions; it considers emotion as a pattern of response that is valuable in promoting action because it projects a judgment toward the future.

Whereas the first half of the book emphasizes themes from the ancient roots of rhetoric, the second half deals with contemporary rhetoricians. The emphasis is on symbolic processes and the power to induce social cooperation. Chapters 9 and 10 are devoted to language. Chapter 9 sets forth the contemporary view that humans act by using language. Chapter 10 is concerned with how we experience meaning in and through rhetorical communication.

Chapters 11 and 12 extend language-based concerns into the realm of strategy. Chapter 11 discusses rhetorical form as a strategy, elaborating on how experiences are structured through choice of language. This strategic view of language use is then applied to argument structures in Chapter 12. In a sense, we have come full circle by returning to matters of argument. Yet Chapter 12 does not consider arguments in terms of good reasons, but rather in terms of form. Even the shape we give to our symbolic expressions serves as a means of persuasion.

Chapter 13 concludes by looking at the role of rhetoric in an age of change. It highlights several conditions of the modern era and the relevance of rhetoric to them.

The book's general structure is topical. This structure best affords the flexibility of incorporating insights from past and present. It also allows the book to be used in a course based on rhetorical theory's historical development. Moreover, the topics addressed apply to media other than public speaking, and the text illustrates the relevance of rhetoric to every kind of human communication, in any setting. Combining the inventive stage in developing proofs and the analysis of language as the basis for inducing cooperation, the ideas discussed are interpreted by me for the use and interest of my readers.

I wish to express my gratitude to many students and colleagues who helped and supported me during this project—more than I dare risk to mention by name—foremost among whom are the students in Speech Communication 220 at Penn State. Since 1971 our dialogue has continually refreshed my curiosity about and altered my understanding of rhetorical transactions. My graduate assistants have been invaluable companions in exploring rhetoric. They have used our weekly staff meetings as an opportunity to examine rhetorical theory as it concretely applies to undergraduates.

My work on this project was aided considerably by my friend and former student Susan Apel, who generously provided a retreat to work on the initial draft, and by Susan Whalen, whose criticisms and encouragement helped smooth the bumpy patches and who composed the Instructor's Manual for the book. I also benefited greatly from comments by Jeff D. Bass, Baylor University; James B. Benjamin, Southwest Texas State University; Martha Cooper, Northern Illinois University; Lois J. Einhorn, State University of New York at Binghamton;

David A. Thomas, University of Houston; and Beth M. Waggenspack, Virginia Polytechnical and State University.

I am indebted to Gerald Phillips for his professional friendship, help, and guidance in the development of this book and for his comments on its drafts. I am grateful as well to Louise Waller and Susan Goldfarb—for seeing it through completion. Diane Roan also aided materially with her efficient and patient typing of different versions of the manuscript.

Finally, I wish to thank my wife, Jean Hauser, for her understanding and charmingly Irish sense of persuasion, but mostly for her understanding.

Gerard Hauser

INTRODUCTION TO
RHETORICAL THEORY

The Eventfulness of Rhetoric

It can almost go without saying that communication is vital to our everyday lives. References to communication as the problem or the salvation of our age have been common since the first quarter of this century. It is recognized as essential in business, in the professions, in science and technology, in interpersonal relations, in community affairs, in political processes, in institutions of all sorts. Most of these writings subscribe to the *Cool Hand Luke* school of thought. They survey the foul-ups, mishaps, misunderstandings, discontents, frustrations, and even carnage that mark bungled attempts at social coordination and conclude, "What we have here is failure to communicate." Having said that, the analysis usually quits. One reads between the lines, "When you say 'communication problem,' you've said it all."

The only inference we may draw from thinking like this is that if we communicated better, our "problem" would be solved. If we really got carried away, we might imagine some perfectly conditioned communicator sailing through life with nary a problem. We sometimes do think of diplomats in this way, though their memoirs reveal that even diplomats get the blues.

We never notice when people *don't* have communication problems. When we do have communication problems, we want to know what went wrong and how to fix it. We aren't helped very much if our analysis stops with advice to communicate better. That's obvious and too general. We need to know what elements to examine as sources of our difficulty and the alternatives available as possible remedies. In short, we need to know more about what we mean by *communication* and about its specific function in social coordination. While it *almost* goes without saying that communication is vital to our everyday lives, it

1

won't do to stop there. Until we study in greater detail what happens when A communicates for some purpose with B, we risk ignorance of how and why this statement is true.

COMMUNICATION AND RHETORIC

Let's begin at the beginning and ask what kind of beast we have in hand when we study communication, especially the type of communication called *rhetoric*. People commonly use the term *rhetoric* to refer to propaganda or empty speech. But that is not what we have in mind when we investigate rhetoric as an important type of communication. So as a first step, we need to determine the boundaries of our subject and its concerns. This will improve our chances of avoiding some pitfalls that come with terms used in a variety of ways.

A great many disciplines now study communication. Biology, botany, zoology, and anthropology include studies of the diverse exchanges that occur in nature among plants, animals, and their environments. Mechanical and electrical engineering and computer science examine technologically based exchanges among machines, computers, and their operators. Business administration, sociology, and political science examine how institutions communicate among one another and within their subdivisions. Our concern is with *human* communication. We are interested in what happens when at least one person engages at least one other person in *an act of shared meaning and interpretation* through the use of symbols.

Its most basic form includes face-to-face talk of friends and lovers. Human communication may extend, however, to include such complicated business as political campaigns, collective bargaining, and television broadcasting. As a general area of study, it does not eliminate the unintentional or the nonverbal uses of symbolic forms from its study. It includes among its concerns all forms where there is meaningful engagement through shared symbols. Research into human communication and human communication theory are therefore concerned with (1) all the ways in which people experience communication, (2) the processes that define how people engage one another through symbols, and (3) the relationships necessary to sustain shared meanings and interpretations.

There are many types of human communication. These include forms of communication, where people use language to accomplish some goal, like sales or politics. Some forms deliberately focus on expressing internal states for insights and enjoyment. Literature is communication of this sort. Other forms focus on conveying information accurately for precise record keeping, such as research reports. Still others focus on managing language to influence prudential conduct—for example, public speeches. This last category is the subset of human communication referred to as rhetoric.

Rhetoric is an *instrumental* use of language. This means that one person engages another in an exchange of symbols to accomplish some goal. It is not communication for communication's sake. Rhetoric is communication that attempts to coordinate social action. For this reason, rhetorical communication is explicitly pragmatic. Its goal is to influence human choices on specific matters

time

that require immediate attention. Such communication is designed to achieve desired consequences in the relative short run. Finally, rhetoric is most intensely concerned with managing *verbal* symbols, whether oral or written.

Clearly, other communication forms can have practical consequences, and communication designed for an immediate issue sometimes continues to exert influence beyond its specific context and across time. There are times, as well, when we influence practical choices even though we did not intend to do so or are unaware of having done so. Further, symbolic modes other than the verbal, such as music and dance, can also exert influence. The initial description of rhetorical communication is not intended to deny any of these possibilities. Rather, we begin by drawing the concerns of rhetoric narrowly so that at the outset we can have a clear idea of its essential characteristics. Rhetoric, then, is *the management of symbols in order to coordinate social action.*

COMMUNICATION PROCESSES AND RHETORICAL EVENTS

We commonly think of natural and artificial systems in terms of process. We conceptualize life as passing through continuous stages of development from conception to death. We pattern our thinking about machines in terms of how they process information. We talk of the biological processes of organisms, the energy processes of matter, the geological processes of the planet, the astral processes of the universe, and, of course, the social, economic, developmental, psychological, and political processes of humans. Not surprisingly, in the last 20 years we have come to speak of communication in the same way.[1]

Communication has been conceptualized and investigated in terms of the interaction among elements when persons engage one another with symbols. Process thinking *does not* focus on communication as a product or output— speech or address or essay. It *does* focus on such features as these: the internal sequence of cognitions or thinking experienced by symbol users; the impact of environment, broadly conceived, on these changes; the chain of developments whenever we send and receive messages; the continuous oscillation of feedback that places sender-receiver-meaning in a special and ever-changing relationship; the ongoing environmental modifications that receive direct or indirect impetus through symbol use.

Since the use of process thinking is pervasive among communication scholars, it is important that we clarify its significance to rhetorical theory. Should rhetoric be thought of as a process? What alternatives are there? To answer these two questions, we need to consider what we mean by *process* and what it differs from.

Things, Processes, and Events

Processes can be set apart from things and from events. Things exist; events occur; processes go on.[2] *Things* have sensible qualities. We can describe them in terms of attributes like shape, size, weight, color. These are the palpable characteristics that distinguish one thing from another. Whereas things are individually existing entities, their qualities, like color and shape, are not. Qualities serve as identifying attributes of things. Imagine that as a child you spied a canister in your aunt's home. Now, some years later, you wonder if she still has it. If she asks which one you have in mind, you are prepared to specify. "You know which one; the round red one with the silhouettes of the presidents on its side and the White House painted on its lid." These qualities will identify it from among the others she may own.

Events occur. Each takes place at a specific place and time. Each has a beginning and an end that can be noted in time. An event may consist of a single episode (say, a detonation that reduces a condemned building to rubble) or have a set of episodes (say, the individual games in the World Series). Regardless, events are bounded or bracketed in ways that processes are not. Our interest in events, even those with multiple episodes, is in terms of their uniqueness as occurrences. Events have causes and outcomes. But we attend to these features for their specific relevance to an occurrence we can locate in time. We are not interested in them as a continuous sequence, even though they may be part of such a sequence. Take a rainstorm of some duration. It may occur on the East Coast; begin on Monday, May 28, and last until Thursday, May 31; pour with such intensity that rivers and lakes swell, flooding a number of eastern communities and forcing residents to evacuate. There are episodes of rain, rising water, flooding, and evacuation. When our friends call to ask how we fared in the storm, we know which one they mean— the one that occurred between May 28 and May 31.

Processes are continuous. They consist of sequential developments that involve changes. In general, we characterize these changes as causes and effects. But our accounts of causes and effects focus on the continuity of their sequential development and the changes that follow. For instance, we read G. B. Shaw's views on social Darwinism. We ask our friends what they think of the theory. If they ask what we mean by social Darwinism, they probably won't be helped if we answer, "The views expressed by Shaw in several plays and introductions." Probably they are after something more like, "It's a theory that says humans evolve as social creatures better adapted to survive their social environment through the process of social natural selection." The interest here is focused on the continuous selection process as a series of causes and effects that weed out the weaker, socially speaking.

Although processes may have sensible qualities, these are not distinguishing characteristics; continuity of sequential development is. Sensible qualities become relevant only if there is an unexpected appearance or absence of a quality. That may signal a discontinuity—the end of one sequence and the beginning of another. For example, the appearance of leaves on a birch tree is not remarkable in itself. They appear annually as part of the continuous active and dormant periods that are natural to the tree's life cycle. Should the leaves suddenly turn yellow in June and begin to fall, that is remarkable. It is a discontinuity that possibly marks the end of one process—life—and the beginning of another— death.

Finally, there are times when we talk of processes in terms of events and when we talk of events in terms of processes. In the rainstorm example, we may talk of this event in terms of the sequences of causes and effects within the frame: The rain caused the rivers and lakes to rise; these waters overflowed their banks, causing towns to be flooded; the floodwaters caused the citizens to evacuate. We can speak of ancillary or secondary sequences within the frame: Property damage caused by the flooding was in the billions of dollars; the governors in the affected states responded by declaring states of emergency; because of the flood damage, tens of thousands of insurance claims were filed. Ancillary sequences outside the frame may also be observed: The higher prices for produce later that summer were due to the substantial crop losses incurred during the flood; the flood damaged much lakefront rental property, causing losses of resort income in many areas. In these instances we are inquiring about processes that are related to or within the event of the rainstorm.

Similarly, we may treat the process described by social Darwinism as an event if, for example, we inquire into the initial cause of Shaw's theory. We may investigate the events that led Shaw to formulate his views. When did he first publish his views? What do his diaries and correspondence indicate as a likely date when he formulated his views? What happened at that time? Did he read Darwin? Did he have noteworthy discussions? Did he write to friends on the matter? Was the whole business instigated by someone writing to him? Here we are searching for a specific occurrence at a specific time.

If we can speak of processes as events and events as processes, how do we know which one we're considering at any given moment? It all depends on the questions we ask. If we want to know about the causes of some X that can be identified by its date, we are asking about an event. If we want to know about a sequence of developments and changes with regard to its continuity and not its date, we are asking about a process.[3]

Continuity and Discontinuity

Bearing these distinctions in mind, it should be evident that *communication is not a thing*. It is not a physical object, and to think of it as such would lead to many erroneous opinions. However, *communication can be thought of as a process or as an event*. As we noted earlier, the prevailing view for the past 20 years has been to view communication as a process. Process thinking has been essential for research that reveals what occurs in the generation and sharing of symbols and in the scope of communication as a major source of influence on our psychological and social behaviors.

In short, when we think of and study communication, we raise questions of process; they are about continuous sequences of causes and effects. This is especially true in areas where personal and social evolution are grounded in communication. Communication is seen as a process that chains out in a never-ending set of interlocking relationships that create our personal awareness, our sense of other, our public institutions, our cultural patterns. As noted at the beginning, communication is vital to all aspects of our everyday lives.

However, there is a danger of pushing too far the idea that everything is related to everything else. It forces us to conceptualize our experiences as unified and to search for the connections that demonstrate continuity. We start analyzing our communication experiences in ways best described as self-fulfilling prophesies: We find continuity because we assume experience is unified.

The fact is that experience is frequently marked by discontinuities or breaks in the sequence. There are discontinuities in legal processes when the Supreme Court restricts search-and-seizure rules for gathering admissible evidence; in economic processes when the federal budget suddenly starts running successive $100 billion-plus deficits; in the nature of warfare when "Star Wars" technologies are perfected; in scientific knowledge when theoretical paradigms—our conceptual frameworks—are changed; in national self-image when an unpopular and unsuccessful war is fought; in our personal lives when birth and death, love gained or lost, careers made or ruined, and countless other formative experiences disrupt ongoing sequences of causes and effects and introduce new ones in their place. These gaps or breaks in the normal processes of experience are *eventful.* They have initial causes, they occur, and they have outcomes that are consequential for the future.

The discontinuities of experience are as important as the unities when we study communication, especially rhetorical communication. We not only experience communication as an ongoing process but also experience discontinuities in communication. This is especially true when we have a communication breakdown. For example, when the Supreme Court restricts search-and-seizure rules, it changes the way the police may operate. Law enforcement can break down until the police adjust to the new rules. The person who picks your pocket may be freed because the police made an error.

Similarly, when a person you are talking with casually begins to get intimate, communication may break down until you decide how to respond to this unexpected development. At such moments we become painfully aware of the function our symbols play in coordinating social cooperation. At these moments we consciously strive to manage our symbols for specific goals. In short, the moments of discontinuity in our communication processes bring rhetoric into play.

Discontinuity is important in another way to our understanding of rhetoric. In all the areas of experience not narrowly thought of as primarily communication processes—legal processes, economic processes, military processes, scientific processes, political processes, and so forth—the need for discourse arises most pointedly at times when disruptions or gaps occur in the normal course of affairs. Again we find ourselves consciously managing symbols to coordinate social action; we are practicing rhetoric.

The fact is that discontinuity is the culture in which rhetoric germinates, the soil in which it grows. A world without gaps and breaks and discontinuities would be utterly predictable and utterly manageable and without need for consciously controlling the use of symbols to coordinate social actors. Everyone would know his or her part and play the role as scripted by the regular nature of the world. But the human world is not a regular one. It is potholed and bumpy, riddled with unpredictable acts and sudden needs. In the human world, people have *choices;* they alter the course of affairs by the decisions they make. Rhetoric comes into play precisely because choices are advised and decisions coordinated through language.

The discontinuities that invite rhetorical acts also are events. They occur at specific times and places. They have initial causes, develop episodically, and are eventually brought to a conclusion. For instance, the new fire marshal in Hometown, USA, decided during last Christmas season to enforce the city code prohibiting decorated plants over 3 feet tall in public buildings. Since all the Christmas trees in downtown stores, restaurants, and taverns were taller than the law permitted, the fire marshal threatened to fine and even close all the downtown establishments that had decorated Christmas trees on the premises. This act is a discontinuity because it interrupts the traditions of the community; it exists as an event. It occurs at a specific time and place and invites rhetorical acts from those affected—the proprietors of these establishments and their patrons. The initial cause of the fire marshal's act serves to elicit speeches, interviews with the local press, petitions, and even city council debate, each of which is an episode in the development of the event to its conclusion—the marshal was fired, the ordinance was changed, or the local customs were altered.

The rhetoric addressed to the concerns, needs, issues, and alternatives that are present in these events is itself an event. Rhetorical communication takes place at a specifiable time and place. It occurs. Sometimes it occurs as an episode of a single message; at other times it has multiple episodes of debates, campaigns, or other serial messages. Regardless, rhetorical communication can be bracketed in ways that permit us to specify its initial causes, its episodic development, and its eventual outcomes.

For these reasons, a rhetorical approach to the ways in which people engage one another through their uses of symbols takes on a different cast than is typically found in the more general study of communication. While rhetoric can be investigated in terms of process questions, it is essentially manifested as an event. Accordingly, rhetorical theory conceptualizes communication as eventful. This conceptual orientation has important ramifications for the way rhetoric is studied and understood.

Characteristics of the Eventfulness of Rhetoric

Obviously, events are unique occurrences. It would be very difficult to develop a systematic body of thought about matters of this sort unless some meaningful characteristics could be found that were typical of all rhetorical events. These typical features are found by shifting focus from the unique events themselves to an *event type.* By event type is meant *the general characteristic or set of characteristics that distinguishes one group of events from another* (say, rhetorical events from astronomical ones).

As an event type, rhetoric falls within the general category of *action.* This category implies an agent who does something as a result of choices. It is distinguished from the general category of *motion,* which refers to the natural processes

of the physical world. Within the category of action, there is a subset of five modes of action that typify rhetoric and provide a conceptual framework for rhetorical theory:

- Situated action
- Symbolic action
- Transaction
- Social action
- Strategic action

Situated Action   Communication occurs in the context of a complex of forces. Considered rhetorically, it is a specific manifestation of language use at a specific time. That is why we are usually disappointed by speeches that are too general. They fail to take into account our specific interests and concerns; they could have been delivered to anybody at any time under a wide variety of circumstances. Such remarks fail to recognize that rhetoric is addressed to somebody *specific* and is contingent on the dynamics of the given case. The nonrhetorical elements that are a part of the complex, such as prior attitudes, legal restrictions, the deadline for a decision, or existing policy commitments, serve as opportunities or limitations for the management of symbols. They provide an environment within which communicative engagement of another will take place. If we had only the words but not these situating features, rhetoric would lose much of its intelligibility as communication. It would be *just* words. Consequently, the salient factors of the situation in which rhetoric occurs modify and contextualize rhetorical action.

Take, for example, the public reactions when Baby Fae, an infant with a congenital heart defect, received a heart transplanted from a baboon. Concerns over the risks involved and the ethics of the procedure as well as curiosity about this unusual operation, not to mention the numerous decisions made by the physicians at Loma Linda Hospital, were salient factors of the situation in which rhetoric occurred. These factors modified and contextualized statements by the hospital, the physician who performed the operation, members of the medical community, and various spokespersons representing concerned interest groups. These statements made sense because they were *situated* acts—rhetorical acts explicitly aimed at coordinating social cooperation ("endorse this procedure," "Don't use animal organs in this way," and so forth) in a given situation. Finally, they were acts that might not make sense in any other context (say, the community's views on the operation implanting an artificial heart in an older patient). What is pertinent to cooperation in one situation may apply to no other.

Symbolic Action   Humans are distinctive in their ability to use symbols. In communication, this ability is manifested most commonly in language. Languages are arbitrary systems. They are human inventions; they are not dictated by the laws of nature. Languages are the means we use to ascribe meaning to reality. The action in a rhetorical event is the action of uniting with or dividing from each other based on the way we talk about things. Every utterance conveys an attitude—unavoidably, because the symbols of language are arbitrary and refer to reality selectively and partially. In the Baby Fae case, was the heart transplant a legitimate attempt to save a human life or an ill-advised cruelty to a human and an animal? Here, as in all language use, each utterance suggests one point of view toward the world among many. Every attitude is also an incipient act, an act waiting to be done. Attitudes project what the future might be like by the presentations they make in the present. Thus the attitude that regards the operation as *progress* projects a world where animal organs become viable replacements for defective human ones. Those who regard the operation as *cruelty* project a world where all living organisms are regarded as having equal rights to life. As we contemplate these appeals, we join or divide insofar as our symbolic presentations coincide. Rhetoric cannot avoid involving the action of humans seeking agreement on their interpretations of their experiences.

Transaction   The rhetorical event is one in which dynamic symbolic exchanges occur among the communicating parties. Rhetorical theory does not conceptualize one party as active and the other as passive or merely reactive. Although there are communicators who treat their audiences in these ways, their communication is generally deficient or nonrhetorical in character. Propaganda would be an example. An audience, whether it be one person who is a conversational partner or a nation viewing a televised presidential address, is interactive. Audiences form opinions and beliefs, come to conclusions, and express themselves in a variety of ways, both verbal and nonverbal. Rhetorical action is a product of the interactions that occur within a rhetorical event. It is jointly constructed action involving all the participants acting together.

Social Action   Rhetoric is a form of social action because it involves at least one person attempting to engage at least one other person. The specific mode of engagement is through symbols. Symbols are managed to influence the perceptions others have of their situations and to coordinate their subsequent responses in acts of cooperation. In other words, humans cooperate by means of the social act of constructing mutually compatible interpretations of their situations. The physicians at Loma Linda Hospital had to agree that the transplant of the baboon's heart into Baby Fae was a life-saving measure, that the procedure had a chance of succeeding, and that there was no alternative if the infant was to be saved. They could not have viewed the situation from the baboon's perspective and have approved the operation. This means that while events really occur (the operation did take place), their significance in the ways they are perceived and understood (the operation represents progress) and in the ways they are resolved (the operation is ethically justifiable) are social constructs.

Strategic Action   Action for a particular goal is strategic. It is intentional and takes into account what can and cannot be done to achieve goals under prevailing circumstances. So the attending physicians to Baby Fae do not try to *persuade* opponents of this procedure; instead they try to *inform* them. Before people can agree, they must be led to understand. Accordingly, rhetoric is an action event in this final sense because those communicating within the event set goals and frame their messages to meet these goals. They deliberately choose means suited to their objectives, such as the types of appeals used, presentation of self, and engagement of audience responses. Further, strategy is evident in the forms of argument, language, medium of presentation, and other salient features that may shape audience perceptions.

THE RHETORICAL DOMAIN

We have considered the ways in which rhetorical communication occurs as an event and how its eventfulness influences the way rhetoricians, or people who study rhetoric, conceptualize communication. While processes are involved in rhetorical communication, they are subordinated to understanding those factors that define how rhetorical events transpire. Moreover, we found that rhetorical events were of a certain type, called action events. The specific subtypes of rhetorical action highlight that rhetoric is a particular kind of action event: one in which social action is coordinated through the management of symbols.

Rhetoric, like politics, economics, and law, is a practical art. It is concerned with matters where humans must make choices about conducting their affairs. Typically, these are problematic matters where there is no certain course of action to follow—the problems, both worldly and mundane, of everyday life. For instance, we get a C in a course in which we expected an A. We want to persuade the instructor to modify the grade. We plan something to say and we say it. But no matter how hard we try to say the right thing, we can be mistaken. That is why rhetoric is an *art;* its practice, no matter how intelligently executed, does not *guarantee* a favorable outcome. Still, adhering to its precepts usually improves our chances of success. For this reason, problematic matters impel us to consider the alternatives available to us and to use prudent judgment in making a decision. Usually these decisions are about actions we should take, such as passing a zoning ordinance, finding a defendant innocent or guilty, investing our money or spending it, or even where we should go for a family vacation. At other times the decisions may be more subtle in character and handled by means less obvious than overt deliberation, such as a lad's bolstered confidence from the manner in which his mother speaks to him, a couple's sense of their relationship by the language they choose to narrate shared experiences, a politician's manner of speech and dress to assure constituents that she is still one of them. Regardless of its form, rhetorical theory is concerned with the relationship between our management of symbols—especially language in spoken or written discourse—and the choices that people make in managing their affairs.

The special focus of rhetorical theory is on the use of symbolic forms, especially persuasive appeals, to engender social cooperation. Its subject matter includes the techniques of managing symbols as well as what transpires through their management in a rhetorical transaction. These two interrelated dimensions indicate that rhetoric is both a method and a practice. As a method, it has a set of principles that are observed in its proper usage. A master of the art follows these principles when constructing appeals. These appeals are ones you study in courses on message preparation. They are also of use in the critical analysis of messages because they provide guidance in determining how a message was adapted to a situation, an audience, and a goal and how it managed available resources in ways that were of some consequence in shaping an outcome. As a practice, rhetoric achieves its finished artful form in the actual performance of a communicative transaction. A master of the art is adept at commanding personal resources of thought, strategy, and language to give ideas effective expression. The study of actual performances is frequently the subject matter of courses explicitly devoted to analyzing communication. Such studies are useful for understanding the way communication shaped specific practical choices. They are also useful as a source of data for advancing our knowledge of what happens when A communicates for some purpose with B. So the study of rhetoric includes two concerns: (1) the methods followed in constructing intentional discourse—an intellectual discipline of sorts—and (2) the way symbolic performances influence practical choices—a social practice of sorts.

Practical choices necessarily involve questions of value. Since values are involved, the personal and social stakes in these matters run high. We are confronted with choices because values differ among people, and their relevance is affected as circumstances change. Outcomes are not predetermined because wherever we have choices, we also have freedom. Humans decide how their social world will develop. So we always run the risk that our decisions may be mistaken or faulty or that we may be misled. We risk choosing a world with social realities that are actually harmful. However, there are no better alternatives in social exchanges among people who prize freedom and respect the legitimacy of different points of view.

A study of rhetoric thus takes us to the very core of our humanly made realities. An enlightened rhetoric can lead us to a world of hope and decency and mutual respect. An uninformed or devious rhetoric can lead us to a world of despair and obscenity and intolerance. Understanding the nature of rhetorical communication can enhance the role each of us necessarily plays as social actors who contribute to the shape our world takes.

SUMMARY

We have been discussing rhetoric a way of thinking about human communication as a conscious art. Rhetoric is conscious because it is a way of planning talk or writing and executing the plan in order to accomplish human goals. It is an art because it is uncertain. In the following chapter we will talk about how we think when we engage in rhetoric.

NOTES

1. For example, Carroll C. Arnold and John Waite Bowers, eds., *Handbook of Rhetorical and Communication Theory* (Boston: Allyn & Bacon, 1984), review research across the

areas of specialization in communication. Noteworthy is the prominence of "process" as an anchoring concept.

2. See Henry W. Johnstone, "Rhetoric and Death," in E. E. White, ed., *Rhetoric in Transition: Studies in the Nature and Uses of Rhetoric* (University Park: Pennsylvania State University Press, 1980), pp. 61–70. My discussion borrows heavily from Johnstone's fine presentation.

3. Ibid., p. 62.

chapter 2

Rhetorical Thinking

Our world is noisy with words. It is not just that everybody's talking at us; it's also that we're talking at ourselves. Try to silence your mind. It's nearly impossible. Supposedly it takes years for seminarians at Buddhist monasteries to master their minds to the point where they can have internal quiet.

For all their noise, words are not just sounds or the representation of sounds on a page. They are symbols; they refer. Moreover, they refer in particular ways of tone and emphasis, of connotation and suggestion that give meaning to their references. Words are essential for thinking about what we see and feel and experience. Words also are essential for expressing these thoughts. When joined in a coherent language system, they bring forth the emotional, ethical, and intellectual contents of our minds in ways that interpret experience and share meaning. Because others can share meanings, the symbol system of our language allows us to act through words. We use language to coordinate our social environments to suit our needs. When they don't suit our needs, we use language in attempts to induce cooperation in rearranging them.

Most social disciplines recognize the importance of language to human behavior. It is quite common to find research that focuses specifically on how people use words, how they act with verbal symbols. Take cultural anthropology. Most researchers in this field try to insinuate themselves into the culture they are studying by learning to talk the natives' language. They assume that until you talk like a native, you can't think like a native. You can't know why people do the things they do unless you know what they mean by their acts. Clinical psychology is another case in point. It assumes that until clients verbalize their problems, they will be unable to deal with them. People develop effective strategies for coping with problems through the introspective talk of therapy—the talking cure. Similarly, in sociology, several schools of thought consider the development and quality of social institutions to be a function of verbal interaction. A great deal of what we have come to understand in this century about the human condition of individuals and societies is tied to the ways people use language. Language is the means by which our species constructs its interpretations of reality.

Because language is so powerful in shaping our perceptions and responses to our environment, we have always regarded it with caution. In addition to the many ways that language exerts positive influence, there is always the danger that its dark side will gain the advantage. For example, here is a statement by David C. MacMichael that appeared on page 2E of the *New York Times* on June 17, 1984. Mr. MacMichael, a former Central Intelligence Agency analyst, was challenging the Reagan administration's policy in Central America.

> The whole picture that the Administration has presented of Salvadoran insurgent operations being planned, directed and supplied from Nicaragua is simply not true. There has not been a successful interdiction, or a verified report, of arms moving from Nicaragua to El Salvador since April 1981.
>
> The Administration and the C.I.A. have systematically misrepresented Nicaraguan involvement in the supply of arms to Salvadoran guerrillas to justify efforts to overthrow the Nicaraguan Government.
>
> It's hard to believe, if we know so much about all these shipments, that we haven't been able to capture one plane or boat. It's even hard to believe that in the last two years one of the planes hasn't crashed or one crate of guns hasn't been dropped mistakenly into a tree.

Mr. MacMichael's concerns are shared by most politically aware Americans, their agreement or disagreement with his assessment notwithstanding. Developments in Central America are, if anything, eventful. Throughout the region there are revolutions and counterrevolutions. Each new episode has ramifications for the United States and its neighbors. For this reason, there is a great deal of discourse on the matter.

Collectively, the speeches, testimonies, reports, and position papers assessing Central American politics are more than a hodgepodge of individual statements. Each statement presents regional affairs in a way that invites us to perceive and think about Central America's turmoil in a particular way. Each counterstatement does the same. Collectively, these statements form a dialogue. The dialogue is itself a mode of thinking. The action events that coordinate meaning and interpret reality are symbolic and social. Our thinking is not hidden inside us. As a group, it is present on the surface of the collective statements that interpret these affairs as threatening or nonthreatening, as justifying military support or neutrality. In brief, our thinking as a group is contained in our symbolic acts.

Mr. MacMichael's concern is that we have not been told the truth and therefore have not formed appropriate conclusions. If the facts about El Salvador have been distorted to justify hostilities against the Nicaraguan government, the public has been hoodwinked. Whether or not Mr. MacMichael is correct, his observation highlights concretely the general concern we all share about the credibility and fidelity of verbal presentations, especially ones that influence our practical decisions.

From antiquity we have wrestled with truth and falsehood, certainty and probability, knowledge and opinion, reason and passion as problems of discourse. Each is a concern for the quality of thinking that is present in and invited by speech and writing. Though not unique to rhetoric, this concern for the type of thinking involved in making and experiencing rhetoric helps us clarify the distinction between rhetoric and other modes of communication that people employ to manage their affairs.

We have indicated that rhetoric is eventful because it occurs at a specific time and place for a specific reason. One of its features is that rhetoric makes appeals. It provides reasons to believe, feel, and act in a particular way. Consequently, rhetorical discourse is a mode of thinking, like other verbal forms. In this chapter we want to clarify the type of reasoning that is involved in rhetoric. In the first part of the chapter, we will consider rhetoric as a social practice: What type of thinking is involved in the eventfulness of rhetoric as it is actually presented? In the second part we will consider rhetoric as a method: What type of thinking is involved when we think communicatively in terms of the eventfulness of a matter? In both cases we will develop our discussion historically to help us maintain a clear focus and to provide a concrete context for understanding what is unique about a rhetorical perspective toward communication.

RHETORIC AS A SOCIAL PRACTICE

Narrative

To get a better handle on the relationship between theory and practice in rhetoric, let us retreat from the concerns of the present day to consider the way in which rhetoric arose. It is a story with a great deal to offer, not only in terms of insight into the roots of this subject but also in terms of why rhetoric is so important to the work of the world.

Imagine for a moment that we were back in the time of Homeric Greece. Most of us would live in small villages or in the countryside. We would have been farmers, shepherds, sailors, fishermen, artisans, merchants, traders, and managers of the household. Because we lived in communities, even though they were not thriving metropolises, we would have had a beginning dependency on one another to provide goods and services necessary for survival. More than this, we would have required cooperation in order to survive. In the wild, beasts might rip food from the weak, might have indiscriminate sexual relations, might kill prey. But when humans live in social units, the survival of the unit requires that these behaviors not occur. It requires cooperation to provide food for the community, regulation to provide opportunity for sexual gratification for all, and organization to defend one's village against hostile attack.

Cooperation requires agreement among individuals concerning their common interests and, usually, some expression of these interests in terms of norms. For example, you might find your community norms as students expressed in your school's student handbook; if you belong to an organization, they might be expressed in its charter; if you belong to a religion, they might be expressed in documents recording articles of faith. But if you give this matter a moment's reflection, you will recognize that these formal documents are only part of the picture. For example, your college or university is unique, its personality expressed in dress, special events, local hangouts, student attitudes, preferred curricula, and especially traditions. The traditions of your college or university have an "official" expression, which usually is perpetuated by the administration and faculty on appropriate occasions. But schools also have "unofficial" traditions perpetuated by the student grapevine and passed from each class to its successor. Mostly this aspect of tradition takes the form of stories about groups and events and courses and professors and students whose unusual conduct becomes legendary. It also includes accounts of magnanimous acts, of contributions to campus and community life, and of other acts that bring honor to your group or school. To be a member in good standing in the student community requires that you acquire knowledge of the lore: what memorable prank your fraternity, sorority, or campus group played on a local merchant; what the reputation of your chemistry professor is; what to expect from this course; why your sorority or fraternity sponsors a particular event; and so on. Much of our initiation into the norms of our community—our acculturation, so to speak—occurs through such narrative tales.

So it was with the Homeric Greeks. Most of them were unable to read or write. But they did live in communities, did have interests to protect, did depend on one another for vital goods or services, and did find themselves occasionally at cross-purposes and in need of guidance. The Homeric tales were a principal source of this guidance. Narratives told stories that depicted good and evil in conflict, exemplified a challenge to virtue, or illustrated a common problem. Through the resolution of these issues, narratives established paradigms for acting. If you understood the story, then in addition to being entertained, you also were given guidance on how to live in your community by partaking of its traditions.

The Homeric tradition was an oral tradition. Listeners lacked alphabetic skills of reading and writing. So they learned the tales by hearing them intoned repeatedly and used the tales as guides for resolving disputes, solving problems, and doing the right thing. Of course this gave great power to the bards because, as the people who sang the tales, they became the custodians of community traditions. In effect they were the moral teachers of Hellas.

Though norms come to us most dynamically in narratives, they do not exist in narratives. Norms exist in the culture of a community. Narratives are like bridges between a normative culture and the material realities people confront. But these bridges are of a special type, and they require a word more if we are to appreciate the differences between a normative pattern in thinking and other modes.

A narrative is scripted. It tells a particular tale in which the world is represented in one way rather than another. For a tale to be accepted, its boundaries for action must make sense within the intellectual, emotional, and moral framework of the community to which it is addressed. Tales can be false and still be acceptable if they represent the world in a manner that agrees with the vision of the community. But a tale that violates the framework of meaning in a culture, no matter how true its lesson, will likely be rejected. Consequently, narratives work within a tradition and tend to perpetuate the tradition. They *transmit* norms; they do not challenge them. So while narratives can initiate us into normative patterns of thinking, they lack the impulse to be critical of the norms they transmit. Narratives tend not to be reflexive vis-à-vis the culture they transmit. This lack of critical attitude was the basis for a famous attack against narrative tales. I refer to Plato's indictment of the poets.

Dialectic

In *The Republic,* the Greek philosopher Plato attacked the poets for teaching the youth in ways that did not permit critical examination of premises. The poets sang tales, they transmitted culture, they accepted what was believed in the culture as wise, and they taught the youngsters of the community these beliefs. For this reason, Plato banned the poets from his school, the Academy, and replaced them with dialecticians.

The dialecticians did not reject the importance of norms for communal living. But they did think that if the norms were not based on truth, the quality of communal life would be diminished. For example, suppose that through stories in which the brave and strong always prevail, a tradition perpetuates the norm that "might makes right." A dialectician would want to inspect that norm, not grant it as an assumption. What if the mighty person is a bully or places personal gain above communal well-being or through stupidity fights the wrong foe? Such possibilities should be considered to determine whether this norm is valid.

Plato believed that by questioning the opinions of the day, he could expose those that were false and that if people recognized the fallacies in their thinking, they would be forced to cultivate new habits of thought better suited to lead them to the truth. The new habit he hoped to cultivate was the Socratic method of question and answer, called *dialectic.* Dialectic posed objections to all doubtful propositions until the objections were refuted or the original proposition was replaced by one better able to withstand critical examination.

Though Plato believed that truth existed and that we could have insight into it, he did not believe that these truths themselves could be captured in words nor that every person would succumb to the force of insights afforded by dialectic. Thus his dialogues have Socrates acting as a gadfly by "bugging" all the supposed experts in Athens.

Today we call this critical thinking. We engage in critical thinking whenever we want to test the strength of an idea. We do this by raising counterexamples to show where the idea doesn't apply or by searching for inconsistencies or raising arguments of refutation. Like Socrates, we engage in critical thinking with a partner, called an *interlocutor,* and we seek our partner's agreement on which criticisms hold and which don't. However, sometimes we fail to achieve agreement. The same is true in Plato's dialogues. Not every dialogue ends in agreement, and sometimes Socrates comes out second best in the exchange.

The dialogues that do not quite work out the way Socrates intends are revealing of a special characteristic of analytic thought. Its great power is in critically examining assumptions so that we may avoid errors of reason and belief. But the truths that dialectic attempts to establish are themselves dependent on a set of shared assumptions among conversants. For example, Plato assumes that no person consciously chooses to do evil. Thus whenever Socrates engages in a conversation in which moral conduct is the issue, he always argues that if the person whose behavior is in question knew the truth about virtue, that person would cease to act in evil ways. At the conclusion of such discussions, Socrates and his interlocutor are interested in certifying or refuting the proposition in doubt. But they can reach agreement only if the interlocutor shares Socrates' assumption that humans do not consciously choose to be evil. More than this, two additional conclusions follow.

Dialectic works out the truth of an assertion on the basis of certain assumptions. But there is no guarantee that the world is accurately reflected in those assumptions. We can as easily imagine a world in which humans consciously choose to do evil as we can the world Plato presents. For example, it is difficult to imagine that individuals who knowingly cheat—poker players at cards, merchants their customers, citizens on their tax returns—do not know that their actions lack virtue. Regardless of the assumption, the point remains that dialectically established propositions are true only if we grant that the world agrees with the interlocutors' assumptions. Dialectic gives us an analysis of a *possible* world (i.e., what the world is like *if* we grant certain assumptions) without a guarantee that the *real* world we live in is the same (i.e., whether these assumptions actually apply).

In addition to this, there is no guarantee that dialectic will lead to appropriate action in accord with its truths. Dialectic does not always coordinate truth and action because it addresses or reasons without regard for our motivations. Another way to express this is to observe that while we may be unable to refute or may even be convinced by a person's argument, we still may be unmoved to act. For example, we may be convinced by the arguments of Karl Marx about the vices of capitalism but still not become socialists and, in fact, support and reap the benefits from the capitalist system. Dialectic analysis does not necessarily lead to action because it concerns itself with the rational certainty of a claim, while human action springs not from reason alone but from the intersection of reason with experience in ways that engage feelings and values as well. This realization prompts a third mode of thinking, the rhetorical mode, which attempts to intersect the secured premise with the ways people experience that premise in everyday existence.[1]

Rhetoric

In their narrative tales, the Greeks found normative patterns of thinking. These norms provided the necessary stability for communities to share a common orientation to social life. In the critical thought of dialectical oppositions, the Greeks found analytic patterns of thinking. Analytic thinking sought the stability of truths that transcended the uncertainties of day-to-day living. By contrast, rhetoric was much less attuned to the stability of permanence and much more attuned to the flux of change. As the Greek city-state developed and as the participation of citizens increased—especially in Athens—the need to achieve communal consensus on issues of the moment gained in importance. These were issues for which there were no certain answers, issues that depended on whose testimony you believed or which factors were weighed most heavily or what point of view you adopted—matters of *contingency.*

The experience of the Greeks is not far removed from our own. We know, for example, that some matters are really beyond our control; they are subject to the laws of nature. We cannot make lead float in water by itself or decide by human fiat that radioactive isotopes will no longer be harmful to humans or change the ebb and flow of the tides. These are matters of nature. They are what they are and are to be understood and explained if we wish to use them to our advantage. On the other hand, a great deal of our world is not determined by the laws of nature but by the actions of humans. Our laws, our literature, our economic systems are arbitrary in the sense that they were not foreordained by nature but are products of human design. Thus when we are confronted by social problems, there is not an obviously correct action to take. It all depends on what we want to accomplish and what we value and what we will find intellectually, emotionally, and ethically appealing. In a word, such situations are *indetermi-nate.*

Indeterminate situations are clarified once we gain a point of view or a perspective that aids in resolving ambiguities and in interpreting how disparate parts fit together into a meaningful whole. There may be a raging controversy in a community over the proposed building of a shopping mall. It isn't clear that one should be built. Will there be economic benefits because new shops and new jobs will become available? Will there be economic harm because of the business taken from downtown merchants, forcing some to release employees and others to close? What will be the social effects? Will downtown lose its vitality as a cultural center? Will the mall be a hangout for youth gangs, or will it bring new blood and new ideas into town? And what of the proposed site? Is it geologically safe? Will their be sufficient access roads? What will be its impact on surrounding neighborhoods? No matter how much expert testimony is provided, disagreement is certain, and an obvious answer is not likely to emerge until some individual or group makes the type of argument that places the varied issues in a perspective that touches the lives and interests of the community.

For such a perspective to emerge, there must be intersubjective meaning wherein the various parties involved share a language of ideas, sentiments, values, and commitments.[2] There must be a core of experiences shared with or at least known and available to communicators if they are to invest appeals with the support of reasoning, examples, and analogies that will make them existentially relevant to the audience.

The Greeks understood that people could not make intelligent choices about matters that were unintelligible. Conflicting interpretations or vague circumstances had to be clarified first. A shared bias or prevailing concern could resolve this murkiness of unintelligibility. When citizens saw matters in the same light, cooperation, so essential to their ideal of civilized humanity, was possible. The Greeks developed public deliberation, or the practice of rhetoric as the means to achieving cooperation. Deliberation involved understanding the issues and presenting effective arguments for their resolution. The practice of rhetoric made clear what previously had been vague or poorly understood. The persuasive appeals delivered to an assembly of peers could move them beyond their partisan views and to a consensus.

This program of civic participation contained two sets of assumptions pertinent to the way rhetorical thinking intersects dialectically secured premises with people's experiences. One set concerned the assembly, and the other set related to the trustworthiness of persuasive speech. First, they took public opinion seriously. Every citizen might raise his voice confident that his views would be weighed in the whole process of assembly deliberation. The program of public deliberation did not establish a class of leaders blessed with special authority to make decisions, nor did it single out a special group whose opinions were esteemed as inherently superior in worth.

Second, public deliberation was undertaken with confidence that consensus would emerge and that this consensus would resolve the issue in a way that was both effective and practicably wise. In the democratic assembly, many voices were heard. Each spoke as a partisan. Resolution of differences was not automatic; it resulted only from understanding and thought. Since deliberation made issues clear, it allowed the assembly to reflect more precisely on the meaning of propositions advanced. Citizens who listened to these arguments could more knowingly negotiate a shared opinion leading to group consensus.

Third, and pertaining more directly to the speeches of the assembly, the Greeks assumed that there was no division between content and language. While deliberation involved the oral presentation of ideas, the art of presentation was not purely verbal. It included the ideas presented as inseparable from their verbal expression. In the public assembly, content had no meaning apart from its expression and subsequent clarification and testing through argumentation.

Finally, the Greeks did not regard rhetorical virtuosity as a threat to freedom from authoritarian rule. The impulse to improve presentational skills was considered natural among those who aspired to leadership roles. However, rhetorical virtuosity was not synonymous with formulating issues and setting policies. Whatever authority a citizen mustered with an assembly was through the persuasiveness of his appeals, not his use of force. Leadership through persuasion was contingent on negotiating a common opinion; hence the assembly had the built-in check of the public mind.

These assumptions were significant in their implications for a conception of rhetoric and its relation to trustworthy speech. Because they took public opinion seriously, the Greeks believed in the necessity of weighing all sides to discover clearly and precisely the stronger opinion. Deliberation freed them from the narrowness of partisanship. They did not propose a rhetoric of compromise where both sides trade off to the best advantage prevailing circumstances will allow. Instead they advanced a rhetoric of consensus, an affirmation that the common premise will become evident once issues are clarified and proposals tested through argumentation. They envisioned an active audience that listened to both sides equally and weighted its judgment toward the stronger argument. They thought of rhetorical deliberations as seeking a floating balance point somewhere amid the range of expressed opinions. When it was located, the apparently fragmented parts represented by partisan appeals were resolved into a whole represented by negotiated opinion and majority vote.

Second, the outcome of the vote stood as an accepted social truth. The Sophist Protagoras expressed this idea in the aphorism that "man is the measure of all things." He used the word *man* in the generic sense of the citizens in the polis. Their consensus on public matters was a judgment about which arguments they found trustworthy. It stood in the middle ground between absolute criteria (which Protagoras and the other Sophists rejected) and thoroughly relative standards (which they are usually indicted for advancing). Instead, they endorsed a social truth that evolved from the polis and was not captured exclusively by any single partisan view. The assembly found this truth and judged it as such through its consensus. Same as "dialectically secured premises"?

Third, the persuasive force to move opinion floating between the extremes represented in debate depended on what the audience thought of the arguments. Not only must the orator understand his audience, but his appeals required their approval. Approval was conditioned by life in the polis: adherence to its laws, following its customs, participating in its affairs. The only advocacy with public authority was one within the context of public beliefs. Persuasive force did not stem from empty rhetorical technique but from effective expression of the moral commitments made by the polis. The reinforcing effect of city life was the source of commitment to action. Arguments gained rhetorical effectiveness insofar as they captured and helped the assembly to appreciate better what those commitments were.

Finally, rhetoric was thought to lead the assembly from partisanship, with its biased understanding of what should be done, to common opinion in harmony with the morale of the polis. In partisanship, they were unable to grasp the line of action that best captured their basic commitments. Rhetorical deliberation allowed them to reflect more clearly on the matters at hand, on their relationship to civic morale, and thereby to discover what they wanted all along.

Our brief comparison of narrative, dialectic, and rhetoric shows that each bears on practical conduct. Each also invites us to reason differently. Narratives provide stories that are representative of life. They invite us to imagine and project reality in terms of a story line. The images they provide depend on and draw from communal traditions. Because narratives provide vivid verbal pictures of what life is like, they can have enormous power to shape our perceptions of our existential circumstances and the judgments we frame about them.

In contrast, dialectic tries to abstract generalizations rather than depict particular circumstances. Dialectic provides the clash of conflicting ideas about the basic principles of life. It invites us to conceptualize these principles as realities and material existence as dependent on them. The principles it presents are drawn from opinions that are seriously held. Through question and answer it attempts an abstract inquiry into the principles that are the foundations of such opinions. Because dialectic provides a compelling analysis of the rationality of our opinions, it can have enormous power in convincing us that a proposition is true or false within a given set of assumptions.

Rhetoric is unlike narrative in that it does not present ideas in the form of stories, and it is unlike dialectic in that it does not address abstract generalizations. Rhetoric provides appeals that advise us about belief and conduct in a particular case. It invites us to interpret reality in terms of hypotheses about prudent conduct. Rhetoric's appeals depend on and are drawn from audience opinions. Through symbolic inducements designed to intersect ideas with experiences, it attempts to evoke moral, emotional, and rational commitments to belief and action. Because rhetoric appeals to the whole person in terms of specific cases, it has enormous power to focus thoughts and feelings and to shape practical judgments.

Though rhetoric differs from narrative and dialectic in its form of engaging thought, it is not divorced from their basic concerns. Rhetorical events are themselves occurrences situated within larger contexts of a heritage. Consequently, rhetoric is never free from a tradition of assumed values. Further, rhetorical presentations in an open society may be subjected to the scrutiny of critical audiences or to the counterarguments of those who hold different opinions. Ultimately they require premises and reasoning that can ward off refutation during deliberation. However, rhetoric engages values and reason in its own unique fashion by addressing concrete cases in terms that are pertinent to how people experience the hopes and fears of life.

The need for rhetorical modes of thinking remains as important today as it was in antiquity. We still face problematic situations that require common effort to be resolved. We rely on our management of language to reason jointly to commonly acceptable solutions. We seek adherence and commitment to these solutions by projecting their impacts on our lives as feeling and valuing as well as reasoning creatures.

The type of thinking we have outlined as typical to rhetorical events affords us this final insight into the role rhetorical uses of language play in coordinating social action. The overall patterns of our experiences can take remarkably different paths. Some people lead lives devoted to service, some to greed, some to pleasure, some to survival. What is true for the greatest is true for the least: The fundamental questions remain "What does our experience mean?" and "How may we enhance our lives?" People simply wouldn't be people if they did not ascribe meanings to their experiences, if they did not share these meanings with others, and if these shared meanings did not bring about an interpretation of what life has been and what it might become. The hallmark of human intelligence is our ability to use symbols to create and share meanings. Not only do we share our meanings with one another, but we seek consensus on what our experiences mean, and we elicit and promote mutual cooperation on those of our experiences that involve common interests. This is also the impulse for rhetoric.

RHETORIC AS A METHOD

In the fourth century B.C., Aristotle made an observation similar to the one we have been discussing when he noted that everyone speaks in ways that seek to change the minds and hearts of others. Some do it well, some poorly, but all humans speak with this purpose in mind. For him, the fact that some consistently spoke well meant that by observing their behavior we could abstract the principles they followed when persuading. These principles describe rhetorical procedures that constitute a framework for thinking communicatively in terms of a matter's eventfulness. We will outline this framework as our final consideration in this chapter.

Today *rhetoric* is most generally understood as *the management of symbols in order to coordinate social action.* *Management* refers to the *purposive selection and arrangement* of symbols. Rhetoric is discourse by design. *Symbols* refer to any meaningful system of signs that is referential. Music, dance, painting, mathematical notation, cinema, to cite but five, comprise such systems. They can influence our perceptions, attitudes, beliefs, and even behaviors. Thus, in the contemporary sense of the term, they may be regarded as rhetorical at some level and, indeed, are being examined as such by contemporary rhetoricians. Among human symbol systems, language is the most basic. It is also the most pervasive and most complex of these systems and the one most clearly and explicitly used to influence others. *To coordinate social action* implies *influence* of some sort. At the very least it would include the inducement of an attitude, but it can extend to moving others to cooperative physical actions. Thus it includes the wide spectrum of concerns from feelings such as elation or depression reflected in our words, tones, or gestures; through beliefs reflected in our opinions, arguments, and isms; to our physical activities directed toward the management of our social relations (such as soliciting a friend's help or campaigning for a political candidate) and our physical environment (such as riding a bike to conserve energy or changing our diet to promote health). Mostly, we understand the management of social action to be concerned with the choices people make, especially choices about prudential conduct. In sum, rhetoric's basic concern is with how party A (a rhetor) speaks or writes to party B (an audience) to affect that person's choices.

Clearly this concern is related to a number of disciplines. Rhetoric and psychology overlap insofar as psychology studies how the mind processes symbols and how this processing influences behavior. Rhetoric and political science overlap insofar as political science studies how interests are formed and represented to the state. Rhetoric and ethics overlap insofar as ethics studies the consequences of human choices. But rhetoric is not the same as, nor can it be reduced to, these studies. It is concerned exclusively with the dynamics that occur within the boundaries of a message and the options available to performers (rhetors) for managing these dynamics in desired ways. It is, as I have already suggested, a way of thinking.

As a *way of thinking,* rhetoric differs form other disciplines in that it tends to be methodical rather than substantive. This does not mean that rhetoric lacks content but that its content is more concerned with the *hows* of what we're talking about than the *whats* of what we're talking about. This distinction was expressed most clearly when Aristotle observed in the opening sentence of the *Rhetoric* that "rhetoric is the counterpart of dialectic."

The Greek term translated as "counterpart" is *antistrophe*. This is a term that refers to an opposing but complementary movement. For example, in the Greek tragedies, the chorus acts as a moral conscience. As the plot unfolds and the protagonist struggles with a dilemma, the chorus will occasionally come on stage to deliver lines of comment and caution. These thoughts are presented in a back-and-forth manner and are accompanied by the chorus's back-and-forth movement across the stage. Thus a *strophe* is presented—one set of reflections as the actors move across the stage. Then an *antistrophe* is presented—another dimension of reflections, different from but complementary to the first, as the actors reverse direction and cross again to the opposite side of the stage. What Aristotle suggests at the very outset of his work is that rhetoric is a complement to, although different from, dialectic. It shares many of the same traits, although in important ways it is unique. These complementary features help us to understand the methodological side of rhetoric.

First, Aristotle thought of dialectic as a mode of arguing; so is rhetoric. It was a mode of arguing that would occur when experts discussed their subjects in technical fashion. For example, when two physicists, two lawyers, or two photographers engage in conversation about a doubtful proposition unique to their field, they use a vocabulary, invoke a theory, and resort to abstractions that are specialized. Laypeople who are ignorant of the field generally find themselves lost by the discussion. Rhetoric is a mode of arguing suited to laypeople. It presents contentions within the boundaries of lay opinion and experience.

Second, both dialectic and rhetoric are universal methods. They apply to all subjects but have no subject matter that is properly their own. Whenever experts make arguments among themselves, regardless of field, dialectic is the method they use for framing their arguments. Similarly, whenever common people have interests in a matter, they are led to a point where they can render sound judgment by arguments suited to the subject and to them. As arguments become more technical, they become dialectical arguments proper to a given field; as they become less technical and more focused on the needs for action, they enter the realm of rhetoric.

Third, when experts speak among themselves, the objective of their inquiry is criticism. When an orator presents an appeal, the objective is persuasion. Dialectic examines opinions and the necessary conclusions that must follow if they are examined systematically. Its issue is always whether this opinion is sound. Rhetoric, on the other hand, examines problematic situations in terms of prevailing opinions. It tries to engage some opinions and refute others in order to urge a particular, partisan judgment.

Fourth, both are in the realm of the *contingent*. This is the realm of circumstance where certainty is unavailable. Rhetoric and dialectic begin with opinions. The dialectician asks the opinion of an interlocutor and then tests it out through critical deliberation of question and answer. The rhetorician begins with audience-held opinions and uses these as a basis for constructing arguments. Because both begin with opinion, they are in the realm of thinking, where conflict is possible because we lack absolute certainty about the matters at hand. There is a stronger and weaker, a better and worse, but not necessarily a true or false solution to the problem. Consequently, the results of dialectic and of rhetoric are probable solutions. In dialectic, these probabilities may reach the point of virtual certainty. This would occur when we failed to find counterarguments to refute an opinion. In rhetoric, the likelihoods are less certain, always subject to the quality of the audience judging the remarks and the uncertainties of situations that are subject to last-minute changes—as happens, for example, in politics or business all the time.

By contrasting rhetoric and dialectic, Aristotle brought out quite a bit about the methodical character of communicative thinking. We learn that rhetoric is a method for framing popular arguments intended to be persuasive. It is a method that can be used on any subject; it has no subject matter of its own. It begins with the opinions of the audience and builds arguments from them to support a partisan proposition. Because it is a method that relies on opinions, it gives us conclusions that are likelihoods, not certainties. This is not a weakness of the method of thinking communicatively, however. Rather it has to do with the contingent and uncertain character of rhetorical events.

So that the abstract character of this theory does not get the upper hand, let us illustrate these points in terms of an example. This will help us to make concrete the distinctions we have been drawing. Let us consider how the current debate on nuclear arms might involve both dialectic and rhetoric.

The public discussion on nuclear armaments comes to us from several quarters: cinema, television, journalists, novelists, elected officials, scientists, organized movements, even clerics. The issues are ones of policy, but the choices made in the policy arena are influenced by other issues: scientific, political, military, moral. These antecedent issues, unilaterally or in tandem, have a great deal to do with whether we support placing nuclear weapons in Europe, going forward with a MIRV system, investing tax dollars in a laser defense, and so forth.

Perhaps the first question that we face in these controversies is about what will happen if a nuclear war is fought. Clearly, only a small minority of people would be for abandoning all modes of national defense. To be able to defend ourselves from attack is not the issue. Rather it is whether a nuclear defense is one we should maintain and develop. To deal with that issue, we must first know what will happen when a nuclear device is detonated. This is a technical question and requires a technical answer. But it is also a question with profound impact on all citizens. They have an interest in this matter. Moreover, because ours is a representative democracy, our representatives will make the ultimate decision—one for which they are responsible to their constituents.

To get the technical question addressed, we would go to those who are experts in nuclear physics and ask what will occur if a nuclear bomb is detonated. Suppose that our roomful of experts began a discussion that dealt with nuclear theory. Someone offered an opinion about the nature of a nuclear reaction.

Someone else disagreed with the theory. Soon the physicists fell to debating the matter in the technical terminology of nuclear theory. While most of what they said would probably escape us, we could nonetheless recognize that in debating these ideas, the physicists were not being peevish or ornery. They were being critical in their thinking. This is the concern of dialectic. Dialectic is a mode of arguing that occurs when experts deal with technical but doubtful propositions in the area of their technical competence. The aim of these arguments is to find the truth value of the opinions professed.

After listening to this debate for a while, we interrupt and ask the scientists if they could please speak in ways we might understand on the issues we wished to resolve. So our first question is, What happens when a nuclear bomb is detonated? The theory of atomic reaction is relevant here but not as a theoretical subject, only as a subject that helps us better to understand what will happen. Our scientists might now speak of the chain reaction of a nuclear explosion, of the various stages in the reaction, of the aftermath of the reaction. They might make all of this more concrete by providing an example. "Suppose we exploded a 20-kiloton device at 10 feet aboveground over the intersection of Main and Allen in Buffalo, New York. Here's the destruction that would occur. . . ." This is the talk of laypeople. It makes concrete the anticipated outcomes of an act. As we hear the account unfold, we find ourselves better able to appreciate why a nuclear weapon is unlike any other weapon devised by man and why we have an intrinsic interest in the discussion of nuclear weapons. In other words, rhetoric is the mode of arguing used when laypeople must be addressed about issues that affect their lives and require them to make an intelligent judgment.

A second feature of rhetoric and dialectic also emerges from what we have said thus far. The science of physics has within its subject matter the study of atoms, including what happens when the energy in their nuclei are released. This is *not* the subject matter of dialectic or of rhetoric. Remember, dialectic and rhetoric have no subject matter of their own. They are *universal methods* that cut across substantive fields and can be used by any of them. Thus to know physics is not necessarily to know how to make an effective critical argument. Dialectic is the method one must investigate to learn that. Nor does the expert on physics necessarily know how to make a persuasive argument. Rhetoric is the method to be mastered for this.

Now let us suppose that we next call in a group of scientists and engineers skilled in ballistics and radar. We want to know about ICBMs: how long it takes to get from point A to point B, how much time is required to intercept a missile, what the probabilities are of hitting or missing such missiles with our antiballistic missiles, whether the trajectory of an alien missile can be detected in time for us to respond. Here again, the scientists and engineers may have conflicting views. Some believe that missiles launched from the USSR can be detected in time to respond; others disagree, basing their arguments on certain atmospheric varia-bles. Soon this becomes the focus of the debate, and the experts exhibit the same pattern observed earlier, talking in the technical vocabulary of their fields and attempting to test out colleagues' opinions.

Again we intercede and ask them to put their opinions and arguments into language we might understand. One scientist says that there will be no problem detecting the missiles fired from the Soviet Union because they must be fired at such and such a trajectory and will travel at a determinable speed and therefore the arc of the missile's path can be detected. Moreover, we can detect its path in time for us to launch a defense missile to intercept and destroy the Soviet weapon. A second scientist says that while this is true, there are some problems. One has to do with the fact that the Soviet missiles have multiple warheads (are MIRVed); though one missile goes up, several come down. That complicates the detection and interception problem. Second, should the Soviets explode a missile above American airspace, it will have an effect on the atmosphere that neutralizes transitors and microchips. In other words, our entire electronic system will be shut down.

As we reflect on these deliberations, some additional similarities between dialectic and rhetoric emerge. Both begin with opinions: the expert opinion on radar and the atmosphere, the lay opinion that we must provide for defense. In both cases, arguments advance by including opinions as parts of the arguments: The scientists call on the opinions of other scientists and their theories to build their appeals; when they talk to us, they draw not only on experts' opinions but also on those we hold (e.g., we wish to preserve the species, money spent in protecting us from attack is money well spent, a solution that is technically impossible is no solution). In short, both methods deal with questions about which opinion is used in finding an answer.

Finally, we notice that questions of opinion are not ones that permit true-or-false answers. They are questions that are contingent in nature. They depend on what we want to accomplish, on whether or not elements beyond human control intervene, on how accurate our opinions are, and on the emotional and ethical commitments of people whose cooperation we seek. In such matters, judgments have to be made, frequently by people who lack specialized knowledge, on the basis of what seems to be the likely outcome of one decision over the other.

These methodological considerations were summarized by Aristotle when he defined rhetoric as "the art of discovering the available means of persuasion in the given case." That definition best captures the sense in which rhetoric serves as a method for thinking about communication. Let's analyze each part of the definition, starting with the word *art*. The Greek term is *technē*. It means a body of principles that describe a practice. Whatever is a *technē* or an art can be studied and learned and practiced correctly because its constitutive elements can be observed and set down. Specifically, it is an art of *discovering*. A synonym would be *observing* or *finding*. It is an art concerned with systematically searching for the *available means of persuasion.* A rhetor seeks what can be communicated in ways that will be consequential. These are not all means of expression, only those available for the issue at hand and for the audience addressed. Moreover, it is not everything available to be said that is sought, but among the possible "sayables" only those that are persuasive *in the given case.* That is to say that rhetoric is an art of the moment. It is concerned always with the novel, with the specific audience, with the special concerns most appropriate at this time for these people on this matter. It is not a method that seeks to address the ages but one that seeks to address people who must make choices that affect their lives on problems that bear on their present interests.

In addition to these features, two others are implied by Aristotle's definition. First, he did not define rhetoric as an art of persuasion but as the art of discovering what is available to persuade. By defining it as he did, he recognized that practitioners of the art may not be successful but that failure may not be their fault or the fault of the art. He recognized that some situations may not permit success for the rhetor any more than a physician doing all that is medically possible can save every patient's life. Second, because it is an art of discovering, rhetoric is seen as a purposive art. It is goal-oriented thinking about what will work, and it requires skill not only at finding materials but also at selecting from among the materials those that are most likely to succeed.

SUMMARY

We began this chapter by discussing language as inherently persuasive. It invites us to perceive and respond to the world in a particular way. Individually, our language actions on any given issue are eventful, each occurring at a specific time and each being of interest as an episode or part of an episode that contributes to the event's final resolution. Because there is dynamic interaction among these discursive acts, they constitute a dialogue. They are a mode of thinking that is visible and, one hopes, legible in the symbolic acts themselves. In this chapter we have tried to clarify the nature of rhetorical thinking by considering rhetoric as a social practice and as a method.

We saw that as a social practice, rhetorical thinking deals with what is expressed or expressible. Thoughts and feelings that are inexpressible are not dealt with in rhetorical thinking. Its domain is the surface of discourse. Rhetorical thinking is joint thinking that arrives at its conclusions through transactions between the audience and the communicator. It is particularized thinking that is marked by immediacy. It addresses situations that are real or purported to be real. It is, finally, holistic and necessarily partisan because it brings rationally defensible propositions into contact with existence and human experience. It necessarily involves interests, values, beliefs, and feelings, as well as more objective and dispassionate reasonings in a whole, complex pattern of response.

We saw that as a method, rhetorical thinking is concerned with finding things to say that will advance our purpose with an audience. It is a method that cuts across subjects; it is universally available in any area where people are addressed for purposes of coordinating social action. It is thinking that is based on shared opinions and aims to persuade by building arguments that show the likelihood of a conclusion. It is not inferior to science or technical reasoning, however, because it deals with subjects of prudent conduct where the best we can do is frame a likely solution. The method of rhetorical thinking is about how best to communicate to an audience for a given objective. It is essential for the management of our social affairs.

NOTES

1. Richard Weaver, *The Ethics of Rhetoric* (Chicago: Henry Regnery, 1953), p. 28.
2. Charles Taylor, "Interpretation and the Sciences of Man," in Paul Rabinow and William M. Sullivan, eds., *Interpretive Social Science: A Reader* (Berkeley: University of California Press, 1979), pp. 25–71. See especially pp. 43–53.

chapter 3

Rhetorical Opportunities

Humans communicate for a variety of reasons. They celebrate a joyous occasion, like the birth of a child or the marriage of friends, by going to a church or synagogue and joining in a religious ritual. They recognize friends on the street by greeting them with a nod and a stock phrase. They enjoy each other's company by sharing social moments, such as a meal, and fill their time together with conversation. They support a legislative proposal by expressing their views through a letter to the editor.

Is each of these acts rhetorical? We might say that in the broadest sense of the term each is, since each induces attitudes through the use of symbols. But we have drawn our net closer than that, indicating that rhetoric's primary concern is to influence. Influence pertains to choice, and choice arises as a conscious act only in situations that are thought to be problematic in some way.

In the case of a marriage, for example, the officiating cleric is not persuading the couple to exchange vows, nor the couple each other. The invited guests witness the ceremony, but their witness is extrinsic to the religious and civil union being forged. The couple would be equally as married had they exchanged vows in a private ceremony with only the cleric and the required number of witnesses. Yet it is undeniably true that by the words that are spoken and the presence of invited guests, the assembly is engaging in a complex symbolic act. Depending on their relationship to the couple, they are participating at some level in a ritual of sharing: the joining of two families, the reaffirmation of a set of religious beliefs expressed by the ceremony itself, or the most general union of expressing best wishes to the newlyweds by virtue of attendance. Insofar as the rubric of the ceremony reminds us of this, the ceremony may be a rhetorical act. We may, for example, be induced to cease our gossip about the bride's family, to be more generous in the future in providing the couple emotional support, or to adopt a more reverent attitude toward the institution of marriage. Nor would any of us be surprised if these exact themes were developed in the homily, as the cleric urged the guests to use the occasion as an opportunity for commitment and reaffirmation.

Whenever humans use language, it is very difficult to rule rhetoric out. At some level we can always find the impulses to influence. Yet if the concept is spread so far that everything becomes rhetorical, we end up with an empty concept. One way in which this problem has been addressed is by looking at rhetoric in functional terms. This is not the only approach to rhetoric, but it is one of the fundamental approaches we can take toward the subject. The most influential statements of this view have come from Lloyd Bitzer in essays dealing with the concept of a *rhetorical situation*.[1] In this chapter we will consider a functional orientation to rhetoric by explaining the situational perspective.

DEFINING THE SITUATION

Have you ever heard someone summarize a set of circumstances by exclaiming, "That was a situation!"? By that exclamation the person attempts to set off a unique experience from the mundane and the ordinary. "This was unusual," the remark seems to imply. "There were novelties involved, choices to be made; I wasn't sure how it would turn out."

We can find situations of all types that would merit such a characterization: Confronted in the wild by a crazed moose, how will we escape injury? Just before a social gathering we discover that our supply of refreshments is low and the stores are closed; how will we avoid embarrassment? Out for a sail, the weather suddenly turns and our motor fails; how will we get to port? Granted an interview with a candidate for office, the interview threatens to go beyond our deadline; how will we end it diplomatically? The list of such situations, real and imagined, could go on and on, each of us supplying our own examples.

The significance of these cases depends on how we define them. Indeed, the very fact that we regard each as a situation, in the sense of something that is out of the ordinary, is a product of the meaning we attach to the event.

Clearly, situations occur in space and time. But these are rarely the coordinates that make a set of circumstances the object of conscious reflection. Knowing that there was a lengthy meeting on a specific date and time in the Oval Office of the White House between Richard Nixon and his chief counsel John Dean is significant only within a complex of circumstances that we call "Watergate" and what these spatiotemporal dimensions tell us of the former president's role in the obstruction of justice. Conceivably, the meeting could have occurred in Philadelphia, and it could have occurred a week earlier or later, without altering the Nixon-Dean transaction as a significant situation. But it is not conceivable that we could alter the *meaning* of Watergate, from the crime of breaking and entering to a legitimate political prank, without changing the definition we would ascribe to the Nixon-Dean conversation.

Although situations have a spatiotemporal definition, their relevance to symbol-using animals requires that *physical space* and *chronological time* be translated into *social space* and *psychological time.* This transformation is marked by two characteristics: emergence and relativity.[2] *Emergence* refers to the meaning of a referent across time. Because meanings develop in relationship to their contexts, they are dynamic and unfold as surrounding events alter. *Relativity* refers to the relationship of the subjective perspective humans bring to bear. As an individual's orientation changes, due to a change in perspective or a shift in role, one's definition of the situation alters.

For example, suppose that upon graduation you secure a job at a modest salary and without much responsibility. You might find yourself stressing positive, mostly future-oriented aspects of your position: It's providing good experience; this is a growing firm; there are opportunities for advancement; I'll be making valuable contacts; and so on. A year later, if your salary increases and your responsibilities grow, the positive aspects of your position are easier to accentuate. If this continues throughout your career, the meaning of your first job will emerge as a very shrewd move on your part. On the other hand, if nothing improves after a year, you will likely be unhappy, and unless your employer is providing some aspect of job satisfaction beyond remuneration and responsibility, you will likely look for another job. If you are unsuccessful and your position doesn't improve, a negative meaning will emerge. You are likely to think that accepting this job was a dreadful mistake. The meaning of the job at time 1 is not the same as at time 2. Its meaning emerges as factors change or remain the same. Its meaning is dynamic.

Moreover, meanings are relative to the perspective and role of the perceiver. Our perspective will be influenced by such factors as level of involvement, ability to create emotional distance, strength of commitments, ethical beliefs, and level of information and knowledge. Our role will influence what we see as the imperatives and consequences relative to our role demands, what we see as our relevant modes of involvement, what we expect of others, and the like. For example, a chief surgeon may expect that routine postoperative procedures will be carried out by a resident. The resident may think that because the surgery was serious, the surgeon should be consulted before a procedure is initiated. Because their roles are different, they are ascribing different meanings to the same objective elements in the situation. The surgeon may be miffed because he has been interrupted to tend to a routine diagnosis that calls for a standard procedure. The resident may be confused because he thought he should report to his superior before acting.

In defining any situation, then, we are confronted with the reality of dynamics and flux. Meanings emerge and are relative. It is important not to lose sight of this, for humans act on the basis of how they define situations. It is these situational definitions that at the most primitive levels evoke patterns of approach and avoidance, responses of territoriality and self-preservation, not to mention the more sophisticated responses of a symbolic order. Were we unable to define a situation, we would be unable to act because it would lack meaning for us.

RHETORICAL SITUATIONS

So far we have been emphasizing the idea that situations are meaningful combinations of events, objects, and people and that they call for action. Without action, the unique dynamics of the interacting factors would continue unchecked, leading to results that in some way are undesirable to those involved. The action we choose depends on our definition of the situation. Some situations are defined in ways that call for physical effort as the appropriate action; others are defined in ways that call for symbolic action to address, partially or completely, the concern at hand.

For example, we wish to grow vegetables in our backyard. Before we can harvest a crop, we must till the soil, plant the seeds, water the garden, thin the seedlings, mulch the garden, pick the weeds, fertilize the plants, and so forth. Our efforts are dictated by nature: If there is sufficient rain, we do not have to water the garden; if not, we do. If we don't hoe and mulch the garden, weeds will grow and compete with the plants for nutrients from the soil. If we let the weeds grow unchecked, they will eventually overtake the garden, diminishing the yield from some plants, destroying others. To prevent this from happening, active intervention is required. But our intervention is typically physical effort, not symbolic. Talking about the ravages of drought or strangulation by weeds will not nurture the plants; regular watering and weeding will. Such problems present us with situations that call for action of a typically nonrhetorical sort if their defining imperfections are to be remedied.

On the other hand, some problems are of the sort that discourse can partially or completely resolve. These are *rhetorical* situations. Rhetorical situations are ones that call for functional uses of discourse to adjust people, objects, events, relations, and thoughts. Rhetorical situations are ones in which either we must change people directly by persuading them to think, feel, believe, understand, or act in a particular manner, or we must change the physical environment indirectly through the intervention of human cooperation. Rhetorical situations, then, are ones uniquely suited to the instrumental uses of language.

In his pioneer essay on this topic, Lloyd Bitzer defined a rhetorical situation as

> a complex of persons, events, objects, and relations presenting an actual or potential exigence which can be completely or partially removed if discourse, introduced into the situation, can so constrain human decision or action as to bring about the significant modification of the exigence.[3]

At first reading, this may seem like a complicated definition, though it is easily understood on a moment's reflection. Let us consider the constituents of this definition and what they imply for our understanding of rhetoric.

First, *rhetorical* situations are "complexes," or situations that contain multiple features. These features include the persons involved, the events that involve them, the object of their conscious attention within the context of the salient events, and the relations among the persons, events, and objects. For example, imagine that we are observing women in a diving competition. The women dive from a platform, perform various "tricks" between takeoff and entry, and receive scores from judges who evaluate how well they did. This might be labeled a "competitive situation." We know that each dive has required months of practice, that conditions like the diver's athletic skill, power to concentrate, and control of her body in executing the mechanics of the trick all come into play. But these are also influenced by the environment in which the dive is performed: whether it is windy or chilly, whether the audience is supportive or nonsupportive or even rude and distracting, whether the other divers try to intimidate her and whether this serves to deflate her self-confidence, and the attitudes and preferences of the judges toward certain tricks and certain competitors. All of these factors interact and can serve to influence the choice of which dives to perform and the diver's actual execution. A "complex," or group of interrelated factors, is involved in her dive. Numerous factors interact in every rhetorical situation.

Bitzer goes on to state that this complex of factors presents "an actual or potential exigence." By this he means that these interacting features give rise to a problem of some sort—either in an actual way, where the problem is immediate and requires our attention, or in a potential way, where we face a likely difficulty if we do not act now. Significantly, these problems, or "exigences," are unique in that they can be modified to some extent—"completely or partially"—through "discourse." Rhetorical situations, in other words, are situations that present problems that can be resolved meaningfully through the uses of speech and writing. Problems that require changes of belief or attitude or require cooperation are typically ones in which skill in the management of language can make a difference.

Bitzer's definition suggests that the outcome of skillful management of language is to "constrain human decision or action"—to make human agents aware of the opportunities and limitations present in a situation, so that audiences respond in ways that alter the original problem in some significant way. In brief, rhetorical situations are ones which present problems *that can be resolved completely or partially through the effective use of language.*

We can say more than this, however. Our previous discussion established that the way we define a situation is significant because this provides our parameters for appropriate behavior. When we define a situation as rhetorical, we are not merely saying that it is a situation in which discourse *can* be of some consequence; we are saying also that it calls for a *deliberate* communicative response. As our definition of a situation emerges as rhetorical—one presenting a problem that calls for discourse—we frame expectations of appropriate responses for the people who have an interest in the problem. We *expect* certain individuals, by virtue of their role, to address the problem. We *expect* other individuals, by virtue of their role, to be addressed. We *expect* the ensuing discourse to be functionally relevant to the problem. We *anticipate* that functionally relevant discourse from appropriate sources addressed to appropriate audiences will so engage thoughts and feelings as to alter the environment.

Moreover we *anticipate* that the environment will be altered partially or completely to resolve the impelling urgency that called for communication. Conversely, we *anticipate* that in the absence of such discourse, the pressing demands of the situation will become critical, lead to a crisis of some sort, and eventually deteriorate beyond the point of human repair. In short, the situation will not resolve itself, nor can it be satisfactorily resolved through wholly nonsymbolic means (as can, say, the gardener's drought problem by watering the vegetable patch). Once we define a situation as rhetorical, the emergent meaning of the situation relative to the actors involved calls for discourse as the appropriate mode of human action. Unless a person could claim ignorance of the situation or silence as a strategic choice, failure to respond to a rhetorical situation when in a position to do so would be foolish at best, perhaps even irresponsible.

Finally, by maintaining that rhetoric can "bring about the significant modification of the exigence," we adopt an explicitly functional view of rhetoric. While this is not the only view one may take, it has utility for analyzing the pragmatic uses of communication. Prior to Bitzer's essay, rhetors were advised to analyze their audience, the occasion, and the possibilities of subject matter. Then, on the basis of these analyses, they were instructed to select the options best suited to their goals. This view was most memorably expressed by Donald C. Bryant, who spoke of the function of rhetoric as "adjusting ideas to people and . . . people to ideas."[4] Bitzer's conception of a rhetorical situation does not contradict this view, but it captures better the complex interaction of factors that bring rhetoric into being and shape its development and outcomes. In a later essay, in which he enlarged upon his conception, Bitzer summarized the functional nature of a situational perspective toward rhetoric in these words:

> The situational view of rhetoric takes as its starting point the observable fact that human beings interact functionally with their environment. This is not an inevitable starting point. Typically, stylistic rhetorics commence with the relation between the nature and resources of language on the one hand and the intentions or meanings of the speaker on the other. The scientific rhetorics of the eighteenth century commenced with the relation between natural psychological processes and communicative intentions and activities. These and similar approaches either dismiss the relations of persons and their messages to environment, or regard this relation as secondary. The situational view, however, seeks to discover the fundamental conditions of rhetoric—of pragmatic communication—in the interaction of man with environment. This inquiry therefore looks toward a starting point similar to that examined by Kenneth Burke, who observed that experience presents divisions that can be bridged through identification and remarked, "Out of the division and the community arises the 'universal' rhetorical situation."[5]

This brings us to the constituent elements that provide the basic conditions for rhetoric.

CONSTITUENT ELEMENTS OF RHETORICAL SITUATIONS

Every rhetorical situation is composed of three elements: an *exigence,* an *audience,* and *constraints.* Analysis of these features helps to determine the defini-

tion of a given rhetorical situation and further serves to indicate what is required
to make a fitting response.

Exigence

Bitzer defines an *exigence* as "an imperfection marked by urgency." Any undesirable element in a situation can satisfy the demands of this definition. Sometimes
an exigence may be as common as the mundane interactions we conduct to
negotiate our way through everyday life: We must say cordial and supportive
words to roommates, coworkers, friends; we make pleas for cooperation in performing team activities; we request favors; we offer arguments for particular ways
of solving social problems; and so forth. At other times it may take on importance
of greater magnitude: Senators deliberate on legislative matters; lawyers plead
legal cases; trustees make arguments establishing policies for complex organizations in both the private and public sectors. Whenever there is a defect that can
be redressed in meaningful ways through talk, the exigence becomes the focus of
rhetoric.

In any rhetorical situation, there can be a number of exigences present,
making analysis sometimes complex and the framing of a fitting response a matter
of judgment. For example, as the United States Congress deliberates on military
aid to nations in Latin America, there are a number of exigences to be addressed:
Rebel troops are attempting to overthrow an existing government; there is evidence that these troops are being aided by regimes in the region hostile to the
United States; there is reason to believe that without our assistance, governments
friendly to the United States will be defeated, thus it is in our interest to aid these
regimes; there is evidence of human rights abuses by regimes we support, which
raises questions about the morality of aiding governments intolerant of people
who do not do their bidding; there is evidence of serious economic and social
problems in these nations, raising concerns about the type of aid best suited to
help the people of this region.

Each of these conditions exists in observable ways; they are not the products of imagination. Each is a condition that may be regarded as an imperfection marked by urgency and could, of itself, be a sufficient call to bring rhetoric
into existence. Yet in this situation there is one exigence that will eventually
serve as the controlling exigence in the minds of the participants, giving definition to the situation and demarcating the range of viable responses. If the controlling exigence is seen as the threat of a communist takeover, insofar as we
oppose communism, we are compelled to provide assistance. If the controlling
exigence is seen as human rights violations, we are compelled to withhold aid
until more humane policies are adopted. Significantly, as Congress deliberated
this very matter in May 1984 with respect to El Salvador, its eventual course of
action was to combine these concerns by granting aid, but with the stipulation
that it could be stopped by the president if, in his view, El Salvador was not
acting in good faith to eliminate human rights violations. For representatives
voting on this matter, the concern with communist takeover dominated, yet the
human rights issue was of such magnitude that their legislative action would

have been unresponsive to the subordinate but powerful exigence of El Salvador's human rights policies.

The exigence, then, is the imperfection in the environment that calls rhetoric into being. It may be simple or complex. For rhetoric to be fitting, it must address this imperfection in meaningful ways.

Audience

A second defining feature of a rhetorical situation is the *audience*. A common misunderstanding of audience is to include in it anyone who has access to the message. That understanding ignores two very important features. First, rhetoric is *addressed* communication. It speaks to some individual or group *in particular*. Second, it seeks a specifiable *response* from the audience. Bitzer attempts to include these features by eliminating mere hearers or readers from this set. He says, "Properly speaking, a rhetorical audience consists only of those persons who are capable of being influenced by discourse and of being mediators of change."[6]

This definition includes two salient features. Audiences consist only of the individuals who are *capable of being influenced*. Such individuals have an interest in an exigence and its resolution. What would be the marks of such interest? Factual knowledge, experiential knowledge, concern about the outcome, proximity in time, proximity of place, a sense of responsibility for the exigence, and the magnitude of the imperfection may each contribute to audience interest and, thereby, their capability to respond in meaningful ways to the exigence.

In addition, the people in the audience must be capable of mediating change. When people think they cannot influence the outcome, they are less likely to respond to messages; they become excluded from the audience.

Thus, for example, if our alma mater launches a campaign to boost the arts and sets as a minimum a $100 donation, thousands of potential contributors stop listening to the message. Most students do not have $100 to spare. Most assistant professors do not either. Both groups may strongly believe the arts are important to college life, but they have been defined out of the audience by virtue of the situation's requirement for meaningful response. Such an appeal may be sensibly constructed if the fund-raisers have reason to believe they are more likely to reach their goal by securing a small number of large gifts than through mass donations of a small amount and if they know that donors of large gifts are more generous if their philanthropy places them among an exclusive group.

The point to bear in mind is that every rhetorical situation requires the mediating action of an audience. Speakers must make careful choices in determining who is, in fact, within their audience and how their readiness to respond can be maximized.

Constraints

As a third constituent factor, all rhetorical situations have salient *constraints*. These are both the limitations and the opportunities present in a situation that bear on what may or may not be said to the audience about the imperfection they are being asked to redress. Constraints may be *physical,* such as time of day, place where the message is to be presented, occasion for the presentation, medium of transmission, and similar material conditions of the environment. For example, during Senator Edward Kennedy's campaign for the Democratic presidential nomination in 1980, he showed a tendency to speak loudly as he became excited about ideas and issues. When addressing a substantial gathering, this posed no problem. But in a small room he appeared to be shouting, making his speeches sound more like harangues than reasoned appeals. This demonstrates a failure to adapt to the physical constraints of the situation.

Constraints also may be psychological in character. Frequently, these are the more important constraints that a rhetor must acknowledge. Such constraints include persons involved in the situation, who they are and what the audience thinks of them; events surrounding the exigence and bearing on audience dispositions at the time of performance; relations of the rhetor, the audience, and the exigence that can color receptivities; rules that govern what a body may or may not do; facts known or unknown that can inhibit or encourage readiness to believe and act; principles to which a rhetor or an audience is committed; laws that limit or make possible certain modes of conduct in resolving an exigence; images audiences and rhetors have of each other; interests that are enhanced or threatened by resolving the exigence in certain ways; emotions that aid or hinder recognition of the exigence; and a myriad of similar considerations that occur to parties engaged in rhetorical transactions. These factors have the power to influence decisions because what can be believed and what can be done are contingent on the host of psychological conditions that shape an audience's perception and evaluation of discourse. Each speaker has the formidable task of discovering the constraints that will aid in influencing audiences to embark on the desired course of action to remedy the exigence.

We may depict the rhetorical situation as a complex of a controlling exigence, an audience, and a collection of constraints that coalesce to call for a rhetorical response. The rhetoric that is generated must be suited to these factors for it to remedy the prevailing imperfection. Ideally, analysis of the constituents of a rhetorical situation will bring forth a *fitting response.*

LIFE CYCLES AND FITTING RESPONSES

Up to this point, we have been discussing *rhetorical* situations in a way that may suggest they are static, like a hidden object waiting to be discovered. In fact, they are dynamic, evolving, ever-changing states that are dramatically altered the moment a message and a messenger are introduced. To conclude this chapter, let us consider this dynamic interplay in terms of the life cycle of rhetorical situations, the relationship of responses to these stages, and the intentions of rhetors.

Life Cycles

According to Bitzer, a rhetorical situation comes into being, evolves to maturity, decays, and eventually dies. Along the way, this cycle may be retarded or hastened as new dimensions of a situation are unveiled, new issues emerge, and new voices are heard.

Eventually, however, every rhetorical situation passes from the scene—either through the front door of resolution, the back door of disinterest, or the side door of transformation—into a newly defined situation with its own controlling exigence. As it develops, a situation may go through four stages: origin, maturity, deterioration, and disintegration.

for whom?

1. Origin   At this stage, an exigence exists, but the audience and the constraints are still unformed. The public may still be unaware of the situation, so the potential speaker must awaken it to the imperfection at hand and must heighten its awareness of the situation's bearing on its interests. The rhetor is, in effect, involved in defining the situation as rhetorical and salient to those the rhetor would have as mediators of change.

Clearly not all situations survive their birth. Some may be wrongly perceived as rhetorical, some may be miscast and fail to gain notice as related to audience interests, and others are placed before the wrong audience and ignored. But some do hit their mark and generate continued attention.

2. Maturity   At maturity the exigence is at its peak of readiness for rhetoric to address it in meaningful ways. Well-crafted appeals that can alter beliefs and induce actions are capable of altering the environment. Audiences are equally matched in their concern about the situation, their receptiveness to discourse, and their willingness to mediate change. The constraints present in the situation provide means of persuasion that, if properly used, can modify the exigence.

Appropriate responses at this point can bring the situation to its resolution in a decision and a course of action. The resolved situation naturally passes from the scene. At this time, the responses may transform the situation as new issues come to the fore and dominate in defining the situation in the participants' minds. Or rhetorical efforts may fail to seize this moment of maturity, and the situation may begin to move into a third stage where the modifying potential of rhetoric is diminished.

resurrected

3. Deterioration   At this stage, the exigence becomes more difficult to remedy. Other factors, perhaps other people addressing their own needs, may have complicated the situation. Attitudes may harden, making audiences less capable of being influenced by people who disagree with them; interest may weaken as the novelty wears thin, and audiences may shift attention to other matters that appear more urgent. At this stage, actions or attitudes or both have begun to move the definition of the situation out of the rhetorical realm. Without some extraordinary intervening circumstance or inspired rhetorical performance, the situation will pass to its final stage.

transhuman

More tension

4. Disintegration   At this point, the imperfection is no longer perceived as modifiable in whole or in part by rhetoric. The audience capable of being influenced and of mediating change no longer exists. Once a decision has been

does that new evidence no longer exist

made, attempts at rhetorical discourse are thus completely idle since they no longer serve any functional purpose. They lack conditions in the environment that are open to modification through the instrumentality of discourse.

Here is an example. Suppose that there is a proposal to erect a building near some dormitories on your campus. This new building will require that basketball and handball courts next to the dorms be moved. When students first hear of the proposal, they make nothing of it. But if they decide, instead, that they want to take issue with the proposal because they do not believe this is an appropriate location for a building, they have created a *rhetorical* situation. Discussions may follow concerning the wisdom of the proposal. If no final decision has been reached, the situation may mature, with proponents and opponents of the proposed building making appeals to appropriate administrators. Once a decision is reached to erect the building, however, the situation deteriorates. Unless someone decides to take extreme action, such as seeking an injunction against the building, rhetoric will serve no useful function. A disintegrated rhetorical situation will exist because it is too late to speak out against the planned building after it has been constructed. Many speakers are remembered for addressing lost causes, but they had little or no effect on history.

Fitting Response

When we view rhetoric situationally, we are concerned with how our speech and writing are functioning in our environment. Hence we assess rhetorical efforts in terms of whether or not they are suited to modify other people's opinions and actions in order to effect change. Appropriate rhetorical efforts in this regard are *fitting responses.* A fitting response is not necessarily a successful one but one that is suited to resolving the complex of factors that define the situation. We may lose an issue and even a decision while still responding in a fitting way. Clearly, however, determining whether or not any response is fitting requires that we understand how the rhetor's rhetoric reflects his or her definition of the situation and meshes with that of the audience.

We may ask if a speaker has communicated in a way that is capable of correcting a real or potential problem in the environment. For example, if a successful candidate for mayor is accused of election fraud, an appropriate response must address the *forensic* or legal charge that a crime was committed. Are the accusations based on fact? Are the accusers competent? Were there opportunities for fraud? Are there independent election officials to speak against the charge? Is there evidence to suggest that the accused is of high moral character? Speaking of these matters would constitute a fitting response because these are the grounds on which innocence and guilt are determined. Similarly, in building a defense, the accused may determine that there are other matters of potential vulnerability that also deserve clarification so that these potential problems do not materialize at a later time.

An approach to *rhetor-audience interaction* that will permit us some degree of objectivity in considering the audience's role is to evaluate whether rhetoric is fitting in terms of its potential to remedy an imperfection and whether it is fitting in its determination of the audience to be addressed. Because audiences are marked by interest and ability to mediate change, there are four possibilities for assessing the fit of a rhetorical response:

1. Audience has an interest and is capable of mediating change.
2. Audience lacks an interest but is capable of mediating change.
3. Audience has an interest but is incapable of mediating change.
4. Audience lacks an interest and is incapable of mediating change.

Rhetoric addressed to audience 1 is fitting. Rhetoric to audience 2 is fitting only if it is geared to kindling an interest. Rhetoric addressed to audience 3 is fitting only if it is focused on potential exigences in the future, when impediments to mediating change may not exist. Rhetoric to audience 4 is futile and therefore unfitting. In each of these cases, a fitting response is one that is potentially corrective of the imperfection in the environment.

Returning to the case of the proposed building next to the dorms, we would assess appeals to administrators, students, faculty, and townspeople differently. Fitting responses to administrators who were decision makers would take into account the fact that they have interests that must be addressed, as well as their authority to act. Students may first have to be awakened to the fact that their interests are at stake, before they can realize their potential to persuade university officials. Faculty, meanwhile, may be following developments in this matter but have no effective means to voice a collective opinion. The building issue might be a catalyst for rhetoric aimed at securing faculty as well as student representation on the building committee that reviews and approves construction proposals. Meanwhile, discourse addressed to townspeople in general is probably misdirected, since the average citizen does not have an interest in where the university locates buildings on its campus, nor is their opinion sought on such matters.

Saying this, we also have to bear in mind that fitting responses will be influenced by the stage in the situation's life cycle and, in turn, will influence how the life cycle develops. Appeals for student and faculty representation on the building committee are fitting only after a resolution of the controlling exigence has occurred. The issue is primarily about the proposed construction site.

RHETOR'S INTENTIONS

Finally, we must say a word about the role of the rhetor's intentions in shaping rhetorical situations. The major criticism against a situational perspective toward rhetoric is that it appears to rest on a deterministic assumption. The theory seems to suggest that discourse is called into being because the situation exists and that the discourse called into being is shaped by the demands of the situation in ways that are beyond the rhetor's control. This appearance of determinism reflects a process of analysis that stops rhetorical situations at any given moment to account for the elements that are present. As critics, we can freeze situations for analytic purposes. But in actual practice, rhetorical situations are experienced in the dynamics of their life cycle. Significantly, this dynamic is one in which exigences, audiences, and constraints are constantly being realigned by the appearance of messages that are "fitting responses." Moreover, these messages reflect not only the demands of the situation but the interpretive responses of rhetors engaged in intentional acts designed to alter the situation. Once messages and messengers enter the situation and interact with receivers, the situation that *was* begins to change.

By recognizing that situational changes are not the result of natural forces (except in rare cases where some event so alters a situation as to eliminate the need for further rhetoric; if the bridge falls down, the debate over repairs is over) but of symbolic actions that are purposive and that have consequences for listener perceptions, we recognize the role of the rhetor's intentions in the shaping and resolving of situations as they are defined in the minds of listeners. Clearly, what speakers and writers say to listeners and readers cannot ignore the demands of the situation. Obviously, the objective circumstances to be addressed influence the rhetor's goals. In this sense, intentions are shaped by the demands of the situation. The demands cannot be ignored without violating the audience's propriety rules: what they regard as appropriate and meaningful discourse in the situation as they understand it. At the same time, it would be absurd to suppose that rhetors are without purposes that may require redefining the situation.

When Richard Nixon, in his notorious Checkers speech, suggested that since he had made a public financial disclosure it was only fair for the other candidates to follow suit, he shifted the focus from his financial dealings to the more general one of how public officials gain and use their wealth. This argument was calculated for its effect. Rhetors see resolutions that they find desirable and try to define and remake situations in ways that will accommodate the solutions they propose. Nixon's appeal was intended to put his opponents on the defensive. Further, there are times when the situation is not "right" for the rhetoric intended, when audiences do not perceive a situation as rhetorical or have forgotten or are unaware even that it exists. In such circumstances a rhetor may resort to such standard devices as introductions or titles to remind or may introduce new themes as part of an address on more familiar concerns to enhance readiness to perceive or even create exigences in the minds of audiences.

In sum, the life cycle of a rhetorical situation and the fitting responses to each stage are not solely products of the environment to be remedied. The rhetor's intentions also play a significant role in shaping and advancing the ongoing dynamic of rhetorical situations as they work their way toward resolution.

SUMMARY

In this chapter, we have been concerned with a *functional* view of rhetoric. This view emphasizes the instrumental role of rhetoric in changing the environment. Since the environment of our minds, our social relations, and our physical surroundings is significantly influenced by beliefs and ultimately by actions, rhetoric is a major source of influence in shaping the world we inhabit. For rhetoric to function as a source of modification, it must interact with the definition of the situation that exists in the minds of its audience. Simply put, action is guided by our definition of a situation. Lacking a definition, we would be unable to respond.

Rhetorical situations—situations defined as ones that can be modified through discourse—were seen to have three constituent elements: an exigence, an audience, and constraints. Moreover, the specific situation addressed was seen to assume its definition through the dynamic interplay of these constitutive elements. This dynamic interplay of elements creates the very possibility for rhetoric to occur and to have *functional* consequences for resolving problems of social action.

Finally, we saw that rhetorical situations have a life cycle. As they pass from origin to disintegration, fitting responses are ones that accommodate audience interests and ability to mediate change while addressing the controlling exigence. In all of this we need to bear in mind, however, that these responses are not mechanical; they are the products of human insight and intuition in response to the problems people face together. Ultimately, for a fitting response to be a satisfying one, it must intersect with the values, ethics, and personal commitments of both rhetor and audience. This is the mark of responsible rhetoric, a concern we will address in Chapter 4.

NOTES

1. Lloyd Bitzer, "The Rhetorical Situation," *Philosophy and Rhetoric,* 1 (January 1968), 1–12, and "Functional Communication: A Situational Perspective," in E. E. White, ed., *Rhetoric in Transition* (University Park: Pennsylvania State University Press, 1981), pp. 21–38.
2. Peter McHugh, *Defining the Situation* (Indianapolis: Bobbs-Merrill, 1968), pp. 23–32.
3. Bitzer, "The Rhetorical Situation," 6.
4. Donald C. Bryant, "Rhetoric: Its Function and Scope," *Quarterly Journal of Speech,* 39 (December 1953), 413.
5. Bitzer, "Functional Communication," pp. 21–22.
6. Bitzer, "The Rhetorical Situation," 8.

Making Commitments Through Rhetoric

History tells us that speech and writing have always been important for forging agreements. Treaties, contracts, laws, alliances, and commercial transactions involve people using words to frame common understandings. More words are used to forge commitments to act in accordance with these understandings. The historical records of these events focus mostly on public transactions.

However, the public stage is not the only one on which rhetoric occurs. In our everyday lives, each of us engages in countless rhetorical exchanges with family, friends, and associates. We seek cooperation in performing tasks; we invite others to offer their opinions; we share events through storytelling and try to relate our version in a fashion that will hold attention and be convincing; we find ourselves offering and receiving suggestions on how to cope with work tasks, relationships, or personal problems; sometimes we enter into negotiations with merchants, union officials, teachers, roommates, or family. Our day is filled with events of these kinds—significant but hardly noticed rhetorical transactions. Just like any event enacted in the full glare of publicity, these everyday rhetorical transactions require the same ingredients for success: common understanding and common commitment.

In Chapter 3 we developed a functional perspective on rhetoric. It was concerned with rhetoric as a means for altering the environment. There is no denying the importance of this role. But the functional view carries with it the danger of distorting our perceptions of rhetoric's relationship to ourselves. The environment of which we speak and the modifications we seek are "out there," external to our personal selves. From this we may form the false impression that rhetoric is a one-way deal: Rhetors act on the world as change agents, but they are immune from being transformed themselves by the same rhetorical transactions. Nothing could be further from the truth; every rhetorical transaction involves personal stakes for everyone involved, including rhetors.

For rhetoric to serve a responsible function, it must be used to advance truth and justice. Rhetoric flourishes in a democratic environment in which people are free to make choices. Our need to choose is what makes rhetoric important as a means for handling personal relations, whether in public or in private. When we make choices, we discover our commitments. When we make choices through rhetoric, we share those commitments with others. In short, *rhetoric makes commitments:* to the self, to others, to the truth value of our ideas, and to a view of what is required for humane social relations. It is this sense of commitment that we shall explore in this chapter. What is the general commitment we make to the type of world worth inhabiting when we choose to alter the environment by managing symbols of language, by using words rather than force? What are the risks inherent in adopting discourse as an instrumentality for creating opportunities, resolving problems, and expressing thoughts and feelings that are important to us? This chapter considers the very personal stakes we accept when we decide to practice rhetoric responsibly and to face the consequences of our decision.

EXPRESSIVE VERSUS INSTRUMENTAL TALK

To begin, we can distinguish discourse that is rhetorical from discourse that is not most obviously and generally in terms of rhetoric's instrumental function. Basically, rhetorical communication is *instrumental communication;* it is explicitly oriented toward goals such as changing opinions and actions.

Not all communication is intended to influence others. Sometimes we engage in *expressive communication,* speaking or writing primarily to vent our feelings. For example, upon striking our thumb with a hammer we may utter an expression of dismay. Our words are not intended to alter the environment of prevailing opinion on nail striking, nor should we have invoked the Almighty to persuade Him to punish the errant hammer for eternity. Our utterance is purely expressive, venting frustration and anger at ourselves and at an inanimate object.

Sometimes language is used in more public ways while remaining expressive. For example, when we receive a poor grade, we sometimes say things to let off steam. We seek a friend and express ire, frustration, outrage at our instructor's grading. Our purpose in venting these emotions is to "get them off our chest," presumably because the expression helps relieve internal feelings, not because the expression will alter behavior. Such communication is self-directed in the sense that it is more concerned with giving expression to our feelings than to changing another's opinion.

Instrumental communication, on the other hand, is designed to modify the environment by the use of appeals to influence conduct. Such appeals are unlike emotive communication in that they are other-directed rather than self-directed. Were we interested in altering the grade that made us angry, we would have spoken to our instructor, not our friend. Though giving the instructor a piece of our mind might be an effective mode of catharsis, it is not likely to secure the desired change. Remarks specifically calculated to persuade her that our answers were stronger than her grade reflects or that her questions were ambiguous and could be answered in more than one way are called for. Rather than communication uttered for its own sake, we would consider our utterance as a means to an end, namely, persuading our instructor to raise our grade.

Rhetorical communication is typically instrumental. When we decide to alter or maintain our environment through rhetorical means, we have made a commitment to communicate purposively with the audience in mind. Audience-oriented communication involves us in the continual effort of adjusting ideas and people to one another. The adjustive function of rhetoric, however, gives rise to two problems. The first problem is that of being true to our own ideas while adapting them to audience readinesses to respond. The second grows from the obvious possibility that instrumental communication may encourage actions that are not necessarily in the audience's best interest. There is a use of language designed to communicate with audiences and a use designed to deceive them. We are concerned with distinguishing between them and with the consequences of choosing to communicate.

ARGUMENT AND SELF-RISK

The process of adjusting ideas to people and people to ideas places heavy stock in arguments. In rhetorical theory, *argument* is a technical term. It does not refer to the activity of people squabbling. Arguments are reasoned appeals based on evidence of fact and opinion that lead to a conclusion. Through arguments, rhetors attempt to provide an audience with a solid basis for holding a belief and coordinating its actions with its belief. Without arguments, rhetoric would degenerate into the excesses of unsupported emotional or authoritarian appeals or become limited exclusively to matters of style. Arguments are the superstructure on which all responsible rhetoric depends.

Since an argument consists of reasons supported by data that lead to a specific conclusion, we can test its value by asking whether or not it can support its expressed inference. This means that an argument's strength is not merely its acceptability to a set of listeners. Telling people what they want to hear, even if false, could pass that test. While common acceptance may be a point of departure, the way arguments get tested is through the give and take of refutation and rebuttal. Strong ideas can withstand objections; weak ones cannot. Thus in seeking to adjust ideas to an audience, we are seeking expressions that will be meaningful to them, appeals that rely on audience opinions, arguments that can make our point in ways that can withstand scrutiny.

The philosopher Henry Johnstone has made the point that when we offer arguments to support our views, we must fulfill certain conditions for our arguments to be genuine. First, we must assume that the audience to whom we offer arguments is beyond effective control. Its members can think and articulate their thoughts; they can reflect on what we say and offer reasoned assessments; if they respond positively, it is because we have secured their agreement. They are not like robots or computers, who perform on appropriate command. They are not small children. They cannot be told what to do, at least in the context of argumentation. They cannot be regarded as objects of manipulation through means of suggestion. Each of these strategies is abandoned when we decide to argue, when we regard our audience as free and as capable of making its own choices. In short, we must regard our audience as human.

A second condition Johnstone points out is that the audience to whom we offer arguments may ignore them, disbelieve them, or even refute them. Consequently, by choosing to offer *arguments* in support of ideas, we run the risk of having our ideas defeated. At the same time, audiences responsive to arguments also risk having their behavior or beliefs altered. If they are unwilling to run this risk they cannot function as a genuine audience. In the terms of Chapter 3, they are incapable of being influenced and therefore fail to meet a necessary condition to be a rhetorical audience. Thus we may characterize people willing to run these risks as *open-minded.*

A third condition necessary for genuine arguments to be made is that the arguer and those responding both have an interest in the outcome of the argument. They are not considering mere possibilities but outcomes with consequences that affect both sides. There is risk because those involved have a stake in the outcome; we do not have a stake in mere possibilities. The specific risk is whether we will be able to maintain our system of beliefs and values, the commitments of mind and of spirit that define the *self,* or whether we will have to change a significant commitment, thereby reassessing the self. This tension between self-maintenance and change is essential for human growth, for getting beyond our individual and immediate experiences, and for inhabiting a common world with others who share our interests.

For example, most students have discussions with their parents about their college major. Sometimes parents question why their child has chosen to specialize in, say, communication rather than accounting. These discussions can become nasty, with father telling son that he must major in something practical and son telling father that he's old enough to make his own decisions. At this stage, effective rhetoric has left the scene. Neither is using instrumental talk designed to persuade; both are instead resorting to assertions and counterassertions that don't take the other's views seriously. Neither is offering compelling reasons for his beliefs.

Should father and son wish to deal with their problem more productively, they must first change their approach toward each other. They must treat each other as capable of reasoning and responding to reason, and they must take each other's views seriously. Further, each must be open to the possibility that he may be mistaken, that his reasons will not withstand objections, and that he may have to change his views on a proper major. Finally, each must recognize that his interest in the matter involves important elements of his belief structure: about education, about careers, about his motivations regarding this issue, and probably about their relationship as father and son.

Arguments that meet these requirements make the outcomes of rhetorical transactions highly personal. Rhetorical exchanges in which we respect the audi-

doesn't manipulate — but does "force" *off choice*

ence's freedom to choose, accept the possibility of being wrong, and have an interest in the outcome can make us self-aware by confronting ourselves with the risk of having to reassess the beliefs, values, and commitments that define us as unique individuals. Without arguments that force us as individuals to consider contradictory views and impulses, we would lack consciousness of a self. The consciousness of our contradictory impulses and their resolution on the basis of arguments tell the self who it is and where it stands.

With respect to the first problem of how far we may go in adapting ideas to audiences without sacrificing the integrity of our ideas, Johnstone's discussion of arguments provides a useful analysis. In every rhetorical transaction, the purpose or goal is to persuade listeners to our point of view. Arguments are addressed to them in ways that are likely to facilitate this objective. Thus the rhetor who argues in ways that sacrifice her ideas is engaged in a specious practice. These are not true arguments because they do not articulate the interests of the rhetor; they do not represent views in which she has a stake. They are mere panderings to the sentiments of the crowd. While false arguments of this sort may result in popularity or power, they misuse rhetoric as an instrumental act by misrepresenting the rhetor's views. Thus rhetorical arguments are always cast with the listener in mind, but such arguments must also reflect the essential views of the rhetor.

does this go far enough?

UNILATERAL AND BILATERAL ARGUMENTS

The second problem we raised at the outset concerned the contrasting use of language designed to communicate with audiences and a use designed to deceive audiences. Again, we can find guidance on this problem from Johnston, specifically in the distinction he draws between *unilateral* and *bilateral* arguments.[2] A bilateral argument is defined as one in which "the arguer must use no device of argument he could not in principle permit his interlocutor to use."[3] In essence, bilateral arguments are ones that avoid tricks, deception, falsehoods, and the like; they observe the Golden Rule, so to speak. A unilateral argument is defined as one in which the arguer uses devices of argument not available for the interlocutor's use. These may include not only gambits and ploys that attempt to elude critical inspection but also role-specific communication, such as directives from superiors to subordinates. Unilateral arguments frequently advance claims in specious ways, although one can imagine situations where unilateral arguments would be essential to avoid chaos.

The concepts of bilateral and unilateral arguments can be extended to characterize a rhetor's mode of communication as bilateral and unilateral. Working from the definitions just offered, *communication* may be defined as "the transmission of messages to another in such a way that it is clear that he is entitled to transmit messages to me in the same way."[4] This would include such features as opportunity for questions and refutation, common access to information, reasoned arguments supported by data, avoidance of devices that would impose unilateral restrictions (such as unqualified appeal to one's authority or refusing to discuss concerns other than one's own). *Unilateral* communication denies the other party equal opportunity of response. It preempts certain modes of transmission for itself. Such techniques as authoritative pronouncements, suggestion, hypnosis, brainwashing, and heavy reliance on presence and personality to carry the message are illustrative of this mode.[5]

For example, when Metropolitan Edison told the people of the greater Harrisburg area that they were in no danger from the nuclear power plant accident at Three Mile Island, they were assuming that they had no obligation to tell laypeople the truth about technical matters. That assumption clearly leads to unilateral communication. When managers employ communication techniques of encouragement or disinterest as a form of behavior modification designed to increase output, they are assuming that the workers are malleable and that they as managers have a right to mold the workers to company specifications. Such communication techniques are clearly unilateral. When student objections to the way a course is being handled are met with the instructor's response that he is personally devastated, he is using his position of authority to change the issue from what aspects of the course may be problematic to his worth as a human being. Again, that's clearly a tactic of unilateral communication.

However, not all instances of unilateral communication are evil. For example, requests for information, ordering from a menu, announcements of company policy, and directions to subordinates are pragmatic exchanges of the sort that usually do not invite or require reflection on the assertions advanced. The use of unilateral communication in such situations is not *necessarily* destructive and, in fact, may be essential for social coordination. When is unilateral communication pernicious? Exactly at times when discussion is appropriate for social coordination, when the issues involved require the mediation of reflection and deliberation. Such situations are ones in which the interacting parties have a stake in the outcome, in which conflicts abide, in which confronting alternatives can give rise to consciousness, in which the points at issue are self-involving. Such concerns lead us to self-insight when bilateral modes of communication are employed because bilateral communication typically forces a wedge between the rhetor and the message. The wedge of bilateral communication is precisely this: the active consideration that the message may have to be revised.

We make these active considerations whenever our previously unexamined assumptions are called into question. Any rhetoric that forces us to attend to ideas and practices that we normally take for granted or had previously ignored is forcing a wedge between our minds and the assumptions we normally make. It allows us to reflect on what we have accepted without question. For example, a rhetorical appeal challenging normal diplomatic relations with South Africa due to its apartheid policies forces us to think about our assumption that the internal affairs of a foreign nation are none of our business. An appeal challenging a previously unexamined assumption that nuclear weapons serve as deterrents to war and therefore must be maintained forces us consciously to reflect on the matter.

Unilateral communication typically fails to drive this wedge; it closes the spaces that might invite reflection by manipulating the audience's beliefs. When the mode of presentation uses devices of language and techniques of appeal that condense the reasoning implicit in the appeal, it disengages rhetor and audience from the mediating exercise of reflection. It fuses speaker, speech, and audience into a composite whole. Conversely, bilateral communication uses a language and appeals that explicitly welcome reflection on the message and the possibilities for its revision to express better a sound and shared opinion.

In rhetorical transactions, then, a unilateral rhetoric would use devices not open to the audience, such as those of propaganda. Because it does not invite reflection on the validity of its premises, it avoids the evocation of consciousness and confrontation with the self. It represses self-aware action, encouraging compliant behavior. Bilateral rhetoric would uncouple a message from the minds addressed, thereby inviting reflection. As Johnstone says:

> Before we can think about any issue, we must first attend to it. The rhetoric that forces it on our attention is the rhetoric of bilaterality, because no one can, in the nature of the case, have a monopoly on it. If I can point out your unnoticed assumptions, you can point out mine.[7]

RHETORIC AND THE SELF

In terms of the originating question, the bilateral-unilateral distinction affords us guidance in differentiating between rhetoric that humanizes and rhetoric that invites unreflective responses. Within this framework, let us now examine some findings that illustrate some of these techniques and their consequences for our self-awareness. We can point to four propositions concerning rhetoric and the self:

1. Rhetoric can reflect a self.
2. Rhetoric can evoke a self.
3. Rhetoric can maintain a self.
4. Rhetoric can destroy a self.

Reflecting a Self

Rhetoric can reflect a self through the types of arguments developed and the language used. Here we are concerned with the self of the rhetor as it is assumed in the way her appeals are developed and their implicit call to audiences to share in this view. With respect to arguments, we can examine the typical manner of reasoning employed by the rhetor to establish major contentions. A twentieth-century rhetorician, Richard Weaver, enumerates four possible modes for such arguments: definition, similitude, cause and effect, and circumstance.[8]

For example, when we examine a sample of messages by a particular communicator, patterns of argument become apparent. Weaver, among others, has argued that these patterns reflect a vision of the world. Individuals who believe that there are "truths" and that we act best when our conduct is guided by these

Not Lincoln's argument!

truths tend to argue from *definition*. Definitional arguments assert the basic nature of their subject (say, Lincoln arguing that by definition, all men are created equal) and base policy on these definitions (thus slavery is wrong and must be abolished).

Next come arguments that are in search of "truths" that have not yet been discovered. These arguments rely on the use of analogy to known or accepted truths to find their way in novel situations where probability is the best we can hope for. These are arguments based on relationships, or *similitudes*. One might find arguments of this sort in appeals that take a more poetic or nonliteral approach to their subject. For example, Swift's *Gulliver's Travels,* Sinclair's *The Jungle,* and Miller's *The Crucible* are instances of fictional messages that were nonetheless commentaries on real conditions of their times. Their persuasion was wielded in terms of the relationships audiences could see between their imaginative worlds (the land of Lilliput, the Chicago stockyards, Salem's witch trials) and the ones they actually populated. This technique is also employed when the rhetor perceives that an indirect approach will be tactful or will best respect the audience's capacity for conscious reflection (as when Martin Luther King, Jr., in his "I Have a Dream" speech, indicted the civil rights practices of the federal government by developing an elaborate analogy to banking: civil rights guarantees are like promissory notes).

A third type of appeal is to *cause and effect*. This view emphasizes the developmental features of a situation rather than its essence. Political arguments of a pragmatic sort urge us to respond because the consequences of present policy are undesirable or the consequences of change are an improvement. It does not focus on underlying principles that could suggest that while pragmatically less satisfying, a course of action is preferable because it is the right thing to do. We can find this pattern in arguments to provide military aid to beleaguered governments friendly to the United States because if we do not support them, communist-backed insurgents will take over. This ignores raising issues related to the types of regimes we are supporting: Are they democracies or dictatorships? Are they open to dissenting opinion, or are they repressive? Do they violate human rights? A more extreme subversion of the cause-and-effect argument is argument from *circumstances*. Its appeal is to the force of immediate facts. It does not offer a cause-and-effect explanation of the facts but takes them as a given, commanding response. We may find this pattern in the argument that the United States should convert to the metric system because the rest of the world uses it. This mode of argument leaves unasked the questions of why we must use the same system as the rest of the world and what will be the results of making such a change. Whereas the first two modes reflect an awareness of self as grounded in its knowledge of being, the second two emphasize the self in relation to processes of change. Significantly, the final tactic of argument does not drive the wedge of bilaterality that urges reflection. It argues that we have no alternative but to respond or be crushed.

Another way in which a self is reflected is through our uses of language. Metaphors, images, descriptive adjectives, and the like reveal an orientation that can be most illuminating. For example, rhetorical critic Edwin Black explored the heavy reliance on a "cancer" metaphor in the rhetoric of the John Birch Society.[9] By arguing that communism is a cancer, the Birchers reflect an image of the self as a victim subjected to invasion by an external source and who, though not responsible for the invasion, must take drastic measures or succumb. Language like this invites a paranoid vision of the world as threatening, of the self as imperiled by alien forces, of external responsibility for the individual's calamities—the alien forces out to get us—and justification for automatic negative responses. This is the language of threat appeal, a unilateral mode of rhetoric.

Evoking a Self

Rhetoric can evoke a self. Sometimes rhetoric presents arguments in ways that force the individual to reexamine assumptions and the self they define. Critical inspection of issues, in other words, can be so profound in its consequences that it leads the person to discover a self. One of the very best illustrations of this occurred during the protest movements of the 1960s and early 1970s. Millions of Americans and Europeans found traditional assumptions about national interests, education, drugs, sex, gender roles, and minority rights called into question. Attending to this rhetoric led substantial numbers of people to become "politicized"—in that they were suddenly awakened to their stake in political processes—and "radicalized"— in that they saw the need for a drastic change from policies of the past. Such rhetoric consciously challenged the basic assumptions on which western European and American society was based or called attention to inconsistencies between "corrupt" policies and "laudable" goals. By defining themselves as different from and put upon by "the system," their rhetoric urged a reconsideration of self. Here is Helen Dudar, in a special report on women's lib written for *Newsweek*, commenting on the personal effects of covering such meetings:

> I came home that night with the first of many anxiety-produced pains in the stomach and head. Superiority is precisely what I had felt and enjoyed and it was going to be hard to give up. That was an important discovery. One of the rare and real rewards of reporting is learning about yourself. Grateful though I am for the education, it hasn't done much for the mental stress. Women's Lib questions everything; and while intellectually I approve of that, emotionally I am unstrung by a lot of it.
>
> Never mind. The ambivalence is gone; the distance is gone. What is left is a sense of pride and kinship with all those women who have been asking all the hard questions.[10]

By her own report, Dudar is led to discover herself through the experience of attending to a rhetoric that questioned in order to persuade: a bilateral rhetoric.

Maintaining a Self

Rhetoric can maintain a self. Not only can rhetoric being us to a new self-awareness, but it can also support and sustain an existing self. In his much cited study of protest rhetoric, rhetorician Richard Gregg[11] provides an apt illustration. Protesters differentiated themselves from opponents as "oppressor groups." The oppressor groups identified were subjected to rhetorical attacks. This mode of self-identification by means of differentiation allowed protesters to enhance their own self-awareness, insulating it from attack by unworthy oppressors and maintaining their sense of self-worth.

While attacks against oppressor groups served to maintain self-identity through differentiation from an external force, internally self-identity was developed and maintained through the myriad of rhetorical transactions that were a necessary part of a protest group's life cycle. Group unity, and the deliberation that manifested unity, provided a powerful experience of identity, as this reflection by James Ogilvy makes plain:

> If one has not shared with others the experience of collectively arriving at a group action without reliance on the tools of voting, compromise and the mechanics of debate codified in *Robert's Rules of Order* [*sic*], if one has not felt oneself as a part of a body whose cohesiveness requires that the entire body grind through the growing pains of resolving and/or fully incorporating conflicts rather than allowing one part to resign itself to compromise with another part, if one has not experienced a totally involving group dynamic for which "decision-making procedure" is an absurdly pale description, if one has not felt an emotionally charged atmosphere in which all one's sensitivities are turned to the progressive disclosure and elaboration of the group's and not just one's own will, if one has never spent a great deal of time with others with whom this kind of experience is possible, then it is extremely unlikely that *desa* [a term for such a collective experience] will admit of translation into terms with semantic referents that would render them more than purely fanciful.[12]

Here we find a former protester emphasizing that the experience of "groupness" among those resisting the establishment was largely a rhetorical experience. The spirit of democracy among group members, the necessity for forging consensus to act as one, their acceptance of freedom to choose and therefore to speak their individual views, and the experience of being open to change and of actually being changed by the views of others were tied to the discursive character of the group. The group was a "life-space" where ideas could appear. We sense that for Ogilvy the group became a place where words could lead to actions that transcended the petty concerns of daily affairs. Ogilvy's view illustrates the experience of participating in a group governed by the ideal of bilateral communication. Bilateral communication reinforced his awareness of himself as a participant in a democratic process and as a being self-consciously reflective about his experiences.

Destroying a Self.

Rhetoric can destroy a self. Finally, we may note how protesters engage in scapegoating, symbolically slaying the selves of their opponents. By identifying what opponents believed and did with immoral opinion or corrupt behavior, protesters effectively defined opponents out of the human race. But they were not alone in this, since establishment rhetors sought identification with those not aligned with dissident factions by using techniques of scapegoating against protesters. Significantly, by engaging in symbolic slaying, both sides used a unilateral rhetoric that protected their respective selves from external attack, from considering the possibility that their respective views were mistaken.

In these four ways—by reflecting, evoking, maintaining, and destroying a self—rhetorical tactics may either bring the self into the risk of reconsidering matters in which it has an interest or seal the self from consciously reflecting on these interests and thereby risking manipulation. In each case the bilateral versus unilateral nature of the exchanges determines whether rhetorical transactions have the potential to enhance self-awareness. As we noted earlier, tension between self-maintenance and receptivity marks the open-minded person.

This tension is especially reflected in protest rhetoric. There is a sense in which Gregg's research is a proof that the ego function of protest rhetoric is to preserve the self by not risking argument. The period he examined had a rhetoric of markedly insular quality, wherein disciples were reinforced and opponents vilified. Their "us versus them" view of the world encouraged separation from adversaries. By dividing the world into opposing camps, it became easier to define the situation as one that was threatening. This threatening definition, in turn, attracted attention and sometimes fear of protesters as aliens in society's midst. When this fear was coupled with the provocative scorn protesters showed for establishment ways, retaliation frequently resulted in the form of police brutalities. These counterreactions only served to reinforce the perception among protesters that this was a nation divided—a final proof that the rhetoric of division was correct.[13] But this type of rhetoric is based on tactics of control. Nowhere do the protesters manifest the *modes* of bilateral rhetoric that would permit meaningful communication between opposing groups. These traits are illustrative of persons behaving out of keen awareness of the risks of dealing with an adversary by engaging in argument and an equally keen awareness of the need to establish uniqueness.

This tension between self-maintenance and change is also present in the protesters' encounters with others in the "movement." Black students during the 1960s and 1970s could reject the appeals of black power advocates as Marxist extremism; women could dismiss feminist appeals as symptoms of middle-class frustration; students could tell radicals that, all things considered, they'd much rather study. In the forums where persuasive appeals were open to question and refutation, protesters did risk themselves.

SUMMARY

We have been considering the role of rhetoric as a source for greater understanding of who we are and what we might become. We have suggested that there are heavy personal stakes for a person who chooses to treat problematic matters in a rhetorical fashion because such a choice opens the possibility of self-discovery but also the possibility of change. In this respect, we focused on the importance of bilateral rhetoric in encouraging self-discovery and self-growth by communicating in ways that permitted a separation between a message and the persons involved in its delivery and reception. Rhetoric has the potential to reflect, evoke, maintain, or destroy a self. The choice between unilateral and bilateral rhetoric plays a significant role in achieving or thwarting these potentialities.

The ramifications of these considerations are profound for the type of world we live in. In an argument, both parties have something to lose—the comfort and security of currently held ideas and opinions. Rhetoric may expose us to the contradictions in our views, both logical and moral, making us painfully *self*-conscious by forcing us to reconsider the grounds for our beliefs. In existentialist terms, a person is his or her possibilities, his or her moral commitments. Thus rhetoric may help make men and women of us by forcing us to become more responsible for beliefs and actions.

Rhetoric also forces us to choose, and choice entails freedom. If rhetoric presents us with alternatives, and if we are compelled to choose, rhetoric is the judge or condemning agency that makes us face up to what we are and what we could be. Rhetoric makes us take on the burden of freedom.

Finally, because of the risk of identity and security involved, rhetoric gives experience a deeper meaning and significance. It amplifies the importance of certain acts, ideas, or beliefs and thus presents the mode of being, the proposition being championed, the relationship of openly speaking and listening parties as a legitimate possibility for those addressed. In so doing it throws them back on themselves, putting them face to face with life and death, with greatness and ignominy.

NOTES

1. Henry W. Johnstone, Jr., "Some Reflections on Argumentation," in Maurice Natanson and Henry W. Johnstone, Jr., eds., *Philosophy, Rhetoric, and Argumentation* (University Park: Pennsylvania State University Press, 1965), pp. 1–10.
2. Henry W. Johnstone, Jr., "Bilateriality in Argument and Communication," in J. Robert Cox and Charles Arthur Willard, eds., *Advances in Argumentation Theory and Research* (Carbondale: Southern Illinois University Press, 1982), pp. 95–102.
3. Ibid., p. 95.
4. Ibid., p. 99.
5. Ibid.
6. Thomas Farrell and G. Thomas Goodnight, "Accidental Rhetoric: The Root Metaphors of Three Mile Island," *Communication Monographs,* 48 (December 1981), 271–300.
7. Johnstone, "Bilaterality in Argument and Communication," p. 101.
8. Richard Weaver, *The Ethics of Rhetoric* (Chicago: Henry Regnery, 1953), pp. 55–114.
9. Edwin Black, "Second Persona," *Quarterly Journal of Speech,* 56 (April 1970), 109–119.
10. *Newsweek,* March 23, 1970, p. 78.
11. Richard B. Gregg, "The Ego Function of Protest Rhetoric," *Philosophy and Rhetoric,* 4 (Spring 1971).
12. James Ogilvy, *Many Dimensional Man* (New York: Harper & Row, 1977), p. 83.
13. Gregg, 87.

chapter 5

Finding Ideas

Wilson + Arnold

review topics vs.
material topics (779)

Aristotle ⟶ vs. Leff *are the "material"*

The book of Ecclesiastes tells us there is nothing new under the sun. Though that may be true in terms of the themes of life, it is equally true that humans are always on the lookout for new solutions to the eternal problems. As often as humankind has wondered about how to keep peace among neighbors, what care to provide the elderly and the infirm, how best to educate the young, and where to draw the line on public reveling, no standard answers have appeared. Each age confronts the perennial problems anew and seeks its own understanding of why they are problems and what to do about them. Though the basic concerns of life may recur, humans are forever searching for fresh insights and effective ways to express them.

Chapters 5 through 8 are concerned with the substance of discourse, the *material appeals.* Material appeals are the arguments and other modes of persuasion developed in the message. These include the reasons offered to support a contention, how these appeals engage audience feelings, and the influence of the rhetor's character on an audience's judgment. In each case our concern is to find materials that will energize our ideas in relevant ways for our audience. In rhetoric, the activity of finding things to say is called *invention.*

Since invention is common to all modes of persuasion, this chapter considers the general method used in rhetoric to generate fresh ideas suited to the speaker, the topic, the audience, and the occasion. This is the method of *topical reasoning.* To set this method in context, we will begin with a general discussion of creativity. From there we will consider the specific need for creativity in goal-oriented communication. Then we will elaborate the method of topical reasoning and its relevance to resolving rhetorical situations.

INVENTIVENESS AND CREATIVITY

The subject of creativity has a long and rich history. From antiquity to the present, each era has explained in its own terms how thoughts and feelings are born and expressed. Why should this be such an attractive topic? Surely not because creativity is essential for art, though the creativity-art relationship is an important one. More basic is the necessary role of creativity in every human's life. Each of us must create in order to give meaning to our experiences. Without creativity, the data of experience would be merely an aggregate of brute facts. We would be no different from other animals, responding to the events of nature and our biological needs as stimuli with sign value at best. Like animals, our senses would command us to eat! avoid! run! The data of nature would lack symbolic meaning. An infant nestled asleep in her mother's arms would be but an organism at rest. The seepage of dioxin into the soil would be no more than matter of one chemical composition mixing with matter of a different chemical composition. The light-headed giddiness of new lovers would be no more than a set of physiological conditions. Through creativity, we transform the brute data of experience into expressions of thoughts and feelings that give them meaning and significance.

Creativity is an act of symbolic expression. As an *act,* it is eventful because it occurs at a particular time and place. Since it is an event, it has temporality, which is open to the historical past and the anticipated future as qualifying and enriching sources of definition. As *symbolic,* it is referential, drawing on the resources of the world to illuminate the meaning of inner experiences. As an *expression,* it is addressed and thereby evokes the depth of individual experiences as sources of relationship and differentiation that provide insight. The only limitations to creativity are the limitations of the self, for the thinkable is a limitless source of meaning and the world an inexhaustible supply of reference.

Symbolic expressions can take a variety of forms, such as words or music or painting or dance. Regardless of medium, since creativity can occur only as an expression, it must place the data of experience in relationship to one another, to the world, to self and other. Each relationship is a manifestation of our uniquely human capacity to create meanings out of nature and its life forms, to share those meanings with others, and through symbolic sharing to create a self and a world. The infant asleep in her mother's arms depicted on canvas may become an expression of vulnerability and innocence, of love and protection; it may become a statement that infants are to be cherished and mothers revered; in a political context, it may serve as an exhortation against abortion. Once we employ symbols to express the data of experience, a world of emotions, thoughts, sentiments, and actions is evoked; for humans, there is no alternative, simply because symbols are naturally evocative and humans are inherently capable of using and responding to them.

So it is with our responses to the physiological reactions experienced when we fall in love and the environmental effects of chemical products. As data, they are what they are. But with symbols we can provide labels for these data that allow us to respond to them with thoughts and feelings. Once expressed in symbols, they become meaningful in ways that create realities for their users. Moreover, because symbols are arbitrary inventions, they can express data in a variety of modes; can place data in a multitude of contexts that establish relationships, each unique in some way from any other; can reveal alternative interpretations of data; can offer a framework—even to the point of becoming an ism with implications for understanding and action.

When we recognize that creativity is the way in which humans make sense of their experiences, all acts of human expression are cast in a new light. Every human becomes a creative agent, not just the select few with special talents. And each human expression becomes an act of construction through which maker and audience interact to determine what they know, believe, value, and feel about a common world. Whenever human expression occurs, the possibility for creativity of some sort exists.

Having said this, some qualifications have doubtless come to your mind. Are banal expressions such as clichés creative? Obviously, they are not very creative, and, if thoughtless mouthings of stock expressions, they may be no more creative than the utterances of a parrot triggered by an appropriate cue. Parrots can speak, not converse. Remember, we have maintained that creativity is an act of symbolic expression. That does not mean that all acts of symbolic expression realize their creative potential.

A second obvious concern is with whether we have eliminated the artist. Not at all. Remember, we have said that the only limitations on creativity are those of the self. Some individuals think and feel and see more possibilities than others. Some have greater skill in the management of symbols than others. Some are more precise in expression than others. Such individuals are called artists because they have mastered a form. But at base their act of creativity is not different from the least imaginative person's in that it rests on using symbols to express the meaning of experience.

Are we always creative? Aren't there times when the use of symbols doesn't involve creativity? Certainly. Each day we engage in hundreds of routine transactions of speech and writing where symbols are used to express the ordinary. For example, our friends and acquaintances know we are still on speaking terms because we use the clichés of speech and writing that signal this fact. These acts are called *phatic communion,* a type of communication in which the act of speaking or writing in a particular form is more important than the literal meanings of the words used. We will discuss this concept at greater length in Chapter 10. Here our point is that we say "hello" to acquaintances, we wish people "a good day," we thank a salesclerk at the close of a transaction, we request the salt at dinner with words that say nothing original but are essential for maintaining cordial relations. Or, for example, at work we may have to log vital weights and measures. This is valuable information, so the form in which the data are recorded is specified by the technical purposes for which they will be used. Though these recordings are no test of our creative powers, they serve a vital function for maintaining accurate files for future reference and decision making. Interestingly, once we learn the appropriate social clichés and the relevant information to record we can execute these communication transactions automatically, without engaging in conscious reflection on what we are experiencing or what it means.

The question of *when* creativity is necessary for us to manage our environment is the key question. While all symbolic acts express meanings, we are most acutely aware of our *need to create* in situations that are out of the ordinary in some respect. Creativity is necessary when standard interpretations and standard responses are not available, when ordinary solutions to problems are not obvious. If your car is out of gas, you have to put fuel in the tank for it to run. You have no choice because the car won't function otherwise. But if your town is suffering unemployment, it is not as obvious what you must do to correct the situation. This is not an ordinary situation with an obvious solution but a problematic one lacking a common interpretation and determined solution. Unemployment problems have a variety of causes, making each one unique. So saying, "Well, let's attract new industry to create jobs" won't do. That's a clichéd response, not an analysis. In brief, such a situation is indeterminate in some important respect that only human creativity can remove. It requires expressions that give the situation meaning.

To bring clarity and resolution to an unusual situation, we must first locate the likely sources of uncertainty that inhibit understanding and action. Typically, problematic situations are marked by tension of some sort: by *conflict,* where competing impulses pull us in opposite directions; by *novelty,* where the circumstances confronting us are outside our frames of reference; or by *ambiguity,* where meanings aren't clearly given but must be selected and developed. Conflict, novelty, and ambiguity heighten our awareness that experiences may be interpreted in a variety of ways, with each alternative projecting a different view of the world and what it might become. Conflict, novelty, and ambiguity also require that we select from among alternative interpretations, our choices being palpably evident in the symbols we select to create meanings for ourselves and others.

The need to select from among alternatives in order to interpret our experiences is evident in every human activity: in work and in play, in public life and in private, in the sciences, the professions, and the arts, as well as in business, industry, and labor. This need is manifested not only in our discovery of new thoughts and interpretations but also in reformulating old ones. We find interpretive selection evident in a Beethoven composition inspired by the sight of a beautiful young woman, in a Count Basie jazz improvisation on a traditional ballad, and in a Leonard Bernstein lecture on a musical genre. We find it in Gunnar Myrdal's brilliantly researched and written scholarly treatment of race relations in the United States, in the irreverent treatment of the same subject by Flip Wilson, and in Jesse Jackson's appeals to redress racial inequities. We find it in an architect's design of spaces intended to encourage people to congregate and in a conversationalist's management of topics for the same end.

Each of these circumstances lacks certainty of meaning and of outcome. In each case choices must be made. Each choice will create meanings by virtue of selecting one symbol over another to express an experience. Lacking true, correct, or sometimes even effective precedents, we nonetheless must resort to symbol selection if we are to make any sense of our experiences. Our symbol choices impose a framework on ambiguous, novel, and conflicting experiences where no set answer will do. Frameworks resolve conflict and ambiguity and place novelty in relation to the known. In this way our symbol choices reflect our interpretations of our experiences.

While our creations reflect the meanings we attach to our experiences, their symbolic character permits others to share them. In this sense creativity is a social activity, and creations are meaningful as social constructs. They bring to others a symbolic structure that is open to appreciation, discussion, modification, action, and the host of possible responses conceivable in the face of symbolic exchanges. Because human creations can be shared, they can give meaning to the experiences of whoever encounters them, even if their experiences are not the same as those of the creator. A good example of this is the comedy of Flip Wilson as it affected white audiences during the stormy days of the late 1960s and early 1970s.

White and black Americans, considered as aggregates, have differing experiences of economic opportunities, political power, cultural expression, family structure, and a host of other indicators well documented by sociological research. How blacks and whites interpret these differences and what responses they find appropriate vary greatly between and within the races. Some group members are consumed by anger and resort to violence, some persist in bigotry and repression, some experience differences as threats to be feared and avoided, some find differences as challenges to be overcome, some resort to pragmatic action, and some drop out. The facts of experience are the same, but their meanings are different. These differences in meaning account for the variety of responses we find, along with their positive or negative impacts on our lives.

In this context, Flip Wilson's comedy was a creative response to issues of the 1960s and 1970s because it exalted his blackness. Several years ago, TV critic John Leonard offered an insightful analysis of how central this exaltation was to Wilson's humor.[1] Consider the characters he portrayed: the sexual predator; the assertive, brassy female; the jive-talking, high-living storefront minister. They are all clichés. More than that, they are ghetto clichés built on sex and rhythm fantasies that were a part of white Americans' stereotypes of blacks during that period. Wilson dealt with these stereotypes by portraying them in the outrageous and hilarious antics of his characters. The fantasies were not sanitized for home consumption; they were not softened to do social work by presenting the black experience as just a "deeper shade of pale." Wilson's routines came off as the innocent hustle of an entertainer who hurled white stereotypes into absurd situations to make us laugh.

But there is more to it than that. As Leonard observed, by making us laugh with stereotypes that are anything but funny, he began to create new meanings for white experiences of black people. Wilson's play with common white views began to take the threat out of blackness. Americans laughed because they recognized the innocent hustle in his characters. They weren't vicious or cynical; they were vulnerable. There were exaggerations, but they needed to exaggerate to stay ahead in their games. Finally, his characters were comfortable. They were laugh-provoking exploiters of white America's myths about black life. In the context of strained race relations, their laughter could only serve to encourage white Americans to see Wilson in a different light than their stereotypes about blacks. Wilson's genius lay in his insights into our vulnerabilities, black or white; to our hopes, black or white; to our needs, black or white. He was black and he was likable, approachable, and unequivocating in celebrating his blackness. Even today, none of his routines tries to demonstrate identity with whites or equality with whites or subservience or superiority to whites. Indeed, these issues and questions are never raised.

Against the backdrop of racial turmoil, Americans were subtly moved to accept Wilson through his characters and thus have their categorizations of "blackness" rearranged. Wilson's creativity helped the white experience of blackness to take on new meaning. His humor encouraged people to think, "We like Flip Wilson; he won't hurt us; he's black; black doesn't have to be fearsome." In this way, we were altered by the man.

The shared character of Flip Wilson's creativity illustrates in graphic fashion how the imaginative expression of experience can influence those who have access to that expression. But the illustration reveals another point as well: The socially shared aspect of creativity is capable of making commentary, of exerting influence, of changing attitudes, beliefs, and opinions. Creativity can lead us to insight and to action. It can function aesthetically and rhetorically. Wilson is not only a comedic artist who entertains, but he is also a rhetor whose specialty is to discover new ways to remold old and commonly shared attitudes and beliefs. In the study of rhetoric, this discovery process is called *invention*.

INVENTION IN PURPOSIVE SPEECH

Invention refers to discovering what might be said on a subject to persuade an audience. It was the first of five *canons* of rhetoric developed and discussed in classical antiquity; the others were *disposition* (or structure), *style, memory,* and *delivery*. The canons served the function of organizing the discussion of rhetorical principles in handbooks on the subject and were seen as the natural process followed in developing a speech from inception of its ideas to actual presentation. Invention, as the first canon in discussion and in the process of developing a speech, received extended treatment, especially by those who were concerned with the content of rhetoric. It was, and remains, an area of study and instruction concerned with creating arguments.

As we have seen in previous chapters, rhetorical events arise when people experience situations that can be better understood or managed through the use of words. When talk or writing can do some good in changing opinions, feelings, or actions, the situation is rhetorical. Situations of this sort are *indeterminate.* They do not have to be as they are; they can be otherwise if people are persuaded to believe and act differently.

In the terms we have been using, rhetorical situations are typically situations that require creativity. The very presence of an imperfection marked by urgency is a sign that novelty, conflict, or ambiguity is a defining feature of the circumstances at hand. There is no certain answer about what to do, nor perhaps even a common understanding of the novelty, conflict, or ambiguity at hand. For this reason we have to make sense out of our experiences of imperfections if we are to resolve them. To do this we require a framework to aid us in interpreting the data confronting us. The inventions of a rhetor provide such frameworks by developing lines of thought or arguments that interpret experiences in a particular way. The question facing every communicator at the outset of developing a message is what determination he or she wishes the audience to make of its circumstances.

Rhetorical modes of communication are expressly purposive in nature. They attempt to influence someone to accept a particular point of view as correct and to act with respect to that point of view. Hence at the outset we need to bear in mind that rhetorical discourse is goal-oriented. Rhetors seek general goals—to entertain, to instruct, to persuade, to motivate to action—as well as specific goals—support the ERA, vote for Jesse Jackson, buy a Chrysler product, think of the accused as a loving father and devoted husband. Goals are established in line with the outcomes a rhetor desires and the perceived readiness of the audience to respond. This is another way of saying that all rhetoric is intentional and is addressed to somebody; therefore, expression is always adapted to what we want to accomplish in light of what we think somebody is ready to hear.

Rhetoric is not general expression but specific to the audience at hand, so we find, for example, that messages designed to elicit the support of true believers may say some things better left unspoken before a more skeptical audience. One would be foolhardy to address the American Council of Catholic Bishops, say, on the topic of birth control and advocate that the church change its restrictions. Because Catholic bishops may be presumed to have opinions and beliefs strongly opposed to birth control, they are unlikely to be moved by such an appeal. More modest objectives, such as tolerance for alternative systems of beliefs, are better suited to their readiness to respond. Closer to home, it would be foolhardy to tell your professor that you missed his test because you had a test in another course. The rhetor who succeeds at opening her audience to considering her point of view will do so because the appeals presented were intentionally designed to influence her specific audience in a particular way. In sum, rhetorical discourse is calculated to encourage an audience to think and feel along a particular bias.

The calculated nature of rhetoric is most responsibly present when a speaker or writer finds the means of persuasion in arguments that provide reasons for believing and acting. Thus rhetors, regardless of setting, always need to create means of persuasion that will gain an advantageous hearing or reading for their ideas. They seek to present ideas as they intersect with audience experiences because these intersections are what determine a matter in the audience's mind. This activity of seeking ways to present ideas efficaciously is called *invention*. Thus we may define *invention* as "the method of finding 'sayables' (symbols) that have the potential to transform some matter or question of an indeterminate nature into one that is determinate in the mind of the audience."

The transformation of an indeterminate matter or question into one that is determinate requires discoveries by both the speaker or writer and the audience. The speaker must know what the audience is able to tolerate. What do they know? and What do they believe? are dominant questions. These will aid the speaker in discovering what may be communicated effectively to this audience on this subject at this time for this end. The members of the audience need to know what the speaker wants from them and what the speaker is prepared to give in exchange. This will aid them in discovering the relationship of the ideas presented to their own experiences and in gaining new insights that help to form a considered judgment. Both aspects involve discovery of how to interpret the events under consideration in a way that will permit an appropriate and effective response.

In actual practice, these respective modes of discovery can be found in the arguments by which a proposition is advanced. The arguments stand as an index to the rhetor's discovery of means of persuasion. The arguments also serve as the stimuli for discoveries, thoughts, and feelings that inevitably accompany an audience's internalizing of a message.[2]

Topical Thinking

Aristotle, who developed the basic method of invention, was aware of this relationship between modes of discovery and argument. In fact, he devoted the first two books of his treatise on rhetoric to the ways in which proofs are found and developed. His approach is useful even today and can help us to understand better how the method of rhetorical invention is practiced.

Aristotle argued that at the heart of every speech was the proof of the statements or claims advanced. Proofs were basically of two sorts. There were deductive proofs, called *enthymemes,* and inductive proofs, called *examples.* We will develop each in greater detail in the next chapter. For now, the important point is that these two patterns of reasoning required *premises* that would support a claim the rhetor wished to advance. The problem every rhetor faced, as Aristotle saw matters, was to find premises that linked the rhetor's claims with the views of the audience. If these linking premises could be found, persuasion was more likely to occur.

Aristotle tells us that we find the premises from which to build arguments through a method called *topical thinking.* Topical thinking is akin to what you may know as brainstorming. In brainstorming you try to imagine or recall everything that is possibly relevant to a subject. Topical thinking tries to do the same. The differences are that topical thinking is systematic and that it uses a specific device of thought called a *topos* to help generate ideas. We need to consider this device in some detail, for it is at the heart of rhetorical invention.

Topos is a Greek word for "place." As it is used in rhetoric, it refers to the place one goes to find arguments. By place we do not mean an actual physical location; it is a metaphor that refers to places in your mind where you would find arguments. That probably sounds obscure. Let's try to make it clearer with some analogies.

First, think of place as a physical location. Imagine, for example, that we are tourists visiting Niagara Falls. Our interest as tourists is to view this natural wonder in as many ways as possible. We might stand next to the Horseshoe Falls and watch the water cascade over the edge. We might ride in the *Maid of the*

Mist tourist boat to see the falls from below. We might walk along the Canadian shore to see the American Falls at a distance. We might travel down into the Cave of the Winds to see the American Falls up close. We might ride in a touring helicopter to see the spectacle from above. In each case we are occupying a different *place* to look at Niagara Falls. Each place gives us a unique view, reveals an aspect all its own, gives us a different perspective on the whole.

A topical place is like a physical place in that it, too, gives a unique perspective or way of looking at matters. The difference, of course, is that a topical place is conceptual; it exists in our mind. Its function is to help us think about a subject to discover what, if anything, may be said about it from the perspective of the place. So the first thing we can say about a topic is that it provides a mental perspective from which we can analyze a subject. It is *analytic.*

There is a second aspect to topical thinking suggested by the metaphor of place. This has to do with place as a location where something can be put. To use another analogy, suppose that you had a cistern as a place in which you could put liquids. Your cistern could store water or wine or gasoline or any other liquid you cared to put in it. Regardless of what you put into the cistern, it would retain its shape and size and chemical composition. As a place, it is not affected by its content. So if you put water in at one time and oil at another, you still have the same cistern. The cistern may be said to have no content of its own but can hold any liquid you care to store in it.

A place for topical reasoning is like a cistern in that it also has no content of its own. It is able to accommodate some contents better than others; those it accommodates well conform to its unique dimensions. But the place is not changed by the material placed in it. For this reason it is able to give shape to a variety of materials without being consumed in the process. It can be used again and again. So a second feature of *topoi,* or places, is that they are *contentless* and therefore can be applied to any material we choose. For this reason, topoi are sometimes referred to as *commonplaces* because they are locations for ideas that are shared by or common to a great variety of subjects—in fact, without restriction to any subject whatsoever.

Finally, the place metaphor suggests a sense of discovery. We sometimes use the term *place* to refer to the spot where an object or a person belongs, as in "put it in its place" or "I feel out of place." Suppose we were to observe a young man in different places. We would see him with his parents, his friends, his teachers, his employer; at a sporting event, the opera, a symphony, a rock concert, the home of a wealthy patrician, the shanty of a beggar; and so on. In each of these places, we would discover different aspects of this fellow's personality, talents, self-awareness, insecurities—where he seemed to feel in place and out of place. Each of these place scenes would be *heuristic;* that is, it would generate some additional bit of information to characterize our subject. This is the third characteristic of topoi. By considering a subject in terms of a topos, we discover new things we might say. A topos has heuristic value because it helps us to discover what can be said about anything put in its place.

Topoi, then, are mental locations that we use to discover what may be said about anything whatsoever. They are contentless in that they have no proper subject that is their own. They can be applied to any subject we choose. They are analytic in that they help us to discover the numerous dimensions of a subject. Finally, they are heuristic in that they lead us to discover new things to say. Rhetorical invention consists in the act of finding the suasive sayables by thinking of a subject in terms of topoi. Having said that, let us try to make the concept more concrete by discussing the ways in which topical thinking is actually employed.

TOPICAL REASONING AND RELEVANT SPEECH

There is a big difference between thinking about a topic for your own understanding and thinking about that same topic in order to communicate relevant ideas to an audience. Thinking about something for your own purposes—say, the costs of a college education—can lead you to form an opinion that makes sense to you but not necessarily to anyone else. Just thinking about rising college costs does not require you to act, nor does it provide reasons for others to act. However, when you think about communicating these thoughts, new dimensions are added. For one thing, you probably think about communicating because you experience some tension that can be relieved by sharing your thoughts and feelings with others. That tension is in you, not in your environment. The impulse comes from within. For another, you probably think about communication when you have an expectation that communication can get results. It is a choice from among nonsymbolic responses, such as mechanical force, and other symbolic responses, such as oaths or screams. When you think about communication, you usually expect that someone out there is able to respond to your message in appropriate ways and, moreover, that their response is essential to relieving the tensions that impel you to communicate. Finally, thinking about communicating is other-directed thought, since the reasons in support of a proposition must satisfy your listeners or readers.

Thus thinking about communicating is not the same as thinking in general. It reflects a commitment to reaching someone, affecting that person in some way, and bringing about action through the mediation of symbols. Deciding what to say is the focus for this kind of thinking. Blurting out our first thoughts or initial feelings is not likely to be as effective as remarks specially chosen to fit the dynamics of the rhetorical situation. For this reason, Aristotle defined rhetoric as "the faculty of discovering the available means of persuasion in the given case." His emphasis was not on persuasion but on *discovering the means* of persuasion. When we search for sayables of this sort, we are thinking communicatively. This type of thinking is always about finding the alternatives best suited to the particular case, about what is most likely to influence our listeners.

Having said that rhetorical thinking was about the *means* with greatest promise in the given case, Aristotle went on to discuss how we discover these means. He developed this analysis in terms of the three types of speaking contexts that dominated public life in ancient Athens. First he considered the kinds of speeches given in the courts. These speeches, called *forensic* speeches, were concerned with justice or injustice, guilt or innocence. These were not speeches by lawyers, because ancient Athens did not have professional lawyers as we know them. If a man was in legal trouble, he had to defend himself. So Aristotle had in mind the kinds of nontechnical appeals average people would make on their own behalf. Speeches like this can be given in other places, but they are fashioned after the courtroom speeches of Aristotle's day. Whenever people accuse or defend actions in terms of justice or injustice, they make forensic appeals.

Next Aristotle considered the kinds of speeches given in the legislative assembly. These were called *deliberative* speeches, and they were concerned with expedience and inexpedience, advantage and injury. These were not speeches by elected representatives, because ancient Athens was a democracy where every citizen could participate in making law. If a man felt that something should be done, he had to advocate it himself. So Aristotle once more had in mind the kinds of nontechnical appeals average people would make to protect their interests. Speeches like these are not restricted to legislative chambers, but they follow the pattern of legislative speaking as Aristotle observed it. Whenever people exhort or dissuade others about the wisdom of some course of action, about its benefits or disadvantages, they make deliberative appeals.

Finally, Aristotle considered the kinds of speeches given on ceremonial occasions. These were called *epideictic* speeches, and they were concerned with praiseworthy or condemnable actions, virtue or vice. They were speeches given by leaders when some event made it important that the community acknowledge or disparage what was done. Leaders were sometimes the people who administered the city or who led the army. But they could also be the head of a family or a person whose wisdom had earned respect. Aristotle had in mind the kinds of nontechnical appeals that deal with the basic values we embrace in our families and communities and that form our bonds to one another. Speeches like these can be given in a variety of places and are very important for establishing and maintaining our sense of community. Whenever people praise or blame actions—of individuals or groups, of the moment or a lifetime—by acknowledging excellence and disparaging meanness, they make epideictic appeals.

Though Aristotle's three causes are limited to his experience and do not include the genres, or speaking categories, of commerce and religion or ends such as instructing or inquiring, what is important for our purposes is the way in which he was thinking about communication. Aristotle analyzed each of these genres because he believed that a successful orator had to have relevant propositions at his command. By organizing his discussion as he did, he implied that you had to know your subject matter in order to have relevant propositions and that these propositions could be organized in some manageable way. In other words, if a person knew about justice and injustice, he would have resources at the ready to make appropriate arguments on matters of law. By reviewing the things that could be said to prove the justness of an act, relevant ones to the given case could be selected and used to develop a defense against the accusations brought.

Aristotle's discussion of this matter in Book I of his *Rhetoric* is developed in terms of the places where one searches to find arguments. He developed two types of places. First there are general places, which applied to any subject matter and provided overall patterns of inclusive thought: Was something possible (or impossible)? Were there past facts that provided the guidance of precedence? Were there predictable future facts whose consequences could be judged desirable or undesirable? Could we estimate the degrees of more and less? These were the general topics Aristotle thought we should consider when thinking about communicating. But as broad and inclusive patterns, they do not provide specific propositions to have handy for given cases.

More specific propositions were derived from the special topics. These were peculiar to a subject; one had to master them to make knowledgeable claims that stood a chance of being taken seriously by an audience. For example, in discussing political matters, one would be expected to deliberate about ways and means, war and peace, constitutional forms, and the like. Today if one were talking about maritime issues, one would have to know about fish and fishing rights, trading lanes, industrial sites, pollution dangers, recreational uses, and so forth. No serious persuasion about our waterways and their uses could ignore such matters. These would be specific topics certain to be considered.

Aristotle's advice, in sum, was to think about communicating by reviewing the possible things that might be said. Examining general themes as well as special propositions would provide a multitude of options. By thinking in these terms, one could select the appropriate lines of reasoning with the greatest promise in the given case. This was a superior way to think about communicating than to imitate what others had said or to deliver adaptations of stock themes. It was creative thinking capable of investing experience with new meaning and of opening audiences to new possibilities for action.

Still, Aristotle's system remains unclear in its precise method of execution. Though interesting work on topoi has been done recently, it has not eliminated the unwieldy aspects of Aristotle's particular system. We can retain his notion for general topics and his notion that rhetoric becomes more precise and persuasive as we use the topics special to a given subject area. At the same time, we can search for a more precise and usable method of topical review suited to our needs today.

One such method has been developed by John Wilson and Carroll Arnold.[3] Basing their idea on Roget's *Thesaurus,* they have developed a 16-item review system that provides cues for recall applicable to all subjects. Their list is as follows.

[handwritten margin notes: → or h-d someone else notice / that / (Nelson P+R 1969) / D'Angelo 1984 p. 63]

A. Attributes commonly discussed
   1. *Existence* or nonexistence of things
   2. *Degree* or quantity of things, forces, etc.
   3. *Spatial* attributes, including adjacency, distribution, place
   4. Attributes of *time*
   5. *Motion* or activity
   6. *Form,* either physical or abstract
   7. *Substance:* physical, abstract, or psychophysical
   8. *Capacity to change,* including predictability
   9. *Potency:* power or energy, including capacity to further hinder anything
   10. *Desirability* in terms of rewards or punishments
   11. *Feasibility:* workability or practicability

B. Basic relationships commonly asserted or argued
    1. *Causality:* the relations of causes to effects, effects to causes, effects
       to effects, adequacy of causes, etc.
    2. *Correlation:* coexistence or coordination of things, forces, etc.
    3. *Genus-species* relationships
    4. *Similarity* or dissimilarity
    5. *Possibility* or impossibility[4]

This list of topics is not intended to function like the special topics; it is intended
to apply to all subjects. It is used by asking if anything useful can be said about
that topic. By proceeding through each, speakers and writers attempt to generate
a substantial list of possible lines of reasoning from which the most promising
ones may be selected. Here's how these topics might work. Suppose that we were
to give a speech urging a job placement center on campus.

> *Existence:* "We don't have a job placement center. Other schools have
> such centers. Seniors have a need for this service."
>
> *Degree:* "It is easier to find a job with the aid of a placement center.
> Schools that provide this service have a higher percentage of seniors
> who graduate with a job than schools without this service."
>
> *Spatial:* "The remoteness of our school from major employment cen-
> ters puts our students at a disadvantage in finding jobs."
>
> *Time:* "Many employers recruit new employees during the spring.
> Having a center on campus will minimize time taken from study for
> a job search."
>
> *Motion:* "It is important for us to be active in shaping employer
> perceptions of our graduates. They will be impressed when they dis-
> cover directly the forward-looking momentum of our curriculum."
>
> *Form:* "Such a center might be modeled after that at Nearby State."
>
> *Substance:* Nothing comes immediately to mind. Move on to the next
> topic.
>
> *Capacity to change:* "Several years ago, we changed our admission
> procedures to recruit new students. We can change our counseling
> procedures to place our graduates better."
>
> *Potency:* "Our school's potential to influence life in our state is ad-
> vanced or hindered by the occupations of its graduates."
>
> *Desirability:* "Better jobs means bigger alumni donations. Bringing
> recruiters on campus can provide valuable information about the fit
> between technical education here and needs out there."
>
> *Feasibility:* "We already possess a counseling service; no elaborate
> new administration is required. Overhead costs would be marginal,
> since staff needs are small and existing facilities can be used for
> interviews."
>
> *Causality:* "In specialized fields, firms seek prospects. Bringing them
> on campus will get them to think of our students as ones they should
> pursue."

Correlation: "Job placement success correlates with recruitment success."

Genus-species: "A placement center would be in keeping with last year's administrative reorganization, designed to improve student services. We have an active placement program to place students in graduate schools. We invite interviewers from medical schools on campus."

Similarity-dissimilarity: "A job placement center is not like an employment agency because the essential features of professional-client relationship and fee structure are absent."

Possibility-impossibility: "Though it is impossible to place everyone, it is possible to improve our placement record."

This list of sayables was composed in approximately 30 minutes. Obviously not everything listed is something that should be said or that could be said. Variables of occasion, audience, speaker, and goal will influence which of our generated items will be retained and which discarded. There is also the obvious need to buttress the items that are retained with evidence of fact and expert opinion to establish the reasonableness of each statement. Moreover, as you read through this list, other thoughts worth developing may have occurred to you. My initial review has not netted everything that might be said. Allowing for these factors, the point remains that by reflecting on the subject of job placement in terms of Wilson and Arnold's review topics, numerous specific lines of thought came readily to mind. These now may be developed further into the actual appeals suited to the demands of a specific rhetorical situation. In sum, these review topics help to uncover and recover information and to structure this information in patterns of thought that will be meaningful and effective for an audience.

SUMMARY

In this chapter we discussed the ways in which speakers and writers find ideas. Their search is for the thoughts and words that will give meaning to events and allow them to share these meanings with others. Our search for meaning is essentially an act of creativity, as much a necessary part of each of our lives as providing for our physical needs. Our creativity allows us to go beyond nature's brute commands to flee danger, to take what will satisfy our physical needs, and so forth. We can invest nature's events with symbolic significance that allows us to mold our human realities. As much as the painter and poet, each language user is necessarily a creative being.

Our capacity and our need to create have a special relevance for rhetorical communication. Since rhetoric arises in situations where alternatives exist, it becomes a means for defining realities and fostering choices. It accomplishes this through arguments that people believe and feel. Thus all rhetorical communicators need a method to help find effective arguments. In short, they need an art of invention. We have discussed this art as one of thinking communicatively through the use of topical reasoning.

In each of the three types of topical systems we have considered—general topics, specific topics, and review topics—the object has been to discover ways whereby we may invest messages with meaning in the minds of listeners and readers. The method of topical thinking is the cornerstone of communication thinking. It is the method for creating the materials from which appeals are fashioned. It involves us in the creative process of discovering what may be said to some end or goal. For this reason, the topical method is essential to rhetoric's function as a means to resolving problems. Ultimately, topical thinking becomes a reciprocal process between rhetor and audience, regardless of setting. It is not just what the rhetor makes but what the audience remakes that emerges as the meaning of a rhetorical transaction. It is not just what a rhetor-artist like Flip Wilson invents but what we do with what he invents—in our heads and hearts and acts—that is at the core of rhetorical arguments.

NOTES

1. John Leonard, "Funny, Funky, and, ah, Flip," *Life,* January 21, 1971, p. 12.
2. Rodney Douglas and Carroll C. Arnold, "On Analysis of *Logos:* A Methodological Inquiry," *Quarterly Journal of Speech,* 56 (February 1970), 22–32.
3. John F. Wilson and Carroll C. Arnold, *Public Speaking as a Liberal Art,* 5th ed. (Boston: Allyn & Bacon, 1983), pp. 83–88.
4. Ibid., p. 84.

chapter 6

Using Good Reasons to Persuade

A noted scholar of rhetoric, Karl Wallace, published an essay in the early 1960s in which he argued that rhetoric was an art of providing "good reasons."[1] By that he meant that rhetoric's business was to find and present the types of reasons that would move interested and reasonable people to accede to a point of view. They would be good reasons for holding or altering beliefs and actions.

The Wallace essay highlights a most important but frequently ignored point about rhetorical communication. Its substance consists in the reasoning we transact together with an audience in negotiating our way through a rhetorical event. When we seek a project extension, argue for a raise, interview for a job, justify our actions, advise a friend, speak out on issues of the day—or attend as an audience to any of these—we are involved in acts that require good reasons. Good reasons allow our audience and ourselves to find a shared basis for cooperating—a basis that is, presumably, intersubjectively valid. They permit us collectively to draw inferences that can withstand critical inspection as blind prejudice cannot. In speaking and writing, you can use marvelous language, tell great stories, provide exciting metaphors, speak in enthralling tones, and even use your reputation to advantage, but what it comes down to is that you must speak to your audience with reasons they understand. In the final analysis, a message is most influential when it provides its audience with good reasons to believe and to act. In rhetorical theory this is called *logos,* and logos will be the subject of this chapter.

ARTISTIC AND NONARTISTIC APPEALS — discussion of ethos

When Aristotle was teaching about rhetoric, he wanted his pupils to be clear on what was a part of rhetoric and what was not. Rhetoric was an inventive art for

71

him. It was best suited to finding the means that would move an audience. It was an art of finding and making arguments. Aristotle recognized that in matters of dispute, arguments are not the only means of resolution. Sometimes, for example, the evidence itself can be so compelling that rhetorical proofs are secondary. He called the proofs developed by rhetorical methods *artistic* and the proofs that were given by the situation and its facts *nonartistic.* Both were sources of persuasion, but rhetoric as an *art* was concerned only with developing artistic proofs.

For example, if you think you have received the wrong change at the drugstore, it is a simple matter for you to demonstrate that this is so. Add the change you received to the total bill. That should equal the money you originally gave the clerk. If it is less, you were shortchanged. A bit of simple arithmetic makes the point. If an accused thief pleads guilty, there is no need for rhetorical appeals to show there was motive, opportunity, ability, and the like. No proof must be invented. There is proof enough in the nonartistic admission. Whenever the facts "speak for themselves," we have sufficient grounds to make a decision without rhetoric. The facts do not require artistry when they are clear and compelling. Yet they can be persuasive nonetheless. Rhetoric is needed at times when and in cases where the facts don't speak for themselves. When they are ambiguous, conflicting, incomplete, inconclusive, and yet a decision or action is called for, we turn to rhetoric to create proofs that will allow us to form a judgment. These are artistic proofs, and their discovery and development are the proper concern of rhetoric.

Aristotle made an additional point that is also important for understanding what rhetorical proofs do and do not include. He recognized that in a given case there may be factors quite apart from the message presented that influence the audience. For the most part these are the constraints present in a rhetorical situation. They should be taken into account to the extent the rhetor can. But their relevance for judgments based on artistic arguments is limited to what is expressed and how it is expressed in the actual rhetorical performance. Rhetors sometimes overlook such constraints or fail to discover means to compensate for or exploit them. Thus they may enter as nonartistic influences on an audience's assessment. Be that as it may, Aristotle's point was that the *art* of rhetoric is focused on what *in the message itself,* quite apart from attending influences, brings listeners and readers to the point where they are ready to form a judgment.

Aristotle's point is valid today, even though contemporary thought might disagree that the facts speak entirely for themselves. There is no denying that in an age of science, factual data can be compelling. Even more so today, responsible rhetoric requires that the facts be known and be used as evidence to support our claims. But at the same time, we must remember that rhetoric does not invent the facts; it does invent arguments that interpret the facts to give them meaning. This inventing of arguments and their articulation in a rhetorical transaction is the proper subject of the art.

ENTHYMEMES AND EXAMPLES

Each of us regularly draws conclusions from observations. Sometimes we add up individual observations to reach a general conclusion; for example: I have observed Jeff, Barbara, Don, and Molly in the Engineering College. They are all skilled at using the computer. I conclude from this that experience with the computer is required of engineers. The observations and details about Jeff, Barbara, Don, and Molly are referred to as *data*. The process of putting them together to form a conclusion is called *inductive reasoning*.

At other times a general observation is applied to individual data to reach a particular conclusion; for instance: All the student athletes I've met have been competitive individuals. I was just speaking with my student, Galen, and found out that he's on the lacrosse team. From this I conclude that Galen is probably motivated by competition. The observation about student athletes is a *generalization*. The process of applying a generalization to data to form a particular conclusion about them is called *deduction*.

Induction and deduction are the basic patterns of reasoning followed in rhetorical arguments. Arguments that follow inductive patterns are called *examples;* those that follow deductive patterns are called *enthymemes*. These are technical terms that we need to consider in some detail, not only because they provide us with basic patterns that arguments take but also because they provide insight into the ways in which an artistic proof persuades.

Examples

Aristotle originally defined *examples* as "rhetorical inductions." We still use that definition today. They are the form inductive reasoning takes when we make nontechnical or popular arguments to persuade. Induction is a pattern of reasoning that goes from particular cases to a generalization. For instance, when scientists pose a research question—say, the effects of cigarette smoking on the lungs—they run the same test over and over to see if they get the same results. If they do, they form a generalization, such as "smoking cigarettes causes emphysema." We follow the same patterns in everyday life. You observe, for instance, that your roommate becomes irritable before taking an exam. The pattern repeats itself throughout the semester. As finals approach, you have an expectation of your roommate's behavior. On the basis of recurrent experiences of the same pattern, you abstract a general observation: Jones gets testy when studying for an exam.

In a strictly logical sense, such a pattern of reasoning requires controlled observation and extensive enumeration to yield a strong conclusion. Were the cases alike in all salient respects? Was the relationship observed an essential one? Were there sufficient cases to warrant any conclusion at all? Are there counter-cases in fact? Are countercases conceivable? In science such questions are common stock in trade for testing hypotheses and forming scientifically valid conclusions. But the requirements of scientific arguments are not the same as those of rhetorical arguments. The subject matter of rhetorical arguments does not permit the same control of variables or the same certainty for its conclusions as those of science. Rhetorical issues are not decided by general rules of knowledge but by specific decisions of conduct. The judges of rhetorical appeals are not technically trained in either subject matter or formal modes of reasoning. They are generally laypeople who have an interest in how an issue is resolved and a say in its resolution. These considerations were apparently as true in Aristotle's day as in our own and led him to define a rhetorical induction in a unique way.

Aristotle maintained that argument from example did not go from particular to general but from *particular to particular.* In other words, because the given case asks for a decision of a particular nature, the goals of rhetorical arguments are always particular. Examples provide parallel cases that permit an audience to see what they should do *now* based on what happened in similar circumstances in the past. For instance, we inquire of a friend whether now is the time to invest in a personal computer, since such machines are expensive. Our friend reminds us that when color televisions were first marketed their price was high, but after the novelty wore off their prices became more reasonable. Without expressing it, our friend told us that better prices are likely to be available later. We have been invited to draw an inference from a concrete case in the past to the concrete case under discussion.

There has been scholarly controversy over the nature of the inference involved in this type of reasoning.[2] Some have argued that it involves the logic of forming an unexpressed general rule (say, technological innovations tend to be more expensive when first marketed) and then the application of the rule to the particular case (PCs are newly marketed technological innovations; therefore, their price is higher now than it will be later). Others have argued that the reasoning is less like formal logic than a "psycho-logic"—an unmediated recognition of similarities without specifying the logical connections, sort of like mental shorthand (wait; a better price is sure to follow). Regardless of how one interprets the mental connections involved, the important observation here is that only particulars are presented when constructing an argument from example. It does not ask the audience to follow a train of formal reasoning but to reason *from* something *known* in its particularity *to* something *novel* in its particularity, from what happened in the past to what we should expect now or in the future.

Having said that the rhetorical form of induction asks an audience to reason from case to similar case, certain assumptions and implications should be noted.

1. Asking an audience to reason from something familiar to something unknown makes it an active partner in constructing the argument. The audience must understand the example, must recognize its connection to the exemplified, must infer what follows in the given case. Matters are not laid out in the meticulous fashion of a thorough scientific demonstration but in the shorthand of joined minds that share something in common but don't bother to express it: common experiences and interpretations of their meaning.

2. We should avoid presenting too many examples; otherwise, our proof will begin to resemble a formal technical argument and become difficult for laypeople to follow.

3. Examples are best suited to making inferences about the future, such as we do when deciding questions of policy, because they help us to frame expectations of the likely impact of our decisions on the basis of past experiences of a similar sort. They are less useful in settling questions of the past such as occur in judicial proceedings.

4. Examples are best suited to audiences that have not yet formed general rules from which to reason, such as youths and novices. These audiences are much more likely to understand in terms of particular cases that fall within their frames of experience.

5. Examples do not permit the maximum amount of control over how an audience reasons. Examples can be interpreted in a number of ways, resulting in confusion or a missed point or even seeming to prove something unintended. Because they are not the most efficient mode of argument, they are to be used with caution.

6. For this reason, the preferred use of example is not as the main argument but as an illustration for an argument. Placing a well-chosen example at the end of an appeal helps secure concretely the rhetor's reasoning in the audience's mind. The preferred mode of argument, then, is not inductive but deductive, the enthymeme.

Enthymemes

Aristotle maintained that the enthymeme was the very heart and soul of rhetoric. Today we still share his opinion; contemporary rhetoric also sees the argument as the essential ingredient for responsible discourse. However, enthymeme refers to something more specific than arguments at large. It is the form the argument takes—the mode of appeal through which audiences are persuaded and the mastery of which is essential to practicing rhetoric as an art.

Aristotle defined *enthymeme* as "a rhetorical syllogism." His meaning, however, has been somewhat obscured by his use of the same term in logic. In logic, an enthymeme is a truncated syllogism, one with either a premise or a conclusion left unexpressed; for example:

Students of rhetoric are interested in persuasion.
I am a student of rhetoric.
Therefore, I am interested in persuasion.

This is a complete syllogism. Expressed enthymematically, it may take one of these forms:

Students of rhetoric are interested in persuasion.
Therefore, I am interested in persuasion.

I am a student of rhetoric.
Therefore, I am interested in persuasion.

Students of rhetoric are interested in persuasion.
I am a student of rhetoric.

In each case, one statement has been suppressed. It is understood so well that it is unnecessary to express it for us to judge the validity of the argument. In logic, the essential feature emphasized is that enthymemes have suppressed premises.

While many times premises are suppressed in rhetorical syllogisms, Aristotle's discussion of arguments suggests that this is not necessarily so in all arguments, nor is it an enthymeme's essential feature. When a speaker says, "As a student of rhetoric, I am interested in persuasion," the essential feature of this statement is the way it involves the audience. It is included in the active process of building a proof from what it already knows and believes or from what it can recognize with ease.

The essential first feature of an enthymeme is usually some point of common ground between rhetor and audience. It may be a belief (communism is a threat), a value (we should be generous to those less fortunate than ourselves), or a goal (I strive to be happy). Because it is *common* ground, it need not be expressed. If the argument is properly constructed, the audience will provide the premises to which it subscribes without their being mentioned.

The essential second feature of an enthymeme is a premise that links the common ground of rhetor and audience to a conclusion. This premise is particular and targeted at the belief (the revolutionaries in Latin America are communists), value (millions of Ethiopians live with the constant pain of hunger; malnutrition is rampant), or goal (controlling nuclear weapons will provide a secure future for our children) we wish to elicit.

The essential third feature is that by making this linkage between the expressed and the unexpressed, the audience becomes actively involved with the rhetor in constructing the argument. They provide premises, they help build the appeal, they cocreate arguments to themselves. In this way, the enthymeme works as a self-persuasive appeal.[3] Because audiences are participating in the construction of the argument, they are actually providing their own good reasons for believing and acting. This is why enthymemes are such strong persuasive devices.

ENTHYMEMES AND GOOD REASONS

The three essential features of the enthymeme just cited make this apparent: It is important to know what the audience believes about the possible ways of expressing (i.e., arguing for) your ideas so that you know which enthymemes will be most effective. This means that you have to analyze your audience to know in advance the types of premises they are likely to provide. Otherwise, contentions are at risk of misfiring, leading to misunderstanding or refutation or flat rejection of the message. For this reason, as we saw in Chapter 5, knowledge of material premises is a great help because these provide specific sayables that are unique to a subject area. People interested in the subject are likely to recognize the relationship of these premises to beliefs and values left implicit in a message. Similarly, review topics provide an index to what might be said or avoided in terms of its promise for involving audiences in the active process of remaking proofs along desired lines.

We may illustrate how this works by examining the type of reasoning found in American advertising. Typically, such messages attempt to link a product with attributes we value. It is good because it makes us *socially acceptable* or because it has *scientifically advanced* features. Such reasoning relies on our acceptance of such values, eliciting them to complete the appeal as a good reason for buying their product.

Several years ago, two researchers conducted simultaneous but independent studies of American value premises. They came to surprisingly similar conclusions and reported their findings in a joint publication.[4] Their findings still provide a handy basic index of common values to which Americans subscribe and to which advertisers may appeal. Here is a summary of basic American values they uncovered:

1. The Value of the Individual
2. Achievement and Success
3. Change and Progress — *do we always value change?*
4. Ethical Equality
5. Equality of Opportunity
6. Effort and Optimism
7. Efficiency, Practicality, and Pragmatism
8. Rejection of Authority
9. Science and Secular Rationality
10. Sociality
11. Material Comfort
12. Quantification
13. External Conformity
14. Humor
15. Generosity and "Considerateness"
16. Patriotism[5]

topoi

special topics

Were we to examine public messages—commercial, political, legal, or of other genres—such values would likely be used quite frequently as unexpressed but necessarily understood and supplied premises to complete arguments. Several such values are enjoined in patterns of argument that conform to the lines of reasoning suggested by the review topics discussed in Chapter 5 in the following advertisement, which appeared in the *New York Times Magazine* of May 27, 1984:

missou point

do you talk to young people through their "channel"/ medium ??

Some
Surprising Advice
to Young People
from R. J. Reynolds
Tobacco

Don't smoke. [1]
For one thing, smoking has always been an adult custom. And even for adults, smoking has become very controversial. [2]
So even though we're a tobacco company, we don't think it's a good idea for young people to smoke. [3]
Now, we know that giving this kind of advice to young people can sometimes backfire. [4]

But if you take up smoking just to prove you're an adult, you're really proving just the opposite. [5]

Because deciding to smoke or not to smoke is something you should do when you don't have anything to prove. [6]

Think it over. [7]

After all, you may not be old enough to smoke. But you're old enough to think. [8]

R. J. Reynolds Tobacco Company

There are eight statements in the ad. Statements 1 and 7 stand as imperatives. The remaining six statements offer reasoning in support of the imperatives. As you read through the ad, the reasoning is extremely truncated. Yet this is typical for advertisements and illustrates in microcosm how enthymemes persuade.

The ostensible audience for this ad is young people. By virtue of its placement in the *New York Times Magazine,* it is sure to be read by a substantial adult audience. Some will be smokers, and to them the copy may serve as reinforcement of their habit. Some will be nonsmokers, and they may find R. J. Reynolds acting responsibly by cautioning young people not to smoke. If nothing else, it may gain them a few PR points with this segment. Still others may read the ad and think it is a slick attempt at reverse psychology. Regardless, we can see that an ad targeted explicitly for one audience reaches several and will have impacts on those audiences because it cannot help but engage values and beliefs that produce closure in conclusions about the message and the maker.

But what of its intended audience? Consider the reasons offered, the unexpressed values they enjoin, and the topic of thinking that advances this reasoning.

Statement 2 reasons from *correlation* between smoking and age. It implies the *value of the individual,* since it claims smoking is not for everyone. It also appeals to *secular rationality,* because if there is controversy, there must be reasons to support competing views.

Statement 3 uses the topos of *desirability:* namely, smoking is not desirable for young people. It implies that the R. J. Reynolds people are "considerate" and, therefore, virtuous.

Statement 4 uses the topos of *causality:* Saying one thing can cause an opposite reaction. Here the value is *rejection of authority.* Rejecting authority could be a way to demonstrate individuality, but . . .

Statement 5 heads off this inference by arguing from *correlation* between independence of thought and not proving something. Here the value enjoined is *external conformity,* and the tension created suggests that *individuality* is more valuable.

Statement 6 uses the topos of *capacity to change:* Make this decision when the time is right. Again the implied value is *individuality.*

Statement 8 uses the topos of *potency:* You have the ability to think. And again the argument relies on the value of *individuality.*

In an overall pattern of argument, this ad implies that it is more important to be an individual than to conform. Individuals make their own choices when the time is right. These implied premises are necessary for a young person to read, without sensing condescension, the explicit claim that the right time to decide about smoking is when you're an adult.

This ad also illustrates in capsule form the variety of reasonings and invitations to complete thought patterns that are typical of enthymematic arguments. Well-adapted arguments involve audiences in argument construction without their conscious reflection on their participatory role. They involve audience members in overall patterns of response that are typical for their group or culture. They provide lines of thinking and valuing that are honored as good reasons to accede to an appeal. Most important, as we have stressed throughout, the enthymematic structure gains accedence through involving an audience in the actual construction of the argument. The audience actually helps to persuade itself.

Consider the kind of situation in which this enthymematic approach might make sense

GOOD REASONS AND ISSUES

Messages can have several persuasive dimensions. To some extent we are usually influenced by our perceptions of the speaker or writer (for instance, our admiration for Meryl Streep's acting ability leads us to accept her views on the quality of contemporary films). At another level our emotional involvement in the topic may sway our judgment (our love for children leads us to fear the spread of communism as a threat to their freedom). Finally, we may find ourselves principally influenced by the reasoning of the arguments themselves (the data and reasoning presented lead us to conclude that downtown stores have lost trade due to congested traffic conditions). The argument of the speech itself, considered quite apart from the emotional involvement of the listeners and their opinion of the orator, is our concern here. In rhetorical theory, this dimension is referred to as *logos*.

The Greek term *logos* has a variety of meanings and is not easily rendered into English. Sometimes its reference to a mode of rhetorical appeal has been translated as "logical proof." But as our discussion of example and enthymeme has indicated, the proofs of rhetoric are hardly "logical" in any rigorous sense. Formal validity is violated all the time in rhetorical appeals, though that does not diminish their persuasive or rational power. Rather than strictly logical appeals, the example and enthymeme are more like a "psycho-logic" because they involve audience interests, values, and readinesses to respond. These biases and commitments are important elements in rhetorical reasoning. The term *proof* also is a misleading rendition. The appeals of popular essays and public addresses certainly are not proofs in the same sense as scientific demonstrations. They are better thought of as *arguments* that urge assent but hardly compel it. Indeed, the *art* of rhetoric resides in the acquired skill of making arguments that show the likelihood of a claim on the basis of what listeners and readers take to be *reasonable,* even if not formally valid, grounds. So, for example, when world leaders threaten to retaliate against terrorist groups, they might have a difficult time proving that taking terrorist lives is logically necessary. At the same time, this extreme course may well be perceived as reasonable within their society's scheme of values. After all, the objective of rhetorical arguments, the logos of the speech

standard

itself, is to reason with the audience to a common basis for assent. In short, through developing good reasons, the rhetor builds a persuasive case.

Detecting a Case

While individual arguments in a message may be more or less reasonable, we need to bear in mind that audiences tend to respond to messages in terms of broad and inclusive patterns of reasoning found in the discourse. For instance, the mayor may offer six reasons why we need a center-city parking ramp. Individually, these reasons may be unimpressive. However, if they complement one another to develop the overall message that a vital downtown benefits everyone, the mayor may have a winning appeal. Taken together, her arguments provide a most persuasive case for this project. The logos of the mayor's speech resides in the cumulative argument of her entire presentation. In rhetoric, the entire argumentation in a presentation is referred to as a *case.* A case consists of the overall management of evidence and reasoning to support a proposition.

The reasoning of the case is toward some end or purpose—the removal of certain tensions of novelty, ambiguity, or conflict that mark a situation as rhetorical. Such reasoning requires carefully chosen remarks, ones suited to the given circumstances or, in Bitzer's terms, a fitting response. How do we select from among all the remarks that we *might* make those that are *most* fitting? To answer that we must determine the issues to be addressed in order to resolve the rhetorical situation.

In an earlier chapter we discussed the concept of an exigence as the central feature of every rhetorical situation. An exigence was defined as an imperfection marked by urgency. Quite obviously, imperfections may be of varying sorts, each requiring different types of responses. We now need to consider the way in which rhetors diagnose these exigences in order to develop appropriate arguments. This method of analysis is called the method of *stasis.*

Determining Issues

Stasis is a Greek term. It refers to a point of suspended animation. It was originally used in Greek physics to refer to the point at which two lines of force would collide and ricochet in a new direction. As Figure 6.1 indicates, line of force A collides with line of force B at point C. The force and angle of their collision deflect them in new directions, A¹ and B¹. Point C represents the point of *stasis:* It is both a *stopping point* for lines of force A and B and a *starting point* for lines of force A¹ and B¹. This concept of simultaneous stopping and starting was borrowed by ancient rhetoricians to describe what happens in the development of rhetorical issues. It remains descriptive of how issues are located and how we must persuade if we are to resolve them.

Imagine a contention as if it were a line of force (say, computer literacy should be required of all college graduates). The line of force would continue to infinity if it encountered no obstacle (since no one disagrees, it shall be a degree requirement). Now imagine a contrary contention as a line of force moving in the

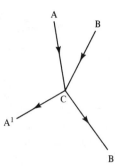

Figure 6.1

opposite direction (computer literacy should not be a degree requirement). When the two collide, their initial motion is stopped, and *stasis* is reached. But there is renewed motion as arguments in support of one view and against the other are developed and presented. Thus, as Figure 6.2 indicates, contrary motions clash to produce stasis. Stasis in turn produces an issue. An issue consists of the clash of ideas that differ about the same thing (whether computer literacy should be a degree requirement). From this clash arises a question that must be decided.

Let's take another example: "A limited nuclear war can be won" versus "A limited nuclear war cannot be won." Here the competing claims bump into each other. Both can't be correct, and a decision is required because our foreign and military posture will be vastly different depending on which view prevails. Hence there is an issue because we have differing ideas about the same thing, and this clash gives rise to a question we must answer as judges: "Can a limited nuclear war be won?"

In terms of our concerns with logos, the presence of a question serves the useful function of focusing our understanding of the rhetorical situation and options for a fitting response. Only remarks that address the issue are fitting. For example, the possibility that Third World nations with unstable leadership might acquire nuclear weapons is frightening. But it is not relevant to this particular issue because it doesn't address the question we must answer.

We determine what will answer our question by examining the essential grounds proposed to support each assertion. As we have reasons offered to support both points of view, an "answer pro" and an "answer con," the question is narrowed to specific points to be decided, as Figure 6.3 illustrates. For example, "A limited nuclear war may be won because we can destroy most of their missiles before they strike and thereby limit the devastation to an acceptable level." "A limited nuclear war cannot be won because their missiles are MIRVed, so there are too many warheads going in too many directions for us to reduce the devastation to an acceptable limit." In making the answer and response, a series of points

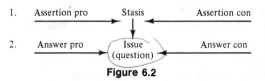

Figure 6.2

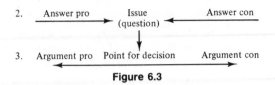

Figure 6.3

become apparent as matters for us to address and resolve in reaching a decision. What are our antistrike capacities? Can we intercept the Soviet missiles before they deploy their multiple warheads? And what, in a nuclear holocaust, is an "acceptable" level of devastation? Whatever the arguments developed in the deliberation of this matter—whether in discussion, partisan oratory, editorial opinion, government position paper, or formal debate—they must address these concerns because given the way the question or issue has evolved, these are the points we must resolve before we can make a decision.

Before leaving this point, one more observation is in order. The point for decision is a product of the specific type of accusation and defense presented. One can imagine, for example, the antinuclear proponent arguing simply, "Even if a massive first strike is contained, no life will survive." This would have shifted the discussion to the nature of a nuclear explosion and its effects on life proximate and distant in the short and long run. Rhetors have choices in how issues evolve, and are guided by their understanding of what evidence and reasoning can be developed persuasively in the given case. Once the point for decision has been determined, rhetors build persuasive appeals designed to sway the judges in their direction. Thus the arrows in line 3 of Figure 6.3 lead away from the point for decision, indicating that the rhetoric is clearly partisan, pro or con, in the attempt to secure a favorable hearing from the listeners or readers.

Classifying Issues

So far we have noted that the exigence of a rhetorical situation can be analyzed with some precision by thinking of it as an issue that arises from competing, clashing viewpoints. These clashing viewpoints create a stasis that must be resolved through effective rhetoric to resolve the situation. The rhetorical participants responding to each other make fitting responses as they address the issue in terms of the question it poses and the points for decision in resolving the question. Having noted this, we can take the model of stasis, or issue analysis, a step further.

In the Roman rhetorics, a great deal of discussion centered on legal oratory because success in legal pleading was an avenue to public notice and an opportunity for entering a political career. But the schema they developed is usable elsewhere, with modification.

The Romans discovered four types of issues, each different from though related to the others and each calling for different types of arguments:

1. *Conjectural issue:* an issue of *fact* (What happened?)
2. *Definitional issue:* an issue of definition or *naming* the fact (What shall we call it?)

3. *Qualitative issue:* an issue of causes and mitigating circumstances (What is the nature of the act?)
4. *Translative issue:* an issue of procedure (Are any rights or procedures violated?)

As a law case develops, it is first necessary to determine what happened—an issue of fact; then what law applies (what shall we call it?)—an issue of definition; then the causes and mitigating circumstances—an issue of quality. These proceed in order, requiring that we argue from fact to definition to quality. The translative issue can be raised at any point, however. For example, at the beginning of the trial, the attorney for the defendant makes a motion to dismiss because the court lacks jurisdiction or a motion for a change of venue because local publicity makes a fair trial unlikely. As the trial proceeds, motions and objections are raised concerning testimony believed to violate legal rules of evidence, and so on. In other words, matters of proper procedure can arise at any time.

The original purpose of this analysis was to locate the precise issue before the court so that pertinent arguments might be invented. We still find it useful for preparing arguments. For example, if the issue is whether something did occur, we require evidence of observation, corroborating testimony, relevant artifacts, and the like. Was a person killed? We have the dead body, we have photos and testimony that it is Jones and that Jones is dead. We have a coroner's report that says Jones died of a bullet wound to the heart. We have the chemist's report that says the powder burns on Jones's clothing indicate a shot fired at close range. We have the ballistics report that says the bullet was fired from a service revolver. These are bits and pieces of evidence that help us resolve a question of fact—Was Jones killed? After all, Jones could be missing and not dead at all, or Jones could be dead but of natural causes. Before the trial may proceed, this issue of fact must first be determined. It will hardly do to argue that Jones was an eccentric or a drug pusher or a regular churchgoer because these matters, even if true, are irrelevant.

Having determined that Jones was killed, the next question is, What shall we call it? Is it murder? Here we have several possibilities. It could be a self-inflicted wound—either an accident or suicide—but the reports of the coroner and the chemist indicate that the distance from which the shot was fired and the angle of entry make it impossible for the wound to have been self-inflicted. Was it murder or self-defense? Arguments are directed to identifying the culprit, placing the gun in his possession, locating him at the scene, proving that he did the deed—all questions of fact. It must be proved that this person had motive and opportunity and was not himself endangered, thereby eliminating the possibility of self-defense and allowing us to call it murder. Finally, the quality of the act may be at issue. The attorney argued that the accused's wife was seriously ill and his children without food, that he was out of work and needed money to care for his family. He was driven to the desperate act of robbery and panicked when his victim resisted. The court should be lenient because he never committed a crime before and because these mitigating family circumstances drove him to a tragic act. Again, relevant arguments here have to do with the quality of what was done. Appeals are fitting insofar as they are relevant to assessing this matter. By knowing the issue, the attorney can be more precise in the inventional process, selecting from among all those things that might be said lines of argument that have the most promise for resolving the points for decision in the audience's mind.

The issue of fact, definition, quality, and procedure are broader in their application than to legal pleadings. Questions of these sorts arise as major issues and subissues whenever there are exigences to be resolved. For example, several years after the near meltdown at the Three Mile Island nuclear generating plant outside Harrisburg, Pennsylvania, controversy remains about whether the environment and the people in the area are in jeopardy. There are questions of fact, such as, "Is Metropolitan Edison, the facility operator, discharging nuclear waste into the Susquehanna River?" If this has happened, questions of definition arise as we inquire into what kind of thing or event this is: "If it is granted that Met Ed is discharging nuclear waste into the Susquehanna River, is this practice regulated by law? Is it considered dangerous? Is the waste considered a noncontaminant if below a certain level?" and so on. Finally, if it exists and has been defined, how are the power company's acts to be judged? "If Met Ed is discharging nuclear waste into the Susquehanna and if this practice is regulated by law or is considered dangerous, are the materials present in legal amounts? Within desirable limits? Avoidable amounts?"

At the same time as we raise these concerns, the spokespersons for Metropolitan Edison will conduct their own persuasive campaign to reassure the public that there is no danger. In all probability, their campaign will attempt to redefine the issue as one of continuing good service and of "no harm, no foul" (i.e., the fact is that we have no documented injury or illness attributable to the "incident"; thus we may diminish the significance of issues surrounding possible contamination of the Susquehanna).

We saw an attempt to control the issues earlier in this chapter when we examined the R. J. Reynolds ad. Notice that the advertiser cast the issue of smoking as one of quality: adult custom, adult choice. The company does not counsel youths not to smoke by raising the issue of fact—namely, that smoking is hazardous to their health. Raising this issue would perform a great public service, but it probably would have adverse effects on the Reynolds company's profits.

One might project the system one final step further, noting that in areas like this where policy is at stake, there are standard or stock issues that must be resolved. These are commonly listed as questions of *ill* (what is the problem?), *blame* (what is the cause?), *remedy* (what can be done?), and *cost* (what resources must be expended?). Typically persuasive appeals develop differently, depending on where we are in policy determinations. Questions of ill require that we discuss the harm involved, the significance of the harm, whether it is persistent or passing, whether it is inherent or accidental. Only after we have resolved that there is harm can we consider blame. This requires examination of the causes, whether they are somehow inherent in present policies and structures, and whether they can be reformed. We must resolve matters of this sort before we can persuasively and responsibly propose remedies. In advocating remedies, we examine whether they will be effective in removing the ill, whether they are technically feasible so that we may implement them, whether they are desirable because they remedy the ill without causing worse problems, whether one solution is preferable to the alternatives, and whether the solution is enforceable and compliance can be ensured. Finally, having selected a remedy, we ask about costs—financial, psychological, moral, and so forth—to determine whether the benefits derived are worth the price we must pay.

By analyzing exigences in this way, thinking about communicating and developing arguments fitting the rhetorical situation can take on a calculated precision. If we know what we are to discuss—what is at issue and therefore what must be decided by our readers and listeners—it is much easier to craft a persuasive message than by proceeding in random fashion or by speaking and writing remarks we would like to make rather than those that need to be expressed if listeners and readers are to find good reasons for believing and acting in the given case.

STASIS IN EVERYDAY LIFE

Our discussion of rhetorical methods and logos have focused on the applicability of thinking about communicating and developing good reasons for resolving public issues. Although the theory of rhetoric was developed to deal with the needs of public communicators, it would be a mistake to limit our rhetorical modes of thinking to the public arena. By way of concluding this chapter, I wish to consider with you one way in which the matters of topoi, logos, and stasis relate to our everyday communication needs. I wish to focus on the times when we are asked by parents, teachers, friends, and lovers to *account* for our behavior. To make the connection between *accounts* and the matters related to good reasons clear, however, we will have to back up a bit to gain a perspective.

In the 1950s, two sociologists, Sykes and Matza,[6] conducted a study of juvenile delinquents. They were interested in how juvenile delinquents saw themselves in relation to social norms. The prevailing theory at that time held that delinquents rejected society and its norms. Their deviant behavior was a sign of this. Sykes and Matza approached this question with a uniquely rhetorical assumption: that people use language to coordinate diverse actions, that motives are not private states but are present in the typical ways that we talk.[7] Working on this assumption, they found evidence that juvenile delinquents were at least partially committed to the same values as everyone else. For one thing, juvenile delinquents frequently exhibited shame or guilt when they violated society's prescriptions. For another, juvenile delinquents gave approval to certain conforming persons, such as law-abiding persons who were "really honest" or selected authority figures like a pious, humble mother or a forgiving priest. Furthermore, juvenile delinquents distinguished between appropriate and inappropriate targets for their deviance. Not everyone was a potential victim.

These signs led Sykes and Matza to hypothesize that delinquents really did subscribe to the prevailing social order and that they had adopted verbal techniques for neutralizing their deviance by supplying verbal justifications for their acts. In short, they could have it both ways: They could hold the same values as the dominant order and rationalize away any apparent violations of that order in deviant acts.

Sykes and Matza uncovered five such verbal techniques:

1. Denial of responsibility—"outside forces caused my behavior" (e.g., social environment).
2. Denial of injury—"the harm is less than alleged."
3. Denial of the victim—"he had it coming, it was rightful retaliation."
4. Condemnation of the condemners—"what hypocrites, the things they do are worse than anything I do; focus on them, not me."
5. Appeal to higher loyalties—"other norms, more pressing and involving a higher loyalty, take precedence" (e.g., sibling pair, gang, or friendship clique has higher demand than the larger society).[8]

These communicative behaviors of juvenile delinquents, while extreme, are suggestive of how normal people behave when their acts are questioned as violating expectations. Juvenile delinquents aren't alone in explaining themselves. This realization prompted another pair of researchers, Scott and Lyman,[9] to develop a theory of *accounts* to cover these explanatory acts.

An account is "a linguistic device employed whenever an action is subjected to valuative inquiry."[10] Scott and Lyman explain it as a statement made by a social actor to explain unanticipated or untoward behavior.

Accounts are called for, in other words, when behaviors somehow disrupt our expectations of amicable relations. When interpersonal communication functions smoothly, this is a sign that we and our interacting partner have a *background consensus* of shared expectations. This background consensus is important to defining relationships. It represents our mutual understandings and expectations of shared commitments. And it allows us to project behaviors that are permissible within the relationship. Because it is a background consensus, we feel no need to discuss it; we implicitly trust that the other party will behave in ways appropriate to the relationship. However, when the background consensus is *violated* by some untoward or unanticipated act, we are offended and may ask the offending party for an account. In other words, the violation of our background consensus and the call for an account create an issue. For the issue to be resolved—for the rupture in our relationship to be repaired—it is imperative that an account be given. If our partner refuses to give an account of herself, she says, in effect, that she sees the relationship differently than we do, that there is no background consensus on this relationship. Equally crucial, we must *honor* the offered account if the relationship is to continue unimpaired. If we do not honor the account, the background consensus remains disrupted.

The idea of accounts, then, captures the way in which the rhetorical theory of stasis applies to interpersonal communication when relationships experience trouble. For friends and lovers, as much as for lawyers and politicians, disagreements arise, issues are formed, and the people involved must make intelligent rhetorical choices if their speech is to resolve their difficulties.

In the theory of stasis, issues are classified into types. So it is with accounts.

Scott and Lyman classify accounts into two types: justifications and excuses. *Justifications* are accounts in which a person accepts responsibility for the act in question but denies the negative quality associated with it. In essence, we justify ourselves when we argue that our act is really acceptable if viewed in the proper light. Interestingly, Scott and Lyman find that the justifications offered in everyday life match up with the justifications Sykes and Matza found juvenile delinquents using. Thus the forms of justifications include:

1. Denial of injury (No harm was done)
2. Denial of the victim (That person had it coming)
3. Condemnation of the condemners (They do worse; don't focus on me, focus on them)
4. Appeal to loyalties (The act is OK because it serves those to whom I am loyal)
5. Sad tales (My sad past justifies my present behavior)
6. Self-fulfillment (I gotta be me!)

Excuses are accounts in which the person admits that the act in question is bad, wrong, or inappropriate but denies full responsibility. Like justifications, excuses take a variety of forms:

1. Appeal to accidents (Forces beyond my control brought this about; it wasn't intended)
2. Appeal to defeasibility, involving some mental element (I didn't know . . . ; I was forced against my will)
3. Appeal to biological drives (Boys will be boys; men are like that)
4. Scapegoating (My behavior was really in response to the attitude or behavior of another—it's that person's fault)[11]

Notice how the types of justifications and excuses found by these researchers function as lines of argument or special topics for developing the enthymemes necessary for giving accounts. Although the theory of topics and enthymeme was developed to account for the rhetoric of public communication, the accounts notion shows how it is equally operative in our private communication within relationships.

The topoi of public address are only as valuable as their effectiveness in reaching an audience. The audience judges whether good reasons have been offered. So it is with accounts. Once an account—a justification or an excuse— is offered, the offended party must honor the account. Scott and Lyman found two basic reasons why some accounts are not honored. First, if the offended party thinks the account is illegitimate, it is rejected. For example, the gravity of the event (say, standing up your date) might exceed the type of account provided ("I was helping my roommate with calculus"), or the motives offered as reasons aren't acceptable ("I would have felt guilty if I didn't help him, he's so poor in that subject"). Second, accounts are rejected if they are perceived as unreasonable. This happens when the stated grounds for the offense cannot be "normalized" in terms of what everybody knows ("Why did you give me the bum's rush on the phone last night?" "Someone was in my room." "So why didn't you say so?" "I didn't think it would be polite."); that is, normal people don't act for the reason given, and everybody knows it.

The analysis of Scott and Lyman can be extended further into the realm of argument tactics to win the issue. Researcher Jackson Toby,[12] working before the essay on accounts appeared, was interested in the same problem: how people restored disrupted social stability. His analysis is complementary to the one we have been considering. Toby focused on how we follow acceptable language behaviors or rules to resolve role conflicts. Role conflicts may extend beyond the interpersonal level to group or even organizational relations. The finding is the same. When conflicts arise, there are set ways in which the issues are treated— topoi for offering accounts. Moreover, implicit in Toby's report of language rules are argument tactics social actors employ to resolve instability. The list of appeals he found, some of which overlap with Scott and Lyman's list, tends to suggest the tactics used to control the issue's development and resolution. Here is Toby's list of things to which we appeal to resolve role conflicts:

1. Hierarchies of role obligations—I had conflicting role obligations and had to place one over the other. Please understand.
2. Appeal to accident—This is regrettable, but matters were beyond my control! There was nothing I could do.
3. Etiquette—Excuse me!
4. Tact—Legitimate deception such as a white lie. I cannot go to the movie with you; I have a previous commitment.
5. Segregation of roles—My role as father is segregated from my role as teacher. If my daughter receives a poor grade she has no complaint against me as her father.[13]

In the foregoing research, the concerns have been with the ways in which people manage their talk under fire in interpersonal situations. The findings of what people do in these interpersonal situations correlates with the general theory of rhetorical invention and logos. We can see the correlations in four areas.

First, when accounts are called for, they require knowledge of and appeal to shared expectations. An account provides a good reason only if it stems from our background consensus on how we should treat each other and reestablishes the disrupted consensus that has jeopardized a relationship. Accounts are basically enthymematic in their structure, therefore, because they argue from shared premises.

Second, the language rules followed in accounting for our role violations are reflective of common behavior patterns our culture uses to avoid interpersonal glitches. They are, in effect, topoi that provide lines of reasoning for repairing sundered or questioned relationships.

Third, justifications and excuses are good reasons offered to resolve an issue in a listener's mind. That a person has been called to account for an untoward behavior indicates that there is an issue in the offended party's mind and that appropriate reasons are required to resolve this issue. Justifications and excuses thus appeal to matters of fact, definition, quality, and even procedure to resolve interpersonal points of stasis.

Finally, when we offer an account, we cannot help but accept the commitments of rhetorical action. To offer an account we must assume a role, with the assets and liabilities it implies. In account giving, as in all rhetoric, we are not just uttering words. We are creating a possible world and inviting others to share in it with us.

SUMMARY

From ancient times to the present, rhetoric has been severely criticized as empty talk or exaggeration or mere bombast. Doubtless history has witnessed its fair share of such performances. As Aristotle noted in the *Rhetoric,* there is no way to prevent foolish, thoughtless, or wicked people from speaking in these ways. But such practices are not genuinely artful practices of rhetoric because they lack the one essential—a substantive argument. In this chapter we have been concerned with how such appeals are formed in responsible rhetoric. We have argued that at the heart of such a rhetoric are good reasons that can give confidence in the rational integrity of what is advocated. Reasons are good insofar as they can withstand critical inspection; insofar as they take the traditions, beliefs, and commitments of the listeners and readers seriously; insofar as they are pertinent to the issues and responsive to other points of view. These attributes of good reasons hold regardless of setting, audience size, or topic of deliberation. They are the essential requirement for trustworthy discourse. Moreover, as we will see in the next two chapters, these are the bases for responsibly invoking character and engaging emotions as means of persuasion.

NOTES

1. Karl Wallace, "The Substance of Rhetoric: Good Reasons," *Quarterly Journal of Speech,* 49 (October 1963), 239–249.
2. See Gerard A. Hauser, "The Example in Aristotle's *Rhetoric:* Bifurcation or Contradiction?" *Philosophy and Rhetoric,* 1 (Spring 1968), 78–90; Scott Consigny, "The Rhetorical Example," *Southern Speech Communication Journal,* 41 (Spring 1976), 121–132; and William Lyon Benoit, "Aristotle's Example: The Rhetorical Induction," *Quarterly Journal of Speech,* 66 (April 1980), 182–192.
3. This feature was first noted in Lloyd Bitzer, "Aristotle's Enthymeme Revisited," *Quarterly Journal of Speech,* 45 (December 1959), 399–408.
4. Edward D. Steele and W. Charles Redding, "The American Value System: Premises for Persuasion," *Western Speech,* 26 (Winter 1962), 83–91.
5. Ibid.
6. Gresham M. Sykes and David Matza, "Techniques of Neutralization: A Theory of Delinquency," *American Sociological Review,* 22 (December 1957), 664–670.
7. C. Wright Mills, "Situated Actions and Vocabularies of Motive," *American Sociological Review,* 5 (December 1940), 904–913.
8. Sykes and Matza, 667–669.

9. Marvin B. Scott and Stanford M. Lyman, "Accounts," *American Sociological Review,* 33 (February 1968), 46–62.
10. Ibid., 46.
11. Ibid., 47–52.
12. Jackson Toby, "Some Variables in Role Conflict Analysis," *Social Forces,* 30 (March 1952), 323–327.
13. Ibid.

chapter 7

The Persuasiveness of Character

In an ideal world where everybody was a model of rationality, a book on rhetoric might have been complete with Chapter 6. In such a world, the art of persuasion would begin and end with finding good reasons. But in the real world, we know that humans respond to more than the reasoning of orators, writers, conversationalists, and other communicators. In fact, a world of reason only might not be ideal after all; reduced to the logical processing of information, we might be no different from androids, dealing with all matters in formal ways. What would a world be without love, passion, frivolity, subjective idiosyncrasy? Our world is a hurly-burly of reason and emotion, of light and dark, of ethical proprieties and conniving machinations. Rhetoric occurs in the real world; it springs from it and addresses it. That is why it is a potent force. That is also why it is sometimes feared.

As the method of communication used by common people to deal collectively with their common problems, rhetorical theory takes into account that in addition to reason, humans are swayed by their emotions, their ethics, their values, their interests, their level of trust (or distrust). So in accounting for what happens when A speaks for some purpose to B, the less trusted elements of persuasion must be considered. These include the persona of the speaker or writer and the emotional states of the listeners. We need to be aware that these may be sources of distorted judgment and hence must be on our guard when we detect them as the basis for appeals. At the same time, we must recognize that humans are not just rational beings. They are also desiring, feeling beings. Our assessment of the rhetor's persona as well as our emotional disposition can aid in making wise decisions. In this chapter we will consider the rhetor's character as a source of persuasion. In the next we will take up the subject of emotional appeals.

THE PROBLEM OF AUTHORITY

In his book *Authority,* the sociologist Richard Sennett recounts the experience of observing the noted conductor Pierre Monteux take command of an orchestra.[1] He tells us that Monteux is a conductor of subtle movements, his baton working in a rectangle of space measuring approximately 12 by 18 inches. A nod, an arched brow, a flick of his eye is all the cue he might provide. Yet so commanding is his knowledge of the music and so self-assured is his manner of expression that these slight movements are all he requires. Moreover, they keep the players on their toes. They have to watch his every move if they are to play the music to the maestro's taste. As the orchestra rehearsed, Sennett observed Monteux sustain a gentle but firm commentary on the performance of each section—perhaps greater energy here to capture force, perhaps more life there lest its beauty escape, always with a simple but sure tone that said, "I know with confidence how this should be played; do as I direct and the music will sound beautiful."

Monteux did not use bully tactics to discipline the orchestra. Absent were the tirades of, say, a Toscanini, designed to strike terror into every member's heart for fear of making a mistake. Yet he acted toward each chair in a manner that indicated that he knew each player's ability. He set the standard each player was to achieve. And if perchance a mistake was made, no words of reprimand were needed; a silent glare conveyed the message: "You have not played up to your ability. You have disappointed me. You have disappointed yourself." His standards, not the musician's peers, were imposed, and Monteux was insistent that each player live up to them. For members of the orchestra, Pierre Monteux had authority. He possessed superior judgment, could impose discipline, had the capacity to inspire fear, and was self-assured.

I begin with this example because each of us has experienced authority as a problem in our lives. Authority is a problem because it can affect us in positive or negative ways. An authority may impose the discipline necessary for us to grow and improve or may provide direction that steers us away from disaster and toward personal success. An authority also can dominate, exercising such power over our thoughts and actions that we abdicate our independence and become subjects to the authority's dominion. In both aspects, our thoughts and actions are influenced because someone has a degree of power over us.

Several disciplines study personal power. Political science, sociology, management science, and psychology come readily to mind. It is also pertinent to human communication. Whenever our decisions are made not on the basis of what is said so much as on who says it, we have recognized that sayer as an authority. In rhetorical transactions, this form of personal power is an important source of persuasion, commonly called *ethos.* But before we turn to ethos itself, we need to illustrate some problems in the way authority is understood to provide a context for understanding ethos.

Sennett points out that there are two major schools of thought on the nature of authority.[2] One school, led by the German sociologist Max Weber, views authority as based on how a figure is regarded by his or her subordinates. If people view a figure as a legitimate authority, they will offer voluntary compliance to that person's will. Authority is imagined to be an attribute a person has that legitimates subjugation. A second school, based on the thought of Sigmund Freud, emphasizes the needs of people to believe something or someone is credible and the ability of an authority to satisfy that need. This challenges Weber's emphasis on the legitimacy of the content as a ground for belief and replaces it with an emphasis on the process—historical, cultural, and psychological—by which people perceive strength in others. But notice that this also imagines authority to be an attribute a person has—in this case, the power to satisfy our needs—that compels subjugation.

Sennett makes a valuable criticism by pointing out that in thinking of authority as an attribute, we make it static and thinglike. We miss the dynamic aspects that accompany the birth and passage of authority. Rather than thinking of authority as a thing, Sennett suggests it is a social construct. It exists as an event in social time and space, the product of an interaction.[3]

We may profit from Sennett's observation in our consideration of ethos. We must avoid thinking of ethos as a quality or an attribute that a person possesses and think of it instead as a social construct. We are sometimes tempted to think that ethos rests on whether an audience believes that the speaker legitimately possesses certain attributes of character. Discussions of ethos under the heading of source credibility frequently treat it so.[4] We may also find it tempting to think that ethos rests on the needs of the audience and its belief that the rhetor can satisfy these needs.[5] These are ingredients of ethos, to be sure. But both views omit the most important aspect present in the original discussions of this subject. Ethos is not a thing or a quality but an *interpretation* that is the product of speaker-audience interaction. Because ethos is dynamic and eventful, its rhetorical presence depends on how arguments and appeals are managed, how the ingredients of needs and perceptions are included in interpreting a rhetor's character through the give-and-take of a rhetorical exchange.

ETHOS AS ARTISTIC APPEAL

Not a day passes that we fail to make some judgment of character. The acts of public officials, employers, coworkers, peers, and friends each in their own way contribute to our experience of these people and our assessment of their moral, emotional, and intellectual dispositions. These judgments linger with us, framing future expectations and coloring our interpretations of one another as social actors. It could not be otherwise, for experience provides us with a guide to understand the events of each day and to frame responses we deem appropriate for negotiating our way through our social contexts.

Every communicator with a previous reputation thus has a reservoir of audience expectations that will be evoked as a matter of course as soon as he or she speaks or publishes. These cannot be ignored, and it would be foolish to do so. For example, if you hear that Gloria Steinem is to speak on your campus, her reputation as a feminist comes immediately to mind. You may see her as a spokesperson for equal rights for all Americans or a protector of women's interests, outspoken in her criticism of a patriarchal culture, sincere in her advocacy.

Or you may see her as overly zealous in her pursuit of women's issues, misguided in her attacks on traditional gender roles, and prone to exaggeration. Ms. Steinem will want to take these views of her character into consideration, building on the positive aspects and defusing the negative. She also can ignore items that are not audience concerns in her case. Unlike some public figures, her private life is not plastered all over the newspapers, she is not rumored to be connected with private interests or partisan economic causes, she has not been implicated in scandals, and she is not regarded as a lunatic. In short, she is not a subject of gossip. Hence she does not have a tarnished reputation to be defended before she can gain a serious hearing.

Yet such factors of previous reputation stand as so many "facts," inartistic arguments for accepting Ms. Steinem as a woman of good character. They are not themselves artistic arguments or appeals unless and until they are in some way incorporated into her speech and become an explicit factor in rhetor-audience interaction. In other words, while a communicator's reputation may precede her, ethos as a means of persuasion is concerned with going beyond the past. It is concerned with the interpretation of character formed through the patterns of interaction that occur in the actual rhetorical event.

As an *artistic* mode of persuasion—an appeal that is deliberate and is based on observed principles—ethos has several features we should bear in mind. First, as already noted, it is an artistic appeal in the sense that *ethos is developed in the message.* It is under the guiding hand of the communicating agent and is the resulting product of choices about *what* to express and to omit, *how* to express these ideas, and *when,* so as to create the proper impression.

Second, because it is developed through the way we talk, *ethos is dynamic.* Ethos is not an attribute but an interpretation based on the way a rhetor behaves in presenting an appeal and the manifold of reactions an audience has to these behaviors. In fact, as a most interesting study by researchers Brooks and Scheidel shows,[6] these reactions change by the moment as audiences receive with pleasure, uncertainty, amusement, fear, agreement, and so forth the specific reasonings and exhortations that comprise the whole of a rhetorical transaction. Only by understanding this dynamic of interactive engagement can we appreciate the essential character of ethos as a social construct, as an interpretation developing through give-and-take, as an event rather than an entity.

Third, because it is developed through rhetor choices of inclusion and exclusion, *ethos is a caused response.* How we appear to others depends on the choices we make in presenting our message and ourselves. In other words, we can guide interpretations of our mental, emotional, and moral dispositions by the ways we argue, including the language we select, the tone we take, and the nonverbal cues we present.[7] The dynamic event of the whole presentation brings the audience to one judgment after another about our character.

For these reasons, rhetoricians have largely endorsed Aristotle's belief that a positive assessment of a rhetor's character could well be the most potent of all the available means of persuasion. Aristotle put it well at the beginning of the *Rhetoric:*

The character [ethos] of the speaker is a cause of persuasion when the speech is so uttered as to make him worthy of belief; for as a rule we trust men of probity more, and more quickly, about things in general, while on points outside the realm of exact knowledge, where opinion is divided, we trust them absolutely. This trust, however, should be created by the speech itself, and not left to depend upon an antecedent impression that the speaker is this or that kind of man. It is not true, as some writers on the art maintain, that the probity of the speaker contributes nothing to his persuasiveness; on the contrary, we might almost affirm that his character [ethos] is the most potent of all the means to persuasion.[8]

In sum, when we cause a positive impression of our character, we gain the great advantage of trust in the midst of conflicting interpretations of issues and evidence. In such cases, where there is no clearly superior argument or where we lack the background to judge which view is more likely, we tend to affirm the views of those whose character is held in high esteem. So the big question becomes one of the basis for forming such judgment. Knowing that, we might better understand both how to cause positive interpretations of character and how to detect when rhetors are behaving in a duplicitous manner.

ETHOS AND THE HABITS OF LIFE

From antiquity to the present, audiences have confronted the recurring problem of deciding whom to believe. In some cases, the difficulty may be that we fear a speaker is lying or in some way attempting to deceive us. In many more cases where we lack sufficient background, we may be uncertain whether a rhetor is truly knowledgeable or merely glib. In still other instances, we must sort through conflicting advice without decisive evidence of fact or prevailing opinion but only our sense of each person's wisdom as a guide. These are determinations of ethos. What leads us to interpret a person's rhetorical appeals as an argument for good character? What counts as good character in matters settled through persuasive discourse?

Habits and Excellence

We can draw a bead on our target by remembering that rhetoric is a civic art. It is used to create and maintain community. It is a method for conducting a public's business, for common people to have a say in decisions of policy and conduct that affect their lives. Though we may be egalitarians in permitting freedom of speech on these matters, as a matter of practice we give our attention to those speakers and writers who show qualities of wisdom in deciding practical affairs.

In antiquity such wisdom was a mark of excellence (*arête* for the Greeks, *virtu* for the Romans). The Greeks, for example, were profoundly aware that living in the *polis* civilized them. They had to set aside the barbaric ways of tribal

life and cultivate political skills to promote the well-being of the community. If
they lived by the law of the wild, they'd end up killing one another. As a man
increased in his civic skills, he gave evidence of enhanced excellence as a human.
The Sophists understood this as a reciprocal relationship between the city and the
man. As the life of the city improved, it elevated the level of each citizen's cultural
awareness. As each man grew in civic virtue, the quality of city life elevated. Thus
city and man reciprocally enhanced one another in an ever-ascending quality of
life.[9] The noted classicist John Herman Randall provides a succinct summary of
this process:

> Any function is well performed when it is performed in accordance with its own
> proper excellence or "virtue." Hence the good of man—human welfare—is the
> functioning of man's various powers under the guidance of intelligence, and in
> accordance with their own proper and respective excellence or "virtue." . . .
> Social organization, the *polis*, provides the means of training in these individual
> excellences, and it also furnishes the field in which they can operate: it provides
> the materials and conditions for training in, and for the exercise of, the good
> life. Ethics and politics are hence two aspects of the same "architectonic"
> science. The excellences or *aretai* of the individual are formed in the *polis*, in
> society, and they can function only in the *polis*.[10]

Excellence was captured in the characteristic ways a person participated in the
affairs of the city. Such virtuosity was formed by individual involvement in public
affairs and required the opportunity of public affairs to function.

Quite clearly, the Greeks had a special type of virtue in mind. It was unlike
the Christian virtues of faith, hope, and charity, for example, which are best
practiced beyond the glare of publicity. They had in mind practical virtues that
would help in forming prudent public decisions.

Such virtues remain important in making sound practical choices. We
recognize their value especially in matters that are emotionally involving and can
lead to the volatile rhetoric that distorts good ideas into dogma. Someone ob-
serves, say, that waste from the local mill is seeping into the water table and
polluting the water supply. This is a serious situation and requires a remedy. But
before one can be found, extremists condemn the mill for lack of conscience and
for exploiting the community. People get upset and clamor for the mill to be shut
down and its management tried on criminal charges. The next thing you know,
the plant does close, 500 workers are without jobs, and no solution has been found
for the pollution problem. It is in situations like this that we seek advice that
avoids the deficiency of doing nothing and the excess of throwing out the baby
with the bathwater. Such advice is a form of wisdom, practical wisdom, and
rhetors who speak in ways that manifest it are interpreted to have sound character.

Aristotle provides us with a plausible analysis of how this interpretation is
formed. In his *Ethics* and *Poetics* he indicates that persons with practical wisdom
act with prudence. These individuals possess a *hexis*, or disposition, to act in ways
that avoid extremes and counsel virtuous acts. By virtue of their experience, they

form a habit of correct conduct. As we observe their public behavior, we see their habits revealed in the choices they make. From observing their habits, we draw inferences about their character, or *ethos*.

In an excellent study of the relationship between habit and character, rhetorician Arthur B. Miller has documented how in language and argument Aristotle connects these two. When he says that ethos is caused by the speech, what he means is that the speaker reveals his habits by the causes espoused, the values endorsed, the actions counseled. These habits are evaluated by the audience in terms of their vision of the good life. The interaction of the rhetor's advice and the audience's understanding lead to the interpretation of the rhetor as a person of character.

Attributes of Character

The habits revealed can be grouped under three headings. First we gauge a person's *mental* habits. We trust individuals who are intelligent. If we believe the person is well informed, has studied a question thoroughly, is clearheaded and reasonable in her beliefs, is able to provide reasons and evidence in response to objections, does not utter foolish or exaggerated or asinine or banal opinions, is her own person and is not easily misled, or has a special expertise through training or experience, we are likely to have confidence in her advice. Conversely, if a person is a sloppy reasoner or slow-witted or uniformed or given to extreme claims or is easily duped, our guard is raised to be cautious of her advice because it may not be thought out.

For example, John Kennedy was regarded as very intelligent by most Americans, even those who opposed him. What were the traits of his rhetoric? First, he had a great capacity for retaining and using facts. He seemed incredibly well informed. Second, the rhetorical figure of *antithesis* dominated his speeches ("not this, but that"). Antithesis suggests analytic precision. This is the habit of a thinking person. Third, Kennedy was fast on his feet. At press conferences he could turn a loaded question back on his interrogator with ease, charm, and wit. He could make a joke out of an absurd question that dismissed the question without attacking the person of the questioner. Kennedy treated a press conference as his personal mental gymnasium, and American voters got the pleasure of watching him strut his stuff as a mental athlete having a good workout. His habit of mind was made apparent by the way he handled himself and encouraged repeated interpretations of him as intelligent.

By way of contrast, presidential hopeful Edward Kennedy committed political suicide in 1980 when he was unable to explain to TV commentator Roger Mudd why he sought the presidency. Kennedy's failure to articulate a clear inspiring mission made his candidacy appear self-seeking. Americans saw this as one more indication that Kennedy lacked sufficient character to lead the nation.

The second assessment pertinent to ethos is of a person's *moral* habits. We trust people who speak with integrity, who show themselves to make virtuous decisions, and who inspire confidence that they know what is right and have the courage of their convictions. We trust these people to be truthful with us and to offer advice that will not bring us to shame or unjustly harm others. In assessing moral habits, we are especially concerned with the virtues of public life. Such virtues include the following:

1. *Justice:* Is there concern that people have what belongs to them? What equity principle is used? Is it used consistently? Are the community's laws respected? Are they adhered to? Or is there blindness to, tolerance of, or even advocacy of injustices where people have what is rightfully others'?
2. *Courage:* Is concern for the right or the noble or the just a higher priority than the convenient? Is it pursued in the face of peril? Is there a habit of doing what is right regardless of its popularity? Or is there cowardice, caving in under pressure, or backsliding from principles that are not popular?
3. *Temperance:* Is there self-restraint in conduct and advice? Is there moderation between deficiency and excess? Is there control of emotions and appetites? Or is there a tendency to self-indulgence in opinions and excesses in advice?
4. *Generosity:* Is there a spirit of giving to others what they need to succeed? Are benefits conferred on others? Is a selfless spirit revealed? Or is there an illiberal, stingy, or selfish habit of conduct?
5. *Magnanimity:* Is there a nobility of thought and outlook? Is there a forgiving spirit? Are insults and injuries overlooked and opportunities to confer benefits sought? Is there a tendency to avoid or rise above pettiness or meanness? Or is the person mean-spirited in thought and deed?
6. *Magnificence:* Is there a sense for the exalted and the grand? Is there vision of what elevates the human spirit? Is there commitment to the highest quality of life? Are the majectic and stately aspects of humanity advocated? Or is there a lowly opinion of humanity and a shabby vision of what we are and what we might become?
7. *Prudence:* Is there sound judgment in practical matters that allows for sound advice on how to act in ways that will accord with these public virtues and will avoid the vices of their opposites?[12]

These virtues should be present in the way the rhetor argues a cause. In other words, virtue is not demonstrated by arguing that we are morally upright. It is demonstrated by arguing in a morally responsible way. Audience assessment of moral habit is inferred from the causes espoused and the reasons given, not from explicitly egocentric appeals. It is a judgment based on the audience's sense of moral habit in evidence as the rhetor treats practical problems.

For example, in his address to the 1980 Democratic convention, Senator Edward Kennedy wished to defend political liberalism as a still viable alternative. He also wished to reassert his position as a leading figure (even the preeminant one) among American liberals. At one point he made these remarks:

> The commitment I seek is not to outworn views but to old values that will never wear out. Programs may sometimes become obsolete, but the ideal of fairness always endures. Circumstances may change, but the work of compassion must

ethos ⟶ something caused...

existential (100)
attribute   (94)   interpretation (94)

entity   (94)   event
(100)
                                        habit
                                          |
                                          |
                                          |
                                        disposition

                                                        [ethos in
                                                         doing⟶]
                                        "demonstrating"
                                        ═══════ (100)

                    disclosed   (384)
                    ═══════   ⟍   the way to handled
                                                ⟍⟍⟍⟍ himself (97)

by what it
═══════
said
════
                                        "the way the orator argues
                                         cause" (98)

continue. It is surely correct that we cannot solve problems by throwing money at them, but it is also correct that we dare not throw national problems onto a scrap heap of inattention and indifference.[13]

Kennedy does not claim that he is a morally virtuous man. But his pleading reveals his values and encourages us to see him as such. Moreover, notice the variety and rapidity with which we are taken through his moral register, as each sentence seems to reveal a different ethical disposition. First we have an appeal resting on *magnificence:* "old values that will never wear out." Next we are urged to act with *justice:* "the ideal of fairness always endures." Then our *generosity* is enjoined: "the work of compassion must continue." Finally, *temperance* is urged: avoid the moral deficiency of "a scrap heap of inattention and indifference." For an audience ready to hear his appeals, the *way* these ideas unfold provides strong encouragement to interpret Kennedy as a man of good character and to place trust in what he says.

Finally, we gauge character by a person's *emotional* habits, especially as they reveal a disposition of good or ill will toward us as an audience. People show goodwill by their concern for our best interests. They are angry at people who insult us or harm us; they are fearful of impending dangers; they are joyful at our successes and counsel us to emulate others who have succeeded. We further test the sincerity of their feelings in terms of the personal stakes they might have in the outcomes. We know people are well disposed when their advice is not necessarily in their own best interests, though it is in ours. On the other hand, we distrust speakers or writers who appear not to offer the best advice, who seek their own advantage through their management of information or their manner of reasoning or the propositions they advance.

Dissimulation or lying is, of course, difficult to detect. It would be impossible, and unjust, to dismiss every partisan pleader as ill-disposed. Partisanship cannot be avoided in rhetorical situations because it is a part of life. Humans have beliefs, isms, and causes they champion and try to get others to affirm and join. The problem is not with partisan rhetoric but with insincere rhetoric. Insincere appeals deliberately distort the facts and true feelings and in this way deceive audiences into beliefs and actions that benefit the rhetor in ways that are never disclosed. This type of deception is difficult to detect, but once detected, it earns our contempt.

Perhaps the most famous example in this century of such rhetoric occurred in the early 1950s when Senator Joseph McCarthy conducted his infamous communist witch-hunt. But cases of this sort are not restricted to politics. We find them in all walks of life. On television, ministers of the "electronic church" promise salvation to those who believe and prosperity to those with the right kind of faith. The contributions of viewers who subscribe to this "give to get" message put millions in the coffers of these preachers and afford them secular power that many clergy find out of keeping with the teachings of Jesus.[14] In business, the Mansville Corporation seeks to separate its asbestos-producing division from the rest of its divisions. That done, it then files for bankruptcy, even though earning a profit, in order to avoid paying the damage claims of workers who contracted asbestosis from using Mansville products. In advertising, the R. J. Reynolds tobacco company advises teenagers not to smoke because it is an adult custom while ignoring the health hazards of inhaling cigarette smoke. The image of responsibility may be distant from the reality, but the fiction is more likely to increase profits.

Interpreting Ethos

The mental, moral, and emotional dispositions of human beings obviously have existences quite apart from the times when we engage in rhetoric. And misjudgments of character may occur in any given case. Be that as it may, the central issue that rhetoric addresses is with what transpires during the speaking-listening or writing-reading transaction. Hence we have focused on the ethos of the rhetor as an interpretation rather than as an existential attribute. We can draw three conclusions about how ethos as an interpretation is formed in rhetoric.

First, ethos grows from arguments and exhortations that are relevant to the subject. Except in rare cases when an individual speaks about himself, as when President Nixon spoke on the Watergate affair, ethos does not get established through direct appeal. Ethos is established by inference. You get a reputation for good reasoning and prudent judgment by demonstrating the appropriate mental, moral, and emotional habits in the types of appeals you make in your speech.

Second, ethos is the product of the interaction between your dispositions to respond as you reveal them in your speaking and writing and the special needs of your audience. Audiences evaluate habits in terms of their own views of the good life. That is why it is important to talk about topics from your listeners' point of view. Your rhetoric directs them to see you in a particular way, but at the same time they bring their own agenda of concerns to bear in forming their responses. If you become an authority for your audience, it is because your mutual interaction has led to a pattern of interpretation appropriate in the given case.

Finally, a rhetorical analysis of ethos avoids trait ascriptions as qualities that communicators actually possess. A rhetorical analysis focuses on ethos as a judgment that is caused by the speech itself. If you regularly meet your listeners' needs by being informed, interesting, succinct, and focused on their concerns, you will encourage them to perceive you as someone worth listening to. Their impression of you is an interpretation, a social construct, not an entity. Ethos is eventful in this respect, as is all rhetoric, occurring in the context of a response to a rhetorical demand. It is time-bound, confined to the configuration of speaker, speech, and audience in a given case. Each new situation calls anew for each rhetor to reestablish ethos through discourse.

ETHOS AND ETHICAL APPEAL

At the beginning of this chapter we noted that the experience of authority is problematic because authority figures can lead us to grow in knowledge and self-reliance or they can dominate us and keep us subject to their wills. No less can be said about communicators who are accorded ethos. Their authority over our judgment can lead us toward wise decisions. But following any leader on the basis of that person's apparent habits can lead us into errors as well.

Determining whether a person is appealing in morally correct ways is never easy. Quite apart from the ethics of a person's views, there is always the question of whether the persuading agent is treating the audience with moral integrity. Thus we need to distinguish between *ethos* and *ethical appeals.* Questions of ethos focus on the perceptions of the speaker caused by his rhetoric. Questions of ethical appeals focus on the issues raised (or suppressed) and the quality of arguments addressed to them. We need a concept of ethical appeal, quite apart from ethos, as a guide for testing the moral quality of rhetorical arguments.

Some philosophers have objected to all rhetorical practices as unethical because rhetoric does not seek the truth but endorsement of a partisan opinion. But that objection is specious because it reduces all matters to issues of true and false. The vast majority of human decisions are ones in which there are no true or false answers, only better and worse. The fascinating aspect of the human world is that we have *choices.* This is the very ground of our freedom, our morality, our humanity. Choice is always reflective of values, beliefs, opinions, desires, and interests. It is inherently partisan. Objecting to rhetoric because persuaders seek endorsement of opinions is to object to the very condition of human existence, an objection that is difficult to sustain.

Partisanship is not the culprit so much as the tactics to which partisans sometimes resort. In the give-and-take of deliberations, the partisan appeals of advocates should balance out against one another. Where matters are presented on their merits, advocates may be expected to emphasize what they find attractive on their side of the issue. But the question we face is whether these presentations are truthful and sincere or attempted seductions.

There is no easy way to ensure that our evaluations of moral character are correct, but we can offer some general guidelines to help evaluate the ethics of a rhetorical appeal. As an overarching guideline, we may adapt to the practices of rhetoric the rule of bilateral argument formulated by philosopher Henry Johnstone: *A rhetor may use no device of persuasion that he could not in princi-ple permit others to use on him.* [15] This rule requires that any practice that would distort our choices is unethical because it would undermine our freedom and our humanity.

The bilaterality principle gives us the basic "sauce for the goose, sauce for the gander" rule in rhetorical communication. Rhetoric, in the sense that it is concerned with all the means of persuasion, can be employed by any person. Presumably, people trained in rhetorical practices will be more skillful in crafting persuasion than those who are not. It is a power that is denied to no one. Further, it is a power that can be enhanced by anyone who undertakes training in its practice. This means that each of us can acquire skills in the use of persuasive means but have ethical limits on how we use these skills. It also means that others can use these skills to persuade us.

We must be mindful of this last fact, so that we are not tricked by those who violate the rule of bilaterality. The bilateral rule is especially helpful because it gives us a way to *think* about what is being said and the manner in which it is presented. Though a checklist of forbidden practices, such as "Don't lie," might be comforting, the problem would be to spot such instances when they occur. There are no easy ways to do that. But we can examine how a rhetor treats an audience and ask whether we could generalize that treatment so that it would be acceptable in principle for everyone to persuade in that fashion.

For instance, when we seek agreement, the bilateral principle requires that we not hide or misrepresent our thinking. We allow our audience access to our beliefs and reasons so that they may form an accurate assessment of their value. Helpful guidelines for making this assessment are provided in a study by philosopher George Yoos concerning ethical appeals.[16] Yoos suggests four rules for audiences to use as tests.[17]

1. *A factor:* "The quality displaying the speaker as seeking mutual agreement with his audience." This factor requires that the reasons we give to our listeners are our real reasons for what we believe. In other words, if we seek agreement, it is unethical to tell the audience only what it wants to hear. When we pander to our listeners, we deny them the chance to reach agreement because we only pretend to share common ground. The A factor also prohibits us from having a hidden agenda, whereby we try to confuse our audience about our true goals. As listeners, we should be suspicious if there are inconsistencies in the speaker's commitments to the reasons offered for mutual agreement.

2. *R factor:* "The quality displaying the speaker as recognizing the rational autonomy of his audience." Every speaker who seeks agreement has an ethical responsibility to honor his audience's right to decide. This means that speakers can't brush aside the audience's criteria for judging. Speakers can't substitute their own criteria without justification. The audience has a right to set its own standards for decision. If the speaker disagrees, he must provide arguments that demonstrate why his standards are better. As listeners, we should be suspicious if the speaker abuses the "common" sense of the audience.

3. *E factor:* "The quality displaying the speaker as recognizing the equality of the listener with himself." The only time that a speaker may speak as one superior to his audience is when there is mutual acceptance of his authority by the audience. It is unethical to act like an authority (to make claims that we expect others to accept simply because we made them) unless the audience recognizes our expertise or we demonstrate it. As listeners, we should be on our guard when someone tries to get us to accept his views on the basis of his word without giving us good reasons to accept him as specially qualified with superior knowledge. We can usually spot such speakers because typically they talk down to their listeners.

4. *V factor:* "The quality displaying the speaker as recognizing that the ends of the audience have an intrinsic value for him." Speakers and writers show that they respect the audience's ends by only committing themselves to the ends they share and want to help become realities. At the same time, they are explicit in presenting their disagreements with the ends they don't share and in accepting the burden of proof for why those ends are inappropriate. Rhetors do not show respect when they

pander to their audiences by giving them what they want. As listeners, we need to be cautious of speakers who disapprove of or dismiss audience goals without offering reasons. Equally, we need to keep an eye on those who seek goals that seem contrary to the audience's but offer no rationale for their choices.

When we seek agreement, bilaterality emphasizes open communication. However, there are a great many rhetorical situations in which communicators are likely to conceal some aspects of their views while emphasizing others. These are situations of *advocacy,* where persuasion and victory are the goals. Typically, we find these where interests are at stake, as in business, politics, law, and even interpersonal relations. Cultural norms regulate what are permissible omissions. For instance, before a big game, the coach may lament about his team's injuries and what a bad week it has had in practice. The other team will be praised as if it were an all-star squad. Few who follow sports take any of this seriously. It's permissible for the coach to bluff in this way. It is not permissible for him to falsify records to play an ineligible student. Similarly, when we deal with salespersons, politicians, and star-struck lovers, we expect the things they say to be extravagant. We do not expect them deliberately to misrepresent the fact that they are partisan advocates.

Thus in advocacy there is a permissible level of deception that is guided by the bilaterality principle. It requires our honesty about being partisans and our adherence to the norms that are conventions for our context. To illustrate how we may use the bilateral rule as a test for ethical appeals, consider the advocacy of Eva Perón as portrayed in the play *Evita.* In its noted song "Don't Cry for Me, Argentina," Eva appeals to the people of Buenos Aires. The song is reintroduced at several places and adapted to the issues of the moment. But always the *manner* of her appeal is the same. After Juan Perón is inaugurated as president, she appears before the crowd. Her appeal, in part, is as follows:

And as for fortune, and as for fame
I never invited them in
Though it seemed to the world they were all I desired
They are illusions,
They are not the solutions they promised to be
The answer was here all the time
I love you and hope you love me

Don't cry for me Argentina . . .
(Eva breaks down; the CROWD take up her tune)
Eva
Don't cry for me Argentina
The truth is I never left you
All through my wild days
My mad existence
I kept my promise
Don't keep your distance

Have I said too much? There's nothing more I can think
  of to say to you
But all you have to do is look at me to know that
  every word is true.[19]

1. Here we have Eva, the poor backwater girl, now a woman of power and wealth, telling the poor workers of Buenos Aires to ignore the facts that she is now rich and famous. Can we generalize the appeal to ignore conflicts between our words and deeds?
2. Here we have common people who are suffering the slings and arrows of an unstable economy being advised that financial well-being is an illusion, that the true answer to their problems is love. Can we generalize the appeal that denies the legitimacy of the audience's goals, that shifts attention from a problem by offering a laudable but irrelevant goal as an answer?
3. Here we have Eva saying, "Don't cry for me, Argentina" and then crying herself. Can we generalize a practice that invites affirmation through sympathy rather than critical appraisal?
4. Here we have Eva concluding her appeal by saying that we will know she is telling the truth just by looking at her. Can we generalize a practice that emphasizes presence and appearance as warrants for belief?

In examining the appeals of a rhetor, just as we have in examining these lines from the song, the bilaterality principle helps us to reflect critically on what we are hearing. While it doesn't identify specific practices that should cause concern, it does help us to determine for ourselves whether we should be concerned. In assessing the ethos of communicators, it can alert us to practices that are symptoms of seduction rather than of intellectual, moral, and emotional virtues and thereby help us to make better choices about the world we live in.

SUMMARY

The advances in knowledge and in technologies that put this knowledge into practice have radically transformed contemporary societies. We are entwined in a complex network of production and services essential to our survival. Most of us have little firsthand knowledge of the whys and wherefores that are the pulse of the late twentieth century. We rely on others to possess this knowledge and on our good judgment to determine whom to believe. Aristotle's claim that our impressions of a person's character may be the most important factor influencing belief is even more true today. We seek individuals with superior knowledge or ability and frequently give them authority in our lives.

In this chapter we have discussed the nature of this authority in rhetoric—*ethos*—and how it is established. Our emphasis has been on the dynamic interaction between a communicator and an audience. Through their transactions within a rhetorical event, the audience forms a judgment—a social construct—that this speaker or writer is trustworthy. Ethos is not an inherent quality a person possesses. It is an interpretation of that person's character based on how the person behaves in light of a specific audience's readiness to respond. Though many factors may influence the trust we place in a person, the strictly rhetorical factors are those present in the message itself: the manifested intellectual, moral, and emotional qualities that we find admirable. Thus ethos is a dynamic attribution that is caused by the rhetorical choices a person makes.

By the same token, though we recognize that rhetor choices may cause a favorable impression, it is not necessarily the case that these appeals are themselves ethical. That judgment depends on the measure of respect extended to the integrity of the people addressed. We test this respect through the bilateral rule, which requires that no mode or means of persuasion be used on others that in principle we would not permit others to use on us. In a world where we seek authorities and invest them with powers that may dominate our lives, the force of ethos is crucial to shaping our private and public realities. Bilaterality as a test of ethos helps to safeguard the quality of our choices about whom to believe and what visions to pursue.

NOTES

1. Richard Sennett, *Authority* (New York: Knopf, 1980), pp. 16–17. One imagines that Sennett, himself a cellist, had this experience face to face as an orchestra member, not as a sideline observer.
2. Ibid., pp. 20–27.
3. Ibid., p. 196.
4. See Gary Cronkhite and Jo Liska, "A Critique of Factor Analytic Approaches to the Study of Credibility," *Communication Monographs,* 43 (June 1976), 91–107.
5. Otis Walter, "Toward an Analysis of Ethos," *Pennsylvania Speech Annual,* 21 (September 1964), 37–45.
6. Robert D. Brooks and Thomas M. Scheidel, "Speech as Process: A Case Study," *Speech Monographs,* 35 (March 1968), 1–7.
7. For example, in the 1960 presidential debates, a majority of viewers who saw the first debate on television thought Kennedy won, while a majority of the radio audience thought Nixon won. The crucial variable was Nixon's nonverbal cues: He was poorly made up, and his heavy beard gave him a sinister appearance. History repeated itself in 1984. In the second Reagan-Mondale debate, Mondale appeared haggard, with dark bags under his eyes. Again, this was the result of makeup plus studio lighting. Viewers translated this as a sign that Mondale was nearly exhausted in a desperate effort to overcome his opponent's lead.
8. Lane Cooper, trans., *The Rhetoric of Aristotle* (Englewood Cliffs, N.J.: Prentice-Hall, 1932), pp. 8–9.
9. Eric Havelock, *The Liberal Temper of Greek Politics* (New Haven, Conn.: Yale University Press, 1957), pp. 191–239.
10. John Herman Randall, Jr., *Aristotle* (New York: Columbia University Press, 1962), pp. 253–254.
11. Arthur B. Miller, "Aristotle on Habit *(εθos)* and Character *(ηθos)*: Implications for the *Rhetoric,*" *Speech Monographs,* 41 (1974), 309–316.
12. As students of Aristotle will recognize, these virtues are discussed in *Rhetoric* I.9. They remain a sound basic list for assessing ideal moral habits that should attract or repel audiences.

13. Kennedy made this speech on August 12, 1980.

14. For example, see William F. Fore, " 'There Is No Such Thing as a TV Pastor,' " *TV Guide* (July 19, 1980), 15–18; Charles E. Swan, "The Electronic Church," *Presbyterian Survey* (May 1979), 9–16; and Allan Dodds Frank, "Mr. Ed and the Gospel," *Forbes* (May 21, 1984), 84–89.

15. Henry W. Johnstone, Jr., "Bilaterality in Argument and Communication," in J. Robert Cox and Charles Arthur Willard, eds., *Advances in Argumentation Theory and Research* (Carbondale: Southern Illinois University Press, 1982), p. 95.

16. George Yoos, "A Revision of the Concept of Ethical Appeal," *Philosophy and Rhetoric,* 12 (Winter 1979), 41–58.

17. Ibid., pp. 50–55.

18. George Yoos, "Rational Appeal and the Ethics of Advocacy," in Robert J. Connors et al., eds., *Essays on Classical Rhetoric and Modern Discourse* (Carbondale: Southern Illinois University Press, 1984), pp. 82–97.

19. Tim Rice, "Don't Cry for Me, Argentina," copyright © 1976 by Evita Music, Ltd. Reprinted with Permission.

chapter 8

The Passions

One of the great triumphs in recent history was the British resistance to the Nazi war machine. The Chamberlain government had followed a policy of military neglect, believing Britain could avoid war through appeasement. The Germans had superior weapons and air power. By rights the British should have been defeated with dispatch. But we know that the opposite happened. Rather than responding out of fear, the British were inspired to confidence that they could defeat the enemy. They offered determined resistance to the Luftwaffe's blitzkrieg and then launched a stunning counteroffensive. The reasons for this doubtless are several, but among them is the stirring oratory of Winston Churchill. In a series of radio addresses, he urged his people to surmount their darkest hour. He raised patriotic feelings, he evoked contempt of Hitler, and he defined the appropriate responses as righteous indignation and noble courage in defense of humanity and the motherland. Victory was never questioned because Churchill convinced his nation that through determined efforts, England would ultimately prevail.

One of the great tragedies in recent American history was the war in Vietnam. Many people questioned what business the United States had getting involved in the first place. The conflict was an old internal one, yet several presidents and several Congresses authorized the use of American troops and materials for the defense of the Saigon government. The reasons for American involvement are complex, and it will be years before historians sort out the facts and provide us with a deeper understanding of how matters got so out of hand. But surely among the contributing factors was the repeated appeal to the "domino theory"—if South Vietnam falls to the communists, the other nations in the region will also fall, one by one, like a row of dominoes. This is a rhetoric of fear.

It arouses concerns for survival and focuses attention on an external force as a threat to our survival.

In both cases, rhetoric played its part in shaping events. Both cases found national leaders pleading for particular kinds of acts to thwart a foe. In both cases, an external source was the focus of attention. In both cases, emotions were aroused, and these guided the actions that followed.

For many, the fact that a speaker can whip an audience into an emotional frenzy has been a reason for condemning rhetoric. How can a mode of communication that leads people to make emotion-based decisions be to their advantage? Reason, not emotion, should be our guide. This celebration of reason over the passions is not just the stuff from which intellectuals make assertions about how to tell fair arguments from foul. In a commonsense way, most people adopt this as a stated view in everyday life. We tend to express distrust of our emotions or, at the very least, imply that we value reason over emotion every time we offer as an excuse for untoward behavior that we were emotionally overwrought at the time.

The celebration of reason over the passions has a history that goes back at least to Plato. In more modern times it has been advanced by the rationalism of Descartes. In essence, the passions are distrusted as the base impulses, desires, or feelings of the flesh. Without the control of reason, located in the mind, we fear that these base impulses will lead us into acts that are bestial in character or that rest on deception or are primitive at best. This separation of reason and the passions is frequently referred to as a mind-body dualism.

This is not the place for a philosophical discussion of the mind-body split. It is enough to say that dualists do not regard the human as a unified or holistic organism and therefore have a difficult time explaining emotions as anything but irrational and untrustworthy. Contemporary philosophy has called this split into question. Present views consider humans to be more than aggregates of anatomic parts. Somehow, in the whole human, what we call "reason" and what we call "emotion" are integrated.

The philosophers are not alone in finding evidence for the holistic character of human action. Psychologists, for example, have devoted considerable study to emotions, attempting to locate them, define them, use them to construct a basic framework from which a scientific theory of human behavior would emerge. However, they do not seem to be able to agree on what an emotion is, nor to find physiological responses that distinguish one emotion from another, nor other evidence that might suggest that emotions can be located within us. In other words, their findings show that even though we can name feelings and describe them, this does not mean that they are discrete entities within us. Emotions aren't things; they are something else—*patterns of response.* These patterns are conditioned by a number of factors, but chief among them are our thoughts, which are connected to language. As the behaviorist John Watson observed many years ago, " 'Thinking' is largely 'subvocal talking.' "[1]

Once we abandon the split between mind and body, the argument that rhetoric is evil because it inflames the emotions seems unconvincing. All thinking involves language; all thinking engages emotional responses. Emotions aren't evil or untrustworthy. They are a necessary part of the holistic pattern by which we process and respond to the experiences of life. The issue is not whether our emotions are engaged but whether appropriate emotions are engaged so that we make wise decisions. In this chapter we will be concerned with how rhetoric addresses the whole person and our testing of the emotional responses it elicits. Although we will list some of the more common emotions that are part of rhetorical situations, we will not focus on describing these emotions. Since emotions are products of language, they tend to be unique. The issue for rhetorical theory is rather how they are brought about through the use of language.

PATHOS AS A PATTERN OF RESPONSE

As we have already seen, Aristotle contended that there were three major sources of influence on audience judgment: the argument of the case itself, *logos;* the perception of the orator's character, *ethos;* and the audience's emotional engagement, *pathos.* We may wonder how it could be otherwise, for to hear something and judge it requires simultaneously that we think about what is being said, who is saying it, and our feelings on the matter. When we think communicatively, each of these factors must be taken into account, as they must when we try to assess and understand what occurred when A communicated for a purpose with B.

The Aristotelian trilogy of logos, ethos, and pathos established a very important point: An understanding of rhetorical effects requires an understanding of the bases for human responses in general. Aristotle had developed a framework for discussing this subject that was essentially cognitive. Interestingly, his views have been revived in contemporary form[2] and provide us with a sensible approach to explain the integration of the three modes of persuasion as they address the whole person. This pattern is called *practical reasoning.*

Practical matters are not solved entirely on their intellectual merits. Though some people may consider whether the propositions advanced are supported by fact and related in a logically valid fashion, such tight inspection is rare. First, a rhetorical argument comes in bits and pieces, requiring us to fill in the blank spaces with common knowledge, ideological commitments, values and goals, and the like. Second, our preferences, needs, desires, and values enter into our evaluation in important ways.

For example, we go to a party and find ourselves feeling "turned on" by some people, "turned off" by others. People who "turn us on" are fun, they're interesting, they make us feel good about ourselves. People who "turn us off" are the opposite. For some of us, an exciting personality may be attractive; for others, a person of gentle sensitivity may fit the bill. Our responses are completely subjective and depend on our needs in the contexts in which we find ourselves rather than on objective discriminators of what produces a "good connection."

Practical decisions are much the same. They depend on the needs, goals, ideology, and desires of individuals in the contexts in which decisions are made. These personal "attributes" express themselves in terms of our physical needs—food, shelter, sexual release—our psychological needs—love, security, self-esteem—and our values.

For example, when young couples fall in love, they face a series of practical decisions of the "What are we going to do?" variety. Do we live together? Do we marry? Do we live together and if things work out then marry? Do we *value* the ceremony? If we want to marry, will it be a civil ceremony or a religious one? If a religious one, whose religion? Are we doing this for us or for our parents? All of these are practical decisions, decisions of action, and they are based on values. If your values were different, your outlook would change, and so might your practical choices.

As our desires, needs, values, and appetites are satisfied or frustrated, our disposition to respond is influenced. We seek to remove obstacles, avoid pain, acquire what brings pleasure, act in ways that will make us happy, stop doing things that make us miserable. All of these can be expressed in a brief but handy form called the *practical syllogism.* This form contains a premise about the agent, a premise about the conditions, and a conclusion that results in action. "I'm the type of person who avoids people who make me envious. Professor Smart's lavish praise of Anne's work has me drooling with envy. I don't want to have pizza with her this evening."

From the perspective of developing rhetorical appeals, it is important that the appeal establish a "proper" relationship between the audience and the point of discussion. If the point is one on which a general avoidance pattern is to the rhetor's advantage, it must be presented in a way that allows the audience to experience it as repelling. The converse is true of points we wish to receive an affirmative response. With these thoughts in mind, let us consider how the emotions are engaged in rhetoric.

PATHOS AND PERSUASIVE REASONING

Common Misconceptions

We began by noting that emotions are not things, and we need to return to that point now to get a better idea of what emotions are. There is a common way of talking that suggests a commodities view toward emotions, as if each human had storage bins and accountant's ledgers to inventory what's in stock. We speak of storing up resentment or having pent-up anger. We use metaphors like "our inner feelings," again suggesting there is some thing or entity inside us. But if emotions were things and could be stored and released, why can't the millions of unhappy souls who lament that they have so much love just waiting to be shared make themselves ecstatic by releasing their love? The fact is that these metaphors mislead, protraying our emotions as something quite apart from us and our bodies as mere vessels for their storage. Emotions aren't "things" one has but actions of a particular sort, as we shall momentarily see.

A second common problem with the way we talk about emotions is the myth we perpetuate that we are passive receivers of the emotional tides of life. Philosopher Robert Solomon maintains that our talking and thinking are riddled with this myth:

We "fall in" love, much as one might fall into a tiger trap or a swamp. We find ourselves "paralyzed" with fear, as if we had been inoculated with a powerful drug. We are "plagued" with remorse, as if by flies or mosquitoes. We are "struck" by jealousy, as if by a Buick; "felled by shame" as a tree by an ax; "distracted" by grief, as if by a trombone in the kitchen; "haunted" by guilt, as if by a ghost; and "driven" by anger as if pushed by a prod.[3]

Here the emotions are placed outside the self, and we find the individual divided as a home of reason fighting off the alien forces from outside. This myth keeps us divided from ourselves and denies us a sense of integrity with regard to our deepest feelings and commitments about life and, more important, ourselves.

In place of these perspectives, rhetoric generally holds an active view of emotions and of the audiences who experience them. Indeed, by embracing the view that audiences are able to form sound judgments, rhetoric separates itself from other persuasive forms (like propaganda) that treat their receivers as malleable clumps to be molded or whipped into a particular behavioral state.

Emotions Reflect Judgments

Rather than viewing the emotions as things or as passively received states, a rhetorical perspective views them as interpretations or judgments. Emotions obviously involve feelings such as helplessness, impotence, honor, power, euphoria, and the like. But when we experience an emotion, our feelings are not nonspecific; they are about something or someone. We don't feel love in general. We love Dad, we love Kirsten, we love our dear friends who have shared so many rich experiences with us. Because emotions are feelings about some object, they represent judgments. X is good, Y is evil; A is pleasurable, B is painful.

If we return to the notion of a practical syllogism, we can clarify the type of judgment involved. Suppose a developer proposes to build a shopping mall on a tract of land that has poor drainage. The geologists tell us that the runoff from rain and melting snow won't be absorbed by the ground, so a retaining wall will have to be built to keep the water from cascading down onto the school at the bottom of the hill. One form of practical syllogism leads us to decide *objectively* that this development is not a sound idea. "If we cover the ground with pavement, there has to be suitable drainage for the water runoff. The Jones farm site does not have suitable drainage. We ought not to build the mall there." But the same set of facts could be construed in a different way: "I'm the type of person who believes children should not be endangered. This mall will endanger our children. I'm angered by this proposal." This syllogism implies a rejection of the proposed mall, but the rejection is couched in a *subjective* judgment about the proposal. The practical syllogism formed puts the object in relationship to the self, and the resulting judgment involves the self. Though not all judgments involve emotions, all emotions are expressions of judgments. Their particular character is that they are self-involving judgments.[4]

When we say that an emotion is the expression of a judgment, several important features are implied. For one thing, all judgments are normative in character. This means that we require criteria to make them. For example, if a friend tells us, "The steak at Louie's is good," we have a judgment. "But what do you mean by 'good'?" we ask. "I'm talking substantial steak—fourteen to sixteen ounces and at least an inch thick. Lean on the outside, marbled in the center. So tender you barely need a knife. They have that *real* charcoal-grilled flavor, and they're cooked just right—seared on the outside and red and juicy in the middle. Yum!" Then again, if your friend is partial to Middle Eastern cooking, you might be told, "These steaks really assult your taste buds. They are sliced thin and cooked to well done, embedded with pepper and covered with the wildest sauce of spices and sautéed vegetables. Yum!"

These judgments, like all judgments, reflect criteria. Sometimes, as in the case of what constitutes "good food," the criteria may be cultural and widespread. But not all judgments require intersubjective agreement, especially ones involving emotions. The whole of humanity may speak as one in telling you that you should not feel anxious or depressed or angry, but that does not alter the fact that you may actually experience those emotions despite assurances to the contrary.

Where emotions are involved, the judgments about subject-object relationship are based on criteria related to self-esteem. These criteria involve our image of what is and of what we think should be, of the present and a projected future. Thus we consider the interaction between what event is transpiring, our self-image, the impact of present events on our self-image, and the implied projection of that relationship into the future. Anxiety does not pop up of the moment, but it includes the fear that the future will be undesirable in some way if events continue as we project them. Love is not a judgment isolated to the present but projects itself to the imagined ecstacy of a future that keeps in touch with love's mystery.

A second feature implied by conceptualizing emotions as judgments is that each emotional experience is in some way unique. We do not have *the* emotion love. Every time we feel love, it is different, depending on whom we love, the circumstances of the experience, our own subjective state of development, and the relationship's special features. These features impregnate our emotions *as they are experienced* because they alter the self-object relationship in terms of its specific circumstances and our projected futures from these circumstances. Emotions, in other words, may have generic labels, but they are unique to the given case.

A third dimension that emerges from our claim that emotions are judgments is their dependence on language. Without language, we would have sensations and could make sign responses, as do other animals. Beaten by a stick, a dog senses danger at the sign of a raised stick and flees—a point not lost on savvy joggers who need to keep the neighborhood beasts at bay. Lacking language, there is no way for dogs to get beyond their primitive sign response. They can't ask or even wonder, "Say, Cowboy, are you engaged in gratuitous thrusting or do you mean to use that thing on me?" But with humans it is different. Language makes it possible for us to create relationships, to create and express the meanings of our experiences, and to alter their meanings by altering the relationships expressed.

You can observe the arbitrary and personal nature of emotional expression by watching the differences in parental responses to the predictable behaviors of their youngsters at the local K mart. To children, K mart is the toy department, plain and simple. They twitch and squirm or, if left unattended, bolt for the toys. Mother Nature's instincts are hard to deny. Not all parents share in this delight. Some find a child's mad dash an inconvenience at best, even a sign of incorrigible misbehavior. Stern looks, commands, chastisement, and rude yanking of tiny arms ensue. But other parents seem to have a more serene perspective on matters. These look on as if in a state of grace. They gush in harmonious exclamations with their tykes and ask questions that help their youngsters express their fantasies. Doubtless they have joined in the children's safari spirit that makes the toy department a source of adventure. The objective bits and pieces of initiating motion are the same in both instances, but the experiences are different: one parent aggravated at the inconvenience, the other enraptured by a child's sense of adventure. The differences stem from the symbolic configuration placed on the experience, altering its meaning and the self-involved judgment encouraged.

Finally, emotions are experienced in eventful ways. They occur in time, they are felt with respect to a referent, they are unique to the configuration of elements in the given case, they are judgments given meaning in language, and they culminate in acts that express these judgments and may terminate the episode. They are, in short, interpretive evaluations about some state that exists in terms of how we think things ought to be and the further actions to which these tend. This is not to deny that we may experience the love of our mother throughout our lives as a process of care and affection and valuing of our worth. It is rather to assert that our consciousness of our mother's love or of any other emotion is tied to a given case, an episode of interaction, a configuration of circumstances, and in this sense is eventful.

The patterns of response we call "emotions" play an obvious and important role in communication. Since these patterns reflect judgments, emotions are not capricious but are tied to the active and ongoing self-involving interpretations we make of our experiences. Knowing that these judgments are normative, unique to their context, language-dependent, and eventful, we may understand more clearly how they are evoked and their propriety in the given case. Ideally, their role is to involve ourselves in such ways as facilitate responsible action. If we return to the Aristotelian observation noted earlier regarding logos, ethos, and pathos as sources of persuasion, we may modernize Aristotle's expression as follows: Rhetoric is the act of interpreting our experiences through symbols for the purpose of making sound practical choice. In any communication, we are moved to such choices by interpretations of experience that are *subject-involved* (logos), *source-involved* (ethos), and *self-involved* (pathos).

Evoking Emotions

With these thoughts on the interpretive character of emotions in mind, we are ready to consider how emotions are developed out of persuasive reasoning. The search for persuasive appeals will take into account the complex of factors that define the given case as a unique rhetorical situation. In understanding how emotions are experienced in a rhetorical situation, we must be mindful of how the factors we have been discussing interact.

Our discussion outlined three factors that seem to be a part of every emotion considered as a thought. First, we noted that the thought has a *referent*. This can be any object of experience: a thing, a person, an event, another thought. Emotions are not free-floating but thoughts with respect to a referent. Second, an emotion is a self-involving judgment called a *feeling*. Feelings can be directed to oneself (as in the case of duty), toward another (such as we experience with envy), or toward a relationship (for instance, love). Again, feelings are not free-floating but directed. Third, the judgments we make in experiencing an emotion are toward the future. This means that emotions are experienced as *telic* (goal-oriented) states. The goal is an act appropriate to the self-involvement experienced. Thus the *experiencing* of emotions includes thoughts about something that arouse feelings of self-involvement and lead to projections of appropriate actions that naturally follow.

You overhear someone gossiping about your friend. In general, loose talk is an annoyance, but this loose talk is about a friend. The *thought* makes a specific coupling of an act (gossip) with a referent (my friend). More than likely, you feel angry. Your friend has been slighted. This is unjust. Your thought is *self-involving* since you care about your friend and her welfare. In a state of anger, you act in ways that are appropriate. You interrupt the gossiper, telling the person to mind his own business. If you are really provoked, you deliver a scathing tongue-lashing to avenge the slight by embarrassing the target before his friends.

The variables that will make these appeals effective will be the same as for all rhetorical appeals: speaker, speech, and audience as they are related in the given case. The essentials for arousing emotions in persuasive appeals are arguments that engage audiences in terms of their experiences. Pathos, properly developed, does not refer to employing loaded language or wild-eyed harangues. It refers to the self-evoking aspects of our total response to the arguments brought before us for our active consideration. Pathos grows from the way in which the enthymemes of the discourse are developed.

Returning to our model of the practical syllogism, each argument developed needs to be evaluated in terms of how it will invite an audience to respond and whether the audience is ready to offer this response. For instance, in May 1983, Congress voted approval of President Reagan's plan to base MX missiles in existing silos. Before that vote was taken, the president defended his plan in a published statement. After referring to the findings of a bipartisan presidential commission that supported deployment of an MX system, Mr. Reagan had this to say:

> The question now before us is whether or not the Congress will join this consensus, a consensus that can unite us in our common search for ways to protect our country and reduce the level of nuclear weapons and the risk of war. Such a consensus is more than desirable, it is crucial to America's future and to the future of all the civilized values we hold dear and would protect from mass destruction.[5]

He invites several responses from his audience: See the commission as responsible; see agreement with them as reasonable; see the fruits of this agreement as desirable and crucial for all you value, including survival.

These responses are *what* he asks of his audience. However, the persuasive success of his appeal depends largely on *how* these responses are courted. Notice two features, the heavy stress on consensus and the projected stakes associated with consensus. All of the responses invited are tied to the "consensus" of the presidential commission. Because we place such high cultural value on consensus, the appearance of widespread and bipartisan agreement makes opposition seem irrational. The role of consensus in the reasoning we are asked to share might be cast this way:

> I'm the type of person who wants to act reasonably.
> Unless I join this bipartisan consensus, I won't be acting reasonably.
> Therefore, I must join this consensus.

This appears to be a good reason. But there is more to this argument than the apparent reasonableness of consensus. Reagan's appeal associates consensus with matters that are extremely important: protecting our country, reducing the level of nuclear weapons, risking war, living a civilized life, possible obliteration of the human race. These matters are highly self-involving. Consequently, joining or rejecting this consensus is made to seem an affirmation or denial of matters that are crucial to our very survival. Such emotions as anxiety, dread, fear, and hope come into play as relevant responses. If we wish to survive, the argument seems to say, we must join this consensus. Our emotion-engaging thoughts might be displayed this way:

> I'm the type of person who wants to have hope for a future.
> Unless I join this consensus, I cannot have hope.
> Therefore, I must say, "Build those missiles!"

For readers already predisposed to his message, Reagan's task is relatively straightforward. By keeping foremost thoughts that they already accept and that support his cause, he encourages not only reasoned assent but emotional reinforcement of this assent.

Whether Reagan's readers were ready to give this response depended on several factors: Did they believe that consensus to build *an* MX system meant adopting *his* MX plan? Did they believe that more weapons would lead to fewer weapons? Did they think the Soviet Union would risk attack if we lacked this system? Would it decrease or increase the likelihood of nuclear war? Those who disagreed in these respects probably resisted the relationships he offered and thus experienced the emotions invited by his appeal to a lesser extent or not at all.

When audiences are not positively predisposed, emotional support may be had only by getting acceptance of new ideas first. Unless an audience can be brought to accept a claim, it cannot experience emotional rapport with the rhetor to act on the claim. The introduction of new thoughts, the placement of existing thoughts in new contexts, or the refutation and removal of thoughts are ways to change the emotional barometer of audiences. Persuaded to change their thinking, their emotional judgments are simultaneously altered.

A handy illustration of the profound impact of new relationships on thoughts and emotions is found in an experiment conducted by the Russian film directors Kuleshov and Pudovkin. They took a close-up picture of the face of the actor Mosjukhin. He was in a quiet pose, and his face was relatively relaxed and expressionless. They asked audiences to view this picture followed by three other pictures: a bowl of soup, a coffin in which a dead woman lay, and a little girl playing with a toy bear.

> When we showed the three combinations to an audience which had not been let into the secret the result was terrific. The public raved about the acting of the artist. They pointed out the heavy pensiveness of his mood over the forgotten soup, were touched and moved by the deep sorrow with which he looked on the dead woman, and admired the light, happy smile with which he surveyed the girl at play. But we knew in all three cases the face was exactly the same.[6]

The reasoning of the audience and the judgment they formed was altered by the juxtaposition of the face with different pictures. The new thought of each picture led to a changed judgment of the feeling involved.

We can see this same principle in our earlier illustration concerning the MX missile system. Several days after President Reagan's observations appeared, the opposing views of Senator Gary Hart were published. Among his arguments was this:

> Each MX we build will mean less emphasis on truly survivable alternatives to today's vulnerable land-based missiles. Each MX we build will mean fewer ships, fewer tanks, fewer fighters and less readiness to face the threats before us around the globe, so that the first rifle shot could mean we would be forced to escalate to nuclear war simply because we were unable to meet aggression with appropriate power.[7]

In order to defuse the emotional support for the MX generated by Reagan's argument, Hart changes the context in which the MX system is understood. Rather than absolute terms, Hart chooses comparative ones. The MX missiles are one of many defense options available. Their expense will lead to shortages in other areas. These shortages will actually increase the danger of nuclear war because the nation will lack sufficient conventional defenses. This point is dramatized by his vision of answering a rifle shot with a nuclear response. Again, because the prospect of nuclear war involves our concerns for survival, it is highly self-involving and has potential for strong emotional response. As in the case of Reagan's appeal, anxiety, dread, fear, and hope are likely responses. But here they are associated with the opposite idea. If we want to survive, this argument seems to say, we must maximize our options for defensive response. The reasoning would go like this:

I'm the type of person who wants to have hope for the future.
Unless we maximize our defensive options, I cannot have hope.
Therefore, I must say, "Do not build those missiles!"

The Reagan and Hart examples illustrate how in speaking and in writing, each thought brought before an audience has the potential to evoke an emotion. To succeed at this, it must intersect with the audience's experience and must be self-involving in some way.

BASIC EMOTIONS

So far our analysis of emotions has been essentially cognitive. We have seen that a *rhetorical* view of emotions considers them to be *judgments* concerning our feelings about the objects of our experience and that these judgments are self-involving. When we communicate, we constantly present others with ideas for their approval or rejection. These ideas are presented in appeals that provide reasons for assent or dissent and simultaneously engage receivers in interpretive acts in which they see the implications of these ideas or thoughts for themselves. Emotions in rhetoric are the products of these interpretations. We also considered how this cognitive model could be portrayed in the form of a practical syllogism. Emotional judgments are experiences of seeing oneself as the type of person who exhibits certain behavior when confronted by an object of a specific sort: "I'm the type of person who defends friends"; "I'm the type of person who seeks revenge when slighted"; "I'm the type of person who is embarrassed when I feel markedly inferior"; and so forth.

Each culture has typical response patterns specific to its members and their times. In Greek antiquity, Aristotle provided a list of 14 basic emotions (Table 8.1). These were emotions common to public life in the Athenian polis. Today we would add to this list. Our culture experiences and expresses emotions that an ancient Greek would not have expressed in public and probably did not experience. Robert Solomon has assembled a dictionary of such emotions (Table 8.2) that includes more than 20 in addition to those discussed by Aristotle.[8] While these inventories are useful for initial understanding of the emotional possibilities we might attempt to explore, it is important to remember that emotions are argued responses specific to our culture and our times. They are not determined responses but interpretive responses. Thus for any analysis of a rhetorical situa-

**Table 8.1 ARISTOTLE'S LIST OF
BASIC EMOTIONS**

Anger	—	Mildness
Love	—	Enmity (hatred)
Fear	—	Confidence
Shame	—	Shamelessness
Benevolence	—	Pity
Indignation	—	Envy
Emulation	—	Contempt

Table 8.2 SOLOMON'S LIST OF BASIC EMOTIONS

Angst, anguish, and anxiety	Frustration	Pride
Depression	Gratitude	Regret and remorse
Despair	Guilt	Respect
Dread	Hope	Sadness
Duty	Indifference	Self-respect
Embarrassment	Innocence	Vanity
Faith	Joy	Worship
Friendship		

tion, the basic emotions available are the ones that listeners and readers may provide by virtue of their acculturation.

Parents, teachers, playmates, and social networks all serve as a school teaching us about ourselves and appropriate interpretations of our experiences. Mother teaches us to be courageous: "You have to go to school today, even though you dread your math exam"; "Be brave and don't cry when you get your shots." Father instructs us in duty: "Mow the lawn before you go swimming"; "Practice your instrument, then we'll watch TV." Many of our emotions (maybe all) are guided by such instruction, whereby we learn the rules for forming self-involving judgments about our experiences. At first we may learn these by rote, but eventually we are on our own to figure out which acts are loving, courageous, generous, and the like, in a given case.

When we listen to rhetoric, our criteria for assessment are continuously engaged. We bring values to bear throughout a rhetorical encounter according to the rules we have learned for their application to our experiences. Each of these standards is a thought with implications for our self-esteem. Audiences cannot offer responses other than the ones that are within their cultural experience. That is why the basic list of emotions is of less use than knowing the typical ways in which the given audience views the events to be considered, the values available to be tapped, the typical ways these values are used by them, and the ones best suited to the present circumstances. Considerations like these guide our judgments of attraction or repulsion. They are the *available* sources of emotion in the given case.

SUMMARY

From earliest times, emotions have been a source of suspicion about rhetoric. When people talk about matters they find important, they become personally involved, and they show it. However, Western societies have tended to value reason over emotion as the proper guide to sound conclusions. By extension, this bias has made us leery of the persuader skilled at inflaming our passions. We fear acting without deliberating a matter on its reasoned merits. Part of the negative associations people have for "rhetorical" communication stems from this fear. Persuaders are suspected of clouding our reason by playing on our emotions. Emotions that have no reasons behind them can be dangerous, leading to rash and even harmful deeds.

The point of this chapter has not been to dispel our cautions with emotional appeals. History contains too many examples of harm from actions guided by passions while lacking in common sense. Rather, we have been concerned with understanding the proper place of emotions in guiding our actions and how this understanding leads to a responsible rhetoric addressed to the whole person—a being that feels as well as thinks.

Emotions are patterns of response; they are specific, directed toward objects of our experience. Their directed character means that our emotions are subjective judgments that we express as feelings. We cannot help but form these judgments whenever the thoughts we entertain involve our selves in some way. We interpret such experiences in terms of what is and what we hope will be as they relate to our self-esteem. The key to all of this, then, is the basis on which these judgments are formed. If they rest on good reasons—the logos of an appeal—our emotions are likely to be appropriate responses, essential for considered action. When a speaker or writer encourages our emotional responses without good reasons, we are likely being manipulated and need to exercise caution. A responsible rhetoric does not separate our thoughts from our feelings; it unites them by addressing the whole person in terms of that person's experiences and the judgments they support. Thus the question is not whether rhetoric engages our feelings—it cannot avoid doing so—but whether our feelings are appropriate in making wise decisions.

NOTES

1. John Watson, *Behaviorism* (Chicago: University of Chicago Press, 1930), p. 268.
2. See G. E. M. Anscombe, *Intention* (London: Oxford University Press, 1957); and G. H. von Wright, "Practical Inference," *Philosophical Review,* 72 (April 1963), 159—179.
3. Robert C. Solomon, *The Passions* (Garden City, N.Y.: Anchor Press, 1976), p. xvii.
4. Solomon develops this point in detail in Chapter 9 of *The Passions.*
5. *Philadelphia Inquirer,* May 29, 1983, p. 1E.
6. Cited in Frank Geldard, *Fundamentals of Psychology* (New York: Wiley, 1962), p. 46.
7. *Philadelphia Inquirer,* loc. cit.
8. Solomon, pp. 282—368.

chapter *9*

Acting with Language

Our discussion in Chapters 5 through 8 has been concerned with the contents of appeals. Our main interest was the method for finding appeals. This included the modes of appeals that persuaded and the ways in which addressed appeals are understood by audiences. The topic of language kept appearing throughout our discussion, as we might expect in a treatment of discourse intended for use. Now we will treat this topic in a systematic fashion. The earlier discussion was heavily influenced by classical treatments of rhetoric because the ancients provided a particularly rich consideration of the techniques for rhetorical arguments. From here on, our perspective will be much more contemporary, drawing heavily on the work of rhetoricians, philosophers, and critics who have broadened the concerns of rhetoric.

The focus of classical rhetoric was persuasion as it occurred in public address. But language can influence our judgment in more forms than formal statements. Whenever symbols encourage us to share our attitudes, they are functioning rhetorically. This broader scope represents a new point of view. Contemporary rhetoricians have captured this new point of view by shifting their focus from persuasion to *identification*. Identification does not supersede our concerns with persuasive appeals. It incorporates them into a larger framework based on the unique uses made of language as the defining feature of our humanity.

In this chapter and the next we will consider persuasive uses of language. We will explain how language used in situated contexts exhibits our motives and encourages others to share them with us—what critic Kenneth Burke calls a *rhetoric of motives.* This theory of language as action will be explained in Chapter

9 and extended to include meaning as a function of situated context in Chapter 10.

ACTION AND MOTION

The moon is one of nature's majestic wonders. Set in its orbit, it circles the earth every 28 days. It is so regular that ever since our species started keeping track of time, the moon has provided a calendar that has never failed. It regulates the ebb and flow of tides. It provides the spectacle of a solar eclipse. Its heavenly course is so predictable that it offers mariners a reliable navigational aid. Were there no humans to observe its cycle, the moon would still go through its phases, still circle the earth every 28 days, still regulate the tides, still eclipse the sun, still follow a trackable path through the night sky. These are descriptive of its place in nature. The moon, in this sense, is in the realm of motion. It is what it is— a clump of matter in orbit around another clump of matter.

These may be descriptive of the moon's harmony with nature, but it serves more vital functions for the human imagination. It is the wellspring of romance, as lovers bathed in moonlight look heavenward in prayer that the mystery will never leave. It is the playpen of science fiction come true, as astronauts hike and bike across its surface to play out the metaphor of America's destiny with the frontier. It is the culprit for lunacy, providing an excuse from responsibility for bizarre behavior. It is the motherlode for poets, songwriters, and fancy Dan wordsmiths who tinker with synecdochic possibilities to express the themes of life or at least tug at the heart. Left to human devices, the moon takes on symbolic significance and is thereby transferred from the realm of motion to the realm of action—the realm of our attitudes, where we attach interpretations to the raw data of existence. It no longer is what it is; it is what we make of it.

All of nature is motion—the earth, the universe, the trees, the fish in the river, the pumping of your heart. All of it is what it is. The term *action* indicates the realm of meaning where symbols are used to refer: dance, painting, speech, languages in general. Something happens to objects of nature when they are transported to the realm of action. Symbols give them meaning that goes beyond their physical properties. Moreover, these symbolically created meanings cannot be reduced to physical properties. B. F. Skinner's pigeons pecking away at their sources of reward are in the realm of motion: They are perfectly explainable in terms of their nonsymbolic or extrasymbolic operations of conditioned response.[1] But put a label on what those pigeons are doing—*behaviorism*—and soon you have controversy on your hands, as in "I ain't no pigeon, Jack!" Transferred into the symbolic realm of an ism, the pigeon becomes more than a pigeon; it is now a claim about the human condition. That statement can't be reduced to the bird pecking away. It is more than the bird, more than motion. Furthermore, the counterclaim makes no sense if taken to mean literally and exclusively that its human author is not a bird. Obviously not, since in the realm of motion there are only affirmatives—things are what they are. It makes sense only as a statement rejecting behaviorism.

Thus we can say that *motion* refers to the nonsymbolic or the extra symbolic operations of nature, as with the earth's rotation, the ebbing of tides, the growth and decay of vegetation, the breathing of mammals. *Action* refers to the type of behavior that becomes possible with the use of symbols. Kenneth Burke summarizes their relationship this way:

1. There can be no action without motion.
2. There can be motion without action.
3. Action is not reducible to terms of motion.[2]

HUMANS ACT WITH LANGUAGE

A contemporary commonplace in the language arts holds that humans *act* with language. The claim is intriguing but ambiguous because it is used in a variety of ways. For instance, there is a school of thinkers who have developed *speech act theory*. They maintain that each utterance has three components: what is said, called a *locution;* what is done in the saying, called an *illocution;* and the psychological impact of what was said, called a *perlocution*. Mostly they focus on illocutions. For instance, when Martha says, "I'll bring the map of West Virginia tomorrow," she has made the speech act of a *promise;* when Kathy says, "Don't vote for him, he's a spendthrift," she has issued a *warning*.

Quite apart from this, there is an anthropological school, started by Bronislaw Malinowski, that views humans as engaged in acts of *communal joining* when they speak. For instance, when you pass a friend on the street, what you say is less important than the fact that you offer a greeting. The function of the utterance is more important than its content. When we call out, "Larry, how're you doin'?" we are not asking for a medical update. If Larry starts complaining about his sinuses and insomnia, we may offer a sympathetic look, but behind this mask our minds are racing to find a graceful exit from this encounter. Our greeting really meant to convey our friendliness toward this person. It was an act of *recognition*. By the same token, were we to look him in the eye and pass in silence, our act would have been a *snub*.

We will return to Malinowski's views in Chapter 10, but for now we note that while these views illustrate that we act with language, they do not indicate *how* we do so. In order to answer that question, we need a functional perspective toward language. While most contemporary rhetoricians discuss their subject in functional terms, the most influential account in terms of *acting* with language is provided by Kenneth Burke. He develops an analysis of how humans act with language modeled after the dramatic action of the stage. This perspective is called *dramatism*.

Dramatistic Assumptions

Dramatism holds that people manage social situations through their uses of language or symbolic acts. Managing symbols is the principal means by which we coordinate our social actions. When we use symbols, we act much as a performer on a stage. These acts are motivated, as are an actor's. We assume that our interlocutors are capable of sharing these motives, similar to an audience caught up in the ebb and flow of a play's dramatic action. When motives are shared, we feel and act as one. It seems, then, that our capacity to use and respond to language or symbols is at the heart of coordinating social action.

At first glance, this claim appears obvious. How else would we coordinate social action except through language? Indeed, we'd be lost otherwise. Less apparent is the reason why this is so. Burke has suggested that we are able to coordinate our social lives only because we construct our social realities through symbols. In short, we are symbol-using animals. Burke's insight is captured in his definition of *man* as

- *the symbol-using* (misusing) *animal*
- *inventor of* (or invented by) *the negative*
- *separated from his natural condition by instruments of his own making*
- *goaded by a spirit of hierarchy*
- *rotten with perfection*[3]

Each of these codicils deserves further inspection because they explain the basis for our human capacity to act with language. This capacity makes rhetorical analysis, when properly understood, among the most powerful tools available for explaining why humans do the social things they do.

Symbol User   The first, and most basic, of Burke's assumptions is that humans are uniquely symbol-using animals. Whereas other animals can emit meaningful sounds or signals in the code of their species, only humans can reflect on this fact. As Burke says, "Cicero could both orate and write a treatise on oratory. A dog can bark but he can't bark a tract on barking."[4] Without the capacity to use symbols, we would be the same as all other animals. But because we can use symbols and reflect on our symbols, we are able to engage in the creative activity of making social realities with our symbols.

It comes as no surprise, I am sure, to hear that humans are symbol-using animals. But the implications of this capacity are far-reaching. For one thing, this talent enables us to reflect on our experience, to abstract meaning from it, to organize and communicate it to others for others to reflect on what we communicate and to communicate back the thoughts they have in response. It enables us to create new understanding by inventing labels for unnamed experiences, especially through the use of metaphor. As symbol-using animals, we are also symbol-making animals. More than this, our symbols can separate us from the nonverbal realm to which they refer. They can evoke confused responses to their cognitive and emotional meanings, rather than to their referents' material properties of existence (as when our isms lead to distorted views of those who practice other isms).

Negativity   Our ability to use language permits us to engage in critical acts. This takes us beyond the implied criticism of an animal who shuns a particular food.

As symbol-using animals, we can make choices that go beyond the factual "is—is not" to the moral realm of "shall—shall not." For example, the formative experiences we have at Mother's knee, such as her admonitions not to pull the cat's whiskers or not to take coins off her dresser or not to tease our sister, taught us a basic moral code. It is not absurd to say that Mother's negatives invented us! As social actors, we possess an identity that was developed through symbolic acts of criticism and encouragement. "Shall—shall not" serves the hortatory or inciting function of urging us to make some choices and avoid others. But these choices themselves are open to criticism. The use of the negative to criticize choices anchors our morality as ethical creatures in our ability to use symbols.

Separation   Choice also implies a condition somewhat removed from our primitive needs for food, shelter, and sexual release. All animals have these needs. Human inventions that take us beyond our primitive state create new possibilities—language inventions not the least. We can use language, like all tools, as an instrument to accomplish ends. Of course, the ends are higher-order abstract needs; they exist only because we have the tools at our disposal to accomplish them. For example, electronic communication creates the possibility for transmitting complex information across space in a matter of moments. Interactive systems permit responses to flow back with lightning speed. There are efficiencies of time, human effort, and precision in data processing not previously conceivable. On the other hand, we risk becoming so reliant on our machines that should they fail us, we would be helpless. The panic that occurs in large metropolitan areas when the electricity goes out is a vivid example. Language as a tool can be equally double-edged, creating the possibilities for survival (as when we are able to understand and manage the forces of nature because we can express them in symbolic ways) and the possibilities for extermination (as when we turn the forces of nature loose in a nuclear weapon).

Hierarchy   Choice also involves us in order—determining what goes with what. Inherent in intelligible uses of symbols is organization, and organization introduces a principle of hierarchy. Symbols array referents in relationship to one another: similarity and difference, up and down. Up and down in turn introduce states, where what is up is guilty of not being down ("They think they're better than we are") and vice versa ("We wouldn't stoop to their level" or "They're not our kind"). In our uses of language we cannot avoid this, because language is riddled with valuing. All statements of more and less, of better and worse imply a hierarchical order. Sometimes we codify these in our laws or religious doctrines; sometimes we engage in social mystification, distrusting people who are different or turning them into deities to be worshiped. Regardless, as symbol-using animals, we are able to create social structures that impose status and place and affect the condition of life as genuinely as any material force of nature.

Perfection   Saying that symbol use involves us in valuing and hierarchy leads to this final observation. As symbol-using (symbol-misusing) animals, we strive to perfect the logic of these orders. For Aristotle, this striving for perfection was contained in his thought that the universe was *entelechial,* with all beings striving for perfection. For Freud, this was contained in a negative sense in the neurotic behavior of compulsive repetition of some earlier unresolved problem. In repeating this agony, the neurotic conforms to a behavior pattern formed early and perfected throughout life. The symbol use or misuse is perfect in both cases, suggesting, as Burke says, that we are "rotten" with the spirit of perfection as we seek the logical extension of some principle, positive or negative. Symbols embody such principles in forms or patterns that we can spend our whole lives perfecting: perfection in work, in relationships, in performing a skill. At a less totally absorbing level, perfection is expressed in our ironic sense of the "perfect idiot" or "perfect fool." As should be evident in this extension of symbol use, we have passed deep into the realm of action, where the forces at play are human motives as they are formed, exhibited, and managed in social intercourse.

Presentation Versus Representation

These codicils clarify what we mean when we say that humans are essentially symbol-using animals. They indicate the great power of symbols to alter our social world. By the selection and use of symbols, we create relationships (as when we make friends by speaking in terms of common interests) and change relationships (as when we embarrass a friend by revealing her secrets to others); we shape perceptions (say, by professing sincere interest) and alter perceptions (by grandstanding); we engage one set of motives impelling us to act for an idea ("I should do this because I'm obliged to"), then engage a contrary set of motives impelling us to act against an idea ("but I must be true to myself first"). Because we are symbol-using animals and because we are uniquely able to respond to symbols, we are able to act with symbols.

Sometimes we have a tendency to think and speak as if our language were only a symptom of some deeper reality hidden inside us. This view treats language as *representational.* This is a typically psychological view of language. It assumes that reality is under the surface and that language is of value insofar as it provides clues to the meaning of the hidden reality. If we want to understand what any communication means, we have to act as detectives, assembling clues to support an inference. While there are doubtless times when we keep our thoughts to ourselves and times when we may deceive ourselves about our true thoughts, feelings, or motives, in general a representational view of language is not very efficient, nor is it well grounded conceptually.

It lacks efficiency because it assumes that nothing is what it says it is, requiring the amassing of substantial clues to support inferences. It is more efficient if we have a model for dealing with the data of communication in its own right.

More important, the tendency to think of communication as *representing* a hidden reality is not well grounded. For one thing, we would have to escape this problem. Either there is a basis for thinking that is not symbolic (a very hard claim to prove), or we'd have to maintain that communication was inherently deceptive. But if it is deceptive, how will we get information that will permit valid inferences about the hidden reality? Except for Freudian slips, it is hard to imagine what this evidence would be. Then, if there is a hidden reality, all inferences from the evidence amassed in communication analysis would be about the past. But this would ignore the fact that people use communication to shape their futures. How could they do that if communication were but a sign of what was inside the communicator?

A more direct route uses the perspective we have been developing. A rhetorical perspective regards communication as a *presentation* of reality. This view holds, first, that communication is the act of *coordinating social actions* through the use of symbols. Symbolic forms express meanings. When we use expressive forms, we *create* meanings with others. For instance, the candidacy of Geraldine Ferraro *means* that Americans give women equal opportunity, or it *means* that the American electorate is sexist. What it means will be a social construct created by the symbolic presentation we make of the 1984 campaign and the shared acceptance of that presentation by others. Rhetorical communication is, after all, addressed activity. It *presents* an image of reality that is responded to as it is presented. In other words, as speakers and listeners, we work together to form the cooperative measures necessary for our social objectives to be met. In fact, even our social objectives are the products of our symbolicity.

Second, communication presents reality through the *organizing and projecting* power of symbols. We are all possessed of a past. But the meaning of that past is dependent on the relationships in which it is placed. For example, the death of a classmate in an automobile accident is tragic. But its meaning is multidimensional: Life isn't fair, she had so much to live for; it is important to drive with special caution at night; you never know when it's your time, so treat everyone with love; and so forth. Symbols take past experiences and organize them in the present in ways that permit projections into the future. Communication is presentational because symbolic forms embody images of reality that invite actions of specifiable sorts. It does not represent a world that already exists (our dead classmate) but presents an image of the world as it is seen (this is a tragic loss) and as it might become (live each day as if it were your last).

Third, the presentational character of communication stems from the *situated context* in which communication occurs. Why we act does not necessarily grow from within us but frequently from how we understand the situations in which we find ourselves.[5] These understandings are contained in the typical ways in which we present these scenes and the motives appropriate to them—a point we will develop shortly. Here the point is that humans act by presenting a scene in a way that delimits appropriate responses.

Dramatism

Understanding the presentational character of communication is valuable because it alerts us to the importance of a message's surface features. These provide basic dynamic connections between speakers or writers and their audiences as they bond in common solutions to common problems. But this insight in and of itself is not usable in a systematic fashion. To systematize it, a model is required.

A *model* is a conceptual structure that shows the interrelationships among relevant elements of some phenomenon of study. We need a model that best shows the presentational character of communication as a symbolic action. When we examine the presentation of messages, it reminds us of how a play is presented. Dramatic presentation can serve as a way to understand what happens when people exchange symbols. This model is called *dramatism.* Dramatism examines the ways in which we use language in the format of dramatic action.

Dramatic action is always situated in a *scene.* The difference between dramatic action and chitchat is that something happens in the scene—there is *action.* This action is not always the physical action such as we expect from Dirty Harry or Indiana Jones. But some event transpires nonetheless in any well-constructed dramatic scene: She *discovers* he loves her; he *rejects* his mother's wishes; they're *masking* their uncertainties through brave talk. Good directors find ways to physicalize this eventfulness of a scene so that the actors' movements as well as their words will add to the impact of the scene. Actions in turn require actors, or *agents,* who can carry them out. And no action could be carried out without means, or *agency,* to do so. All is for some end, or *purpose.*

Dramatism is a functional perspective toward language; it is concerned with how people manage symbols for social coordination. Through analysis of how language is used, we gain insights into the motives that impel human actors to do what they do and to justify it to others.

The dramatistic model formalizes the elements of dramatic presentation with five terms, called the *dramatic pentad.* Burke depicts the elements in this way:

Act: what was done; what communal moments were depicted

Scene: where the act occurred; the context of interaction in time and place and including the conditions for interaction

Agent: who performed the act; the individual or group engaged in some social function through the management of symbols

Agency: the means of acting; how the deed was done, including the medium of enactment

Purpose: the end or goal of the act; the communal values that were certified by engaging in an act.[6]

These five elements permit a complete description of the relevant aspects of a symbolic interaction. Furthermore, because they model human action dramatically, they emphasize the motivational dynamics that explain why a character did what she did. They are conceptual tools used to discover the facts about any communicative act and then put those facts in relationship to one another in a way that provides a plausible explanation for *what* happened, *how* it happened, and the motivational urges that account for *why* it happened.

This last point is important. As we watch a play, we are left unsatisfied if we do not know why the actors are doing what they are doing. We always search for their motivations. Once we get a sense of their motivations, we form expectations of what they'll do next and why. Romeo *loves* Juliet, so we are not shocked to see him calling outside her balcony. Henry Higgins has a *mission,* so we do not find his treatment of Eliza Doolittle inexplicable. Burke maintains that the human arena is precisely the same. We act out of motives. More than that, we impute motives to other actors. We have to if we hope to understand why they are acting as they are.

We use each element of the dramatic pentad in imputing motives. We examine how each contributes to or induces symbolic action. The patterns we discover allow us to draw inferences about a person's *attitude.* Burke says that when we think of communication as dramatic action, "the pattern is incipiently a hexad, in connection with the different but complementary analysis of *attitude* (as an ambiguous term for *incipient* action)."[7] By saying that "attitude is an incipient action," Burke means that every symbolic act conveys an attitude or disposition toward its referent. He maintains that attitudes are projections into the future of images from the past. For example, baseball fans hear that George Steinbrenner has hired a new manager, say Yogi Berra, and think, "Poor Yogi." From the past we have an image of the Yankee owner firing managers to beat the band. "Poor Yogi" reflects an attitude, a projection into the future: "You're going next."[8] Because it is a projection into the future, attitudes are *incipient* acts, that is, acts in their first stages, where their performance is just commencing. Attitudes, in short, are our projections into the future of events in the present based on our experiences from the past. Attitudes are the first stage of the future we anticipate will occur.

At the beginning of this chapter we remarked that contemporary rhetorical thinking has expanded beyond the podium to include all ways and places in which language influences others. Our discussions of dramatism's assumptions about humans as language-using animals, of its view that communication is presentational in nature, and of its modeling human action after the elements of drama suggest why this expansion has occurred. Together these assumptions indicate that we use language to shape our world. Rhetoric's domain extends beyond formal presentations in institutional sites to include any use of symbols that encourages attitudes.

Where does this leave us with respect to our original search for a functional account of *how* humans act with symbols? I believe it brings us to the point at which we are now ready to entertain precisely this concern.

With an expansion of rhetoric's boundaries to include all symbolic activity comes a corresponding need for a construct adequate to explain human symbolic behavior. Burke and other contemporary rhetoricians do not find such constructs in science. Scientific constructs are designed for variables that are regular, predictable, and controllable. These are variables in the realm of motion. However, humans are more than machines in motion. Humans are intentional beings who can create meanings symbolically and who can *act* as well as *move.* At the heart of action is *motive.*

Motives get us into the realm of the individual's merging with groups, the ways in which they merge, the reasons for the mergers, the forms these mergers take, and the "realities" for humans that they delimit. It is the social realm of humans using symbolic forms as means for promoting cooperation. This is our next concern.

MOTIVES AND ACTION

If we took a representational view of communication, we would assume that *motives* are hidden within the individual and that we must engage in the detective's task of collecting data to permit an inference about this inner reality. But the type of inference this assumption requires can never satisfy Sherlock Holmes because there is no basis for confirming or denying the inference, since its referent is presumably hidden. By adopting a presentational view of communication, we assume that people reveal their motives by the ways they bond to one another. Motives are observable in the ways we use language and, therefore, are available to anyone who cares to look for them. Motives are also present in everyone's use of language and are the source material from which rhetoric develops.

The presentational view introduces this important shift: It changes motive from a *psychological* concept that must be inferred to a *vocabulary* concept that can be observed. A vocabulary concept allows us to listen or read and discover why people do and say what they do. In other words, a motive is contained in a term or set of terms that people use to explain what they are doing. Such terms have ascertainable functions for the individual and the group in promoting social cooperation. They are elements in vocabulary that permit interpretations of meaning and intent that are necessary for social action to proceed.

For example, consider this excerpt from a union speech by Edward Keller:

> Our political action agenda must continue, because for public workers it goes hand in hand with the collective bargaining process!!! Let me tell you that our commitment to aggressive political action is as resolute as it ever was, because we have no other choice!! We have other options. We could give up the fight, and we could resign ourselves to second-class citizenship, or we could return to collective begging, and macing, and patronage, but, Brothers and Sisters, they are irresponsible choices. If we opted for them, we wouldn't deserve to be called a Union . . . [*sic*] and we wouldn't deserve to be called AFSCME![9]

Clearly, Mr. Keller wants his audience to continue political efforts. But notice how this language provides a justification that explains these union members' world. He depicts the union in a "fight." If it "gives up," the taboos of "collective begging," "macing," and "patronage" follow. If it fights on, it is "responsible." How does it fight? Through political action. Why does it fight? For advantage in collective bargaining. Who are the fighters? "Brothers and Sisters" who earn their family status only through continued political efforts. All of this is presented to Keller's listeners by the language he chooses to motivate their collective action. His language provides them with an explanation of who they are and what they are doing. In short, he provides them a meaningful vocabulary of motives.

Burke defines motives as "shorthand terms for situations."[10] Although that may seem a peculiar definition at first sight, it is reasonable and rich in meaning when considered in light of what we have been discussing. Why "shorthand terms for situations"?

All action, as we have noted, is situated action. The situations in which actions occur lend significance to those acts and are essential for understanding them. A priest walking to the altar of a church and genuflecting is showing reverence. The same priest instructing a college class and genuflecting toward the front of the room upon hearing a very confused student answer is showing despair. Situation provides us with the context for interpreting the symbolic actions that occur in them.

Not all situations are ones of conscious reflection, however. There are hundreds of acts we perform every day without reflecting on them. They are routine and not marked by conflict. We shut off our alarm and take a shower without thinking. We put on our jeans, the same leg first each day, without thinking. We walk to class without thinking about how to walk or which route to travel. Our minds are elsewhere, worrying about today's exam, determining whether we'll finish a project in time, recounting the stimulating events of last night, conversing with friends. Soon we're at the building, in the room listening to the lecturer. In the hour that passed, we were continuously situated but not consciously aware of that fact.

Consciousness arises in situations marked by conflict of some sort. Impulses pull us in different directions—approach this, avoid that. This is a bind; what shall I do? I can't do both; I'm faced with choice. In situations of conflicting impulses, choice is the essential ingredient. We have to decide what to do. And when we decide what to do, we do so on the basis of a motive. There is an explanation that we can offer. As Mother taught us, "just because" isn't satisfactory because it is ambiguous. Thus consciousness is concerned with motives, because motives move us to choose one alternative over the others. Burke summarizes this point when he asks, "Would not such facts all converge to indicate that our introspective words for motives are rough, shorthand descriptions for certain typical patterns of conflicting stimuli?"[11]

For example, your friend asks you to go to her party on Saturday. But you have a term project due on Monday that is not completed. This weekend is your best shot at meeting the deadline. You think of your professor, who has encouraged you in your work; you think of what a fine course it has been and all that you have gained from it; you think of the consequences for your grade if the project is rushed or turned in late. You decline the invitation. If we ask you why, you would say, "I have an obligation to my course work first." Your statement conveys very clearly a motive for turning down your friend's invitation, one that most of us would expect a friend to understand as a reasonable excuse, a proper motive.

On the other hand, suppose you think about how dull your life has been, how uninspired you are about this project, how much fun you'll have at the party, what a good group of people will be there, how much better you'll feel on Sunday. You'll go. And if we ask you why, you would say, "I needed a change of pace." Again, your statement conveys a motive for attending the party, one most of us have experienced and can understand as a way to release tension and allow us to work more productively because we're refreshed. It would be odd, if sensible at all, to say you went to the party as an obligation. That would suggest an entirely different set of conflicts—between you and your friend, not between your desire to finish a quality report and your need to socialize. Similarly, we would find it odd if you said you didn't attend because you needed a change of pace. You mean you haven't been doing course work lately?

In this case, *obligation* and *change of pace* are shorthand expressions that are used to resolve patterns of conflicting impulses so recurrent in our society that we have special terms for them. They are shorthand for situations of conflict and the ways in which they are resolved. They are words that organize the conflicting stimuli on the basis of images drawn from the past. They project an anticipated outcome from imposing this organization on the present.

Through the processes of socialization, we learn a vocabulary of motive terms. In fact, we learn several vocabularies: of home, family, and neighborhood; of friends; of school; of subcultures. When we learn a vocabulary of motives, we have learned what counts as a legitimate way to resolve life's conflicts for people who use that vocabulary. In a sense, we learn to speak that language and, by speaking the language, to become a member of the group.

Our affiliation through a vocabulary of motives does more than provide us with group identity; it also provides us with an orientation toward the world. Through our use of symbols, we project images of reality. These projections are not of realities themselves as factually existing entities but of *interpretations* of realities. We know, for instance, as a matter of fact that the Protestants and Catholics of Northern Ireland live in a state of mutual terror. We know that large numbers of these people are economically impoverished. We also know from listening to their rhetoric that they each act on their *interpretations* of reality, not on objective facts. Some vocabularies make Protestants the villains, some the Catholics. Some say it is really not a religious issue but an economic one. Some say it is a nationalistic issue at heart: The British are at fault, or the IRA is at fault. As confusing as this swarm of appeals may appear to an outsider, for those in the trenches of this conflict the vocabulary of motives they adopt makes all the difference in the world in determining their allegiances and targets of response.

Finally, we should observe that the concept of motive, when developed as the use of language to coordinate social functions, is quite similar to Aristotle's perspective on special topics. Whereas special topics focused on the material premises that were common to a group, motives focus on the linguistic aspects of common orientation. Both provide the means from which rhetorical appeals are developed. Let us now turn to rhetorical appeals to see how the concerns we have been discussing come to bear.

RHETORIC AND MOTIVES

Kenneth Burke tells us that rhetoric is not rooted in some magical power of primitive voodoo but "in an essential function of language itself, . . . the use of language as a symbolic means of inducing cooperation in beings that by nature respond to symbols."[12] Let us consider this definition as a summarizing statement for what we have thus far considered and as a transition to its rhetorical application.

First, we note that Burke thinks rhetoric is an *essential function of language.* By that he means that you could not have language without rhetoric being present in some way. We are reminded here of how the symbolic action perspective views all language as containing an attitude, which is an incipient act. All language, in other words, has bias in it, and that bias projects toward the future. It is an encouragement to perceive the world in a special way. Language sermonizes, much as a preachment, about our point of view, whether we intended to or not.[13]

Second, rhetoric is a *use of language.* So the study of rhetoric is concerned with the way language functions, with what people do with it. We are reminded that the contemporary study of language emphasizes the function it serves in coordinating social action and that in this respect people act with language. The uses of language are to form bondings of individuals with groups through their shared motives.

Third, rhetoric is a *symbolic means of inducing cooperation.* Consequently, rhetorical studies are not concerned only with the act of social bonding through cooperative exchange but also with how such acts are induced. People are encouraged to bond, not required to do so; they have choices. Moreover, these inducements are symbolic in character. They are not in the realm of motion as, for example, might be the case in the face of a natural emergency (your stove is on fire, so your roommate cooperates by throwing salt on the flames). Symbolic inducements are in the realm of action—human acts of selection, organization, and emphasis through intentional choices of symbols to interpret experiences.

Finally, rhetoric is directed to *beings that by nature respond to symbols.* As symbol-using animals, humans can be moved by symbols. They can use them, reflect on them, embellish or refute them, and act on them as interpretations of reality.

Identification

The primary rhetorical function of symbolic acts is to produce *identification.* This does not eliminate persuasion from rhetoric; it views persuasion as part of a larger, more general whole. Identification does not refer to identification *of,* such as my identification of the picture before me as my son or the sounds outside my windows as birds chirping. It refers to identification *with,* whereby we find that our ways are the same. At the most basic level, such identification occurs when we try to show that our ways are like the other person's: "I was once an undergraduate myself." At its most complex, it can go to the extreme of fusing rhetor and audience together in the cultural ideologies that mark us off as unique groups of people—nationally, religiously, economically, politically, philosophically. Regardless of its depth or sophistication, the basic principle of rhetoric, when examined dramatistically, is the *act* of identifying.

Identification can occur through any symbolic means. It can come through speaking the same language, wearing similar clothing, exhibiting common tastes, espousing the same cause, buying into the same ideology and playing by its rules. Any mode of symbolic action can be the source of identification.

Identification is a *dialectical* term. A dialectical term is one that implies its opposite. So when we say that identification occurs, we simultaneously imply that division has occurred. To be attracted to one view implies that you forgo its opposing views. Always there is the movement in rhetoric of identifying and dividing. But more than that, rhetoric also overcomes or compensates for division. We need rhetorical uses of language precisely because we are not one with each other. Rhetoric makes us one by showing us how our ways are united, as when an older person says, "You may find it hard to imagine, but I was once a student." In this fashion rhetoric overcomes division. Thus the principle of identification creates an ongoing cycle of joining and dividing, creating the need for a new effort to join that will also divide us from something else.

You may witness yourself being tossed about in these rhetorical seas by listening to the types of speeches delivered as keynote addresses at national political conventions. The purpose of these speeches is to give the delegates a chance to shout and holler enthusiastically. How better to do this than to reaffirm what "we" stand for and denounce the folly of what "they" propose? Yet each party's speaker will try to hit themes that the average American believes. We believe that the nation should have defensive capabilities, that our dollars should be worth something, that federal expenditures should be controlled, that individual initiative should be encouraged. We know Republican keynoters will speak on these themes. Insofar as we assent, we may feel ourselves divided from the opposition. At the same time, we believe that the government should not adopt policies that create unemployment, that we have an obligation to ensure equal opportunity—economically, socially, and politically, that we should not reward people or regimes that suppress human rights—Democratic themes to be sure. And we can identify with these appeals as surely as with the Republican speaker's. In both cases we identify and divide in an unceasing process of rhetorical exchanges.

Misidentification

Identification can also be misperceived. We may falsely believe that our ways and the rhetor's are one. In a word, we can *misidentify*. We may misidentify through the various ways in which misunderstanding and false interpretation can occur. We may think we stand for the same ideas, share common values, seek identical ends, only to discover that we have not heard correctly. Most frequently we will encounter this in conversations with strangers or new acquaintances. As our conversation progresses, we seek to understand what the other person says and how it relates to our beliefs and values. It is not uncommon for us to distort these messages toward symmetry of motives, lacking a history of behavior to help us interpret our newly acquired conversational partner's vocabulary of motives.

Misidentification may also occur through deceit and dissembling. Such occurrences require a deliberate management of symbols to create a false sense of unity. When a person engages in self-serving rhetoric or has ulterior motives in seeking our cooperation, misidentification is afoot.

Regardless of intention, we can look at misidentification as a perversion of identification. Whenever rhetoric leads us to change our perception, we identify with something *new* and divide from something *old*. In the act of dividing from a former perception, we have a tacit recognition that a former identification was a misidentification. Sometimes these divisions and simultaneous recognitions of misidentification are stark, as when a person experiences a religious conversion or becomes politically radicalized. At other times they are barely noticeable, as when a person adopts a modification of vocabulary to reformulate the expression of an experience. For example, the characterization of a military action as an "incursion" rather than an "invasion" may go unnoticed by most, but there is a clear difference in the perception each encourages of such an undertaking. Regardless of magnitude, identification and division are present whenever we use symbolic means to induce cooperation because all symbols express an attitude.

Vocabulary of Motives

The rhetorical objective of identification is advanced, therefore, by sharing a common vocabulary of motives. Such a vocabulary gives us a common framework in which to conceptualize our experiences. It provides a common rationale for our perceptions and interpretations of experiences, our expectations of future outcomes, our confidence that we are bonded in a fashion that sees reality in ways that are essentially the same.

Each vocabulary of motives becomes an elaboration of a basic organizing principle that unites these symbols into a coherent whole. Take the vocabulary of capitalism. The capitalist is concerned with the acquisition of *excess wealth* or *profits*. One acquires profits by providing something of *value* for *remuneration*. When the remuneration exceeds the costs, profits are earned. When costs exceed remuneration, *losses* are *suffered*. In order to know whether we are earning profits or suffering losses, we use methods of *accounting*. These will help us determine whether costs outweigh benefits. To account for costs and benefits, accountancy requires a unit of measurement. *Money* provides such a unit. Money is of value as a *medium of exchange*. Work, time, creativity, everything involved in a capitalist enterprise is of *value* insofar as it can be expressed in money. Money becomes the unit whereby we determine how we're doing. The more money we acquire as excess capital or wealth, the more *successful* we are.

Notice how easy it is now to slip into the social realm from the economic. If wealth is the measure of success, the only way anyone can measure my degree of success is by the amount of excess capital I have to spend. If I hoard my money, I do not use it for exchange value; it is not being put to use. If I spend money, I am using it for exchange value, but the exchange value is not just the material goods it purchases but also the social esteem it purchases. By subtle but trackable moves, we arrive at Thorsten Veblen's theory of conspicuous consumption, according to which the wealthy spend money lavishly to purchase recognition of their success.

But the matter does not stop there. Imagine that this vocabulary of economic exchange was used to discuss and make decisions about education. In the language of this vocabulary, we need a unit of exchange. If that unit is the student credit hour, then the more students we enroll in a course, the more valuable that course. Since the benefits of high enrollment outweigh the costs, we should encourage mass-enrollment courses and discourage low-enrollment courses. We will accord high status to departments that pack them in, low status to those with marginal enrollment. We will make decisions about which courses to offer and which departments to support on the basis of their popularity rather than on their merits as contributors to human knowledge. Students will not be considered in terms of their human potential to learn but in terms of their economic value in generating higher credit hours. Soon departments will make decisions based on the "draw potential" of a course rather than its intellectual merits. By adopting this vocabulary, it should be evident, we quickly lose sight of why students go to college in the first place, and we pervert the mission of higher education to discover, criticize, and disseminate knowledge.

The capitalist vocabulary illustrates how identification can involve a whole conceptual schema that articulates a coherent interpretation of reality. Moreover, such interpretations can be broad in scope, finding uses in more than one dimension of human experience. Capitalism provides a vocabulary of motives—a language for coordinating diverse social functions—not only in the economic realm. It can be applied to matters of social status, education, friendship, or politics, to mention a few. Each application may change the form that embodies the vocabulary, but it does not change the underlying principle of profitability.

Let us extend the contention that identification occurs through sharing a vocabulary of motives. Such vocabularies provide conceptual patterns for interpreting reality, and it is our conceptions of what is real that shape our responses. When we identify, we become one in terms of a shared principle. We cannot distinguish ourselves from one another in terms of that principle because we all adhere to it as essential to our orientation toward reality. This oneness in principle that underlies identification is called *consubstantiality,* meaning that there is an essential nature that is shared in common. If we think of profits as the index of success, we are likely to adopt an instrumental (if not materialistic) orientation toward life. We are likely to identify with whatever embodies positive attitudes toward the means that will further our ends. We are likely to define value in terms of personal gain. We are not likely to identify with matters presented as worthy because they have intrinsic merit. We are likely to feel miserable if we don't achieve personal gains that exceed personal costs because we will have failed to achieve success.

By the same token, we can change the conceptual pattern we bring to experience and thereby change our interpretations of reality and the responses called for. If we think of success as, say, making a beautiful thing, we will shift the basic principle from the instrumental (and materialistic) concern with profit to the aesthetic (and spiritual) concern with creativity. We may find beauty in a task well done, in raising children to be caring and sensitive toward their neighbors, in living our lives in ways that bring out the virtues of the people we touch, in writing a poem that illuminates the predicaments of the human condition. We are likely to identify with appeals to virtues of construction. We are not likely to identify with matters presented as worthy because they have utilitarian merits. We are likely to feel miserable if we don't find imaginative release because we will have failed to achieve success.

Each act of identification implies some underlying principle that gives coherence and unity to our conceptions of reality. But because each conception is embodied in a vocabulary of motives, each set of motives also acts as a *terministic screen,* emphasizing some aspects while ignoring others. A terministic screen provides a partial perspective that serves as a mask concealing alternative interpretations we can make if we use a different vocabulary emphasizing other conceptual possibilities and providing alternative underlying principles to unite us.

This uniquely human ability to make, use, and misuse symbols provides the basis for rhetorical acts to continue from event to event, with people identifying and dividing. Each rhetorical act is both an unmasking of the partial and negative aspects of our previous identifications and a creation of a new mask necessarily present in a new vocabulary of motives.

SUMMARY

The dramatistic perspective makes rhetoric central to the study of human behavior. Humans are symbol-using animals. Consequently, we cannot understand human actions without studying their uses of language. When we examine what humans do with language, we discover that they cannot use any symbolic form without communicating an attitude. All attitudes are incipient acts. They provide organization for our images from the past, and they project a future. All languages contain special terms, called *motive terms;* that convey these projections. Rather than looking within to impute motives, we find people exhibiting motives in the typical ways they use language to facilitate social coordination and cooperation. Motive terms provide inducements to cooperation. Thus all language is rhetorical. So when we examine the persuasive uses of language from a dramatistic perspective, we are really studying how the persuasive dynamics inherent in language allow humans to act cooperatively in constructing interpretations of experience and social forms that define the human world. At base we are essentially rhetorical creatures.

NOTES

1. B. F. Skinner is a behavioral psychologist who maintains that all behavior is conditioned response. His contentions regarding operant conditioning rely heavily on studies of the effects of positive and negative reinforcement on the behavior of pigeons.
2. Kenneth Burke, "Dramatism," in Lee Thayer, ed., *Communication: Concepts and Perspectives* (Washington, D.C.: Spartan Books, 1967), p. 336.
3. Kenneth Burke, *Language as Symbolic Action* (Berkeley: University of California Press, 1970), p. 16. This section is based primarily on Burke's discussion in his essay "Definition of Man," contained in this book as Chapter 1.

4. Kenneth Burke, "(Nonsymbolic) Motion/(Symbolic) Action," *Critical Inquiry,* 4 (Summer 1978), 810.

5. C. Wright Mills, "Situated Actions and Vocabularies of Motives," *American Sociological Review,* 5 (December 1940), 906.

6. Burke provides a book-length development of the pentad in *A Grammar of Motives* (Englewood Cliffs, N.J.: Prentice-Hall, 1945).

7. Burke, "Dramatism," p. 332.

8. A projection that proved true between the time these words were written and the time this book was published!

9. Edward J. Keller, *Address to District Council 90 Leadership Conference, December 1, 1984* (unpublished typescript). AFSCME stands for American Federation of State, County, and Municipal Employees.

10. Kenneth Burke, *Permanence and Change,* 3d rev. ed. (Berkeley: University of California Press, 1984), p. 30.

11. Ibid.

12. Kenneth Burke, *A Rhetoric of Motives* (Berkeley: University of California Press, 1969), p. 43.

13. Richard Weaver, "Language Is Sermonic," in Roger E. Nebergall, ed., *Dimensions of Rhetorical Scholarship* (Norman: University of Oklahoma Press, 1963), pp. 49–63.

chapter *10*

Experiencing Meaning in Rhetoric

In 1963 President Kennedy delivered a speech at the Berlin wall. The speech is remembered for his statement, *"Ich bin ein Berliner."* Upon hearing these words, the crowd roared its sustained approval. As you listen to a recording of the address, you sense that deep emotions flowed through the crowd like an electric charge. In the context of East Germany's erecting a physical barricade to isolate West Berlin, his utterance became a commitment of continued American presence and of solidarity in the face of oppression. The audience's enthusiasm was not so much for the actual words as for what they meant. The meaning of his words existed not in their semantic content but in the act they performed. Kennedy identified himself with them as a Berliner, giving special meaning to their beleaguered experiences in the city and to their relationship with the United States.

How Kennedy's speech acquired special meaning for his audience, or how any message acts as a source of meaning for its audience, is a question of central importance to students of rhetoric. As producers and consumers of rhetoric, we seek to understand the functional role symbols play in the management of social action. We know that language is dynamic; it shapes our perceptions and coordinates our attitudes. We require a theory especially suited to explaining these dynamic functions as we encounter them in rhetorical events.

The whole topic of meaning is very complex. We would require a volume of enormous proportions to deal with it in any complete way. Our consideration will necessarily be partial and focus on what is essential to an initial understanding of meaning in rhetoric.

When we ask about meaning from a rhetorical perspective, we are con-

138

an instrumental

cerned with how people act with language to manage their affairs. How do the symbols of messages acquire their meaning for audiences? How do these meanings encourage perceptions of reality? How do these perceptions bear on salient variables in a rhetorical situation, including language itself, to form relevant interpretations of experience? In sum, our questions ask, How shall we understand the way language interacts with itself and with the experiences of audiences to create meanings that pertain to social cooperation?

1) cf. Gregg

2) can you divorce language for cognition?

These questions do not refer to the psychological processes of cognition. They are not about how the mind processes sensations or how the mind perceives patterns because neither of these gets at the concern for how meaning is formed in rhetorical exchanges. Nor are our questions of a linguistic nature. Clearly, utterances that violate the syntactic and semantic rules of the language system will also fail linguistically and rhetorically. They will be incoherent. But linguistic competence is not the same as communication competence, and it is the *communicativeness* of the utterance that is the rhetorician's concern.

MEANING AND CONTEXT

Following the lead of Bronislaw Malinowski, contemporary anthropologists have made an important breakthrough in how to study cultures. They have realized that culture does not *consist* of act and artifact but is *manifested* in act and artifact. Puzzling over how to untangle the webs of culture if one did not find answers in the art and tools of a people, the anthropologists' answer was to go into the culture to see what its members thought they were up to. In other words, one can untangle the web of cultural characteristics by taking the natives' point of view.

An important part of taking the natives' point of view involves studying their utterances. In an important essay,[1] Malinowski maintained that language has meaning only in terms of its context. To study language apart from the context in which it is situated gives us mere figments of meaning. Thus Malinowski proposed that students of language use and meaning should shift their attention from the derivation of words used in a general cultural context and focus instead on how language was used in actual practice. He called this type of situated study an *ethnographic* approach to language. Malinowski outlined two simple guidelines for ethnographic studies. First, you had to know about the culture you were studying. Were these farmers or hunters or industrial workers? Were they of a particular religion? What was their political structure, and how were they organized socially? In other words, one needed a baseline to anchor any claim about how users saw their contexts of utterance, including their relationships to one another as language users who were culturally related. Second, he maintained that you had to determine the situation or circumstances of the utterance because language had no meaning apart from the contexts in which it was used.

When Malinowski examined the natives' uses of language from this perspective, he discovered that they did things with words. In addition to signifying thoughts, language use was an action. Malinowski conjectured that the meaning

Culler — *meaning in context dependent*
context in boundless

of language usage was intertwined with its accompanying activity. Consequently, people could not separate the two. Meaning was embedded in an activity, and activity was enmeshed with the language used.

We can find illustrations of Malinowski's point in our everyday lives. For example, when we pass friends on the street, we offer a greeting. This is called *phatic communion.* The defining feature of phatic communion is not what we say to indicate acknowledgment of the other but simply that we do acknowledge the other. The saying is the act of reaffirming our social bond. As we noted in Chapter 9, "How are you?" is usually not a real question in this context. We are not asking for a medical or psychological bulletin; we are indicating that we acknowledge the other party as part of our social world. We have a variety of verbal and nonverbal ways to do this, but they are one in the act of acknowledgment. People who believe they deserve our nod of recognition would probably feel snubbed if we withheld such signs of sociability. Similarly, when we visit with family we have not seen for a while, we expect to offer and receive special attention. The patterns of inquiry and response that we inevitably adopt are not just to solicit and impart information. They are also symbolic acts that reaffirm our familial bonds.

Acts like these extend throughout our communication on practical matters, even to exchanges in which we are intent on communicating specific meanings. For example, we learn how to convey specific meanings to our family through the activity of managing practical matters with them (say, teaching the value of money by helping a child keep a savings account). This is a participatory form of learning, not the type of knowledge acquired through abstract reflection. When we seek to influence through expressions of thoughts and feelings, we are simultaneously engaged in acts of thoughts and feelings as they are performed by *our* family. By the same measure, when we learn some specialized vocabulary (say, of music), we acquire it through some mode of active participation in that field (by study, practice, and discussion). When we discuss music, we are also acting as musicians (talking to musicians as peers), as musicologists, as critics, or simply as buffs. Malinowski's point would apply to any area where people manage practical matters with language. They learn to perform these tasks by participating in the activity of that domain in given contexts. Consequently, their uses of language become bound to the activity. To use language in situated contexts is to act with language.

Rhetoricians understand "meaning" in a fashion similar to that of Malinowski. His early recommendations regarded language as "situated action." Rhetoricians understand the use of language in context. This means that they do not believe that words alone carry ideas but that meaning lies in an interaction of language and context. Thus, if we want to discover how meaning develops in rhetorical events, we must examine how rhetorical speakers use language.

DYNAMICS OF MEANING

Thus far we have claimed with Malinowski that language means as it is used. Now we will advance that claim a step further to assert that meanings develop through the interaction of symbols within and upon contexts. So that we may be clear on what we are asserting, let us begin with an extended illustration that will aid in understanding how meanings develop through the dynamic tensions among symbols, contexts, and symbol users.

Imagine hearing an instrumental tune for the first time. It is a simple piece with a romantic melody and a rhythm that is easy to detect. It is slow and not really the kind of music to which you tap your feet. You feel it someplace else. It is a duet played by a piano and a bass. The piano is played so that the individual notes of the melody seem accentuated over the chords. The bass is bowed with occasional finger plucking. Its sounds are deep, with an onomatopoeic quality to them. As you listen, the serenity of the piece makes you feel calm, even tranquil. You imagine scenes that fit the mood. One scene stands out—a meadow. You imagine it on a summer afternoon; the sun is high, but there is a cool and gentle breeze. You see patches of wildflowers painting the verdant setting with brilliant splashes of magenta, rust, violet, deep yellow, white, cranberry. You hear cows lowing in a distant field; birds chirp and insects hum lazily in the summer sun. Butterflies seem to hang in the air and then zigzag in drowsy patterns of random flight. The scent of sweet grass perfumes the air. Puffy clouds float across the sky, inviting you to play with their rococo caricatures of creatures and things. It is serene there; the imagined scene fits the music.

You have interpreted the tune. It is your interpretation, forged from interaction between the sounds you hear and the experiences you have had. You interpret it as a song expressing tranquillity. But at this level the meaning dictated by the song is not very specific; without much data, you have constructed a pastoral scene from the context of your own past.

You are curious to see whether your interpretation is on target, so you look at the song title: "Good Morning Heartache." Your interpretation does not fit that title at all! You play the song again, listening to it with the title in mind. Now you hear it differently. The deep and very slow bowing of the bass is not a musical imitation of cows lowing. It is the throbbing of a saddened heart. And the individual notes that stand out so clearly on the piano are not birds chirping or flies buzzing but now are heard as emotions jabbing with piercing pain. The added information of the title brings to mind a different memory. This time it may not be a scene but a recollection of what it felt like to have a broken heart. As you think of sad times, you may recall the wrenching pain that greeted each morning—the feeling of despair at a profound loss, of helplessness because circumstances were beyond your control. You recall how slow your mind felt, how you sensed constriction in your chest that made it difficult to breathe. It is a very sad recollection, befitting the mood evoked by the song heard in this new way.

You may still like the song, even though it is sad, because it seems to express musically what you felt emotionally at a sad time. Further, you may find that the song has helped you to perceive as a gestalt what you only perceived in its particular parts when you were actually in the saddened state. It has helped you better to frame your own experience. The composer's title has altered your interpretation by giving you a context for listening. That context was in turn dynamically interactive with your own experiential history.

Still, since this is an instrumental rendition, you have great latitude in the meaning you construct from the music. The composer may have intended to express sadness, but you prefer your first interpretation. You listen to it in your own way and create your own meaning. Subsequently, you play the song to help yourself feel tranquil.

One day you discover a version of the song with lyrics. The lyrics prevent you from interpreting the song as you choose. The words speak thoughts and feelings that belong to one set of recollections (heartache) but not another (tranquillity). You cannot imagine the bass as cows lowing or the piano as birds chirping. It is definitely a heart-wrenching ballad. Still, you can imagine scenes from life where the words fit. It may be your life or that of friends going through hard times. If you are in the midst of personal trauma, the words may seem to express your feelings. Or you may find that the song recalls a past experience. If the specific event it recalls is distant, the song may give you ideas that help you to pattern and interpret what was previously a jumble of emotions. You find that the music plus the lyrics help you to understand what that past experience means for you. Six months later you may hear the lyrics again and have none of these thoughts. You may be ecstatically happy and so have the more general response of "that's sad" or "that's life" or "I know what she's singing about, I've been there." It makes no difference which of these is your response because the essential point is that the music plus the words are but a part of what the song actually does mean at any given moment. You bring your experiences to bear, and the relationships among sounds, words, past experiences, and present contexts interact to create meaning for you. You have a considerable and essential role to play in establishing the meanings that occur as you listen.

Let us extend our example one final step to make it completely contemporary. One day you are watching a music video show and see a rendition of the song. This rendition translates the song into a visual narrative. A female singer acts out a scene that depicts the lyrics of "Good Morning Heartache." She confronts you with a different image again. You witness a particular setting, with a particular person enacting a scene from her life. The video image is so concrete that it obliterates your previously imagined scenarios for the song. In fact, it even obliterates you from the scene. It is not your story but that person's story. The potential for fantasy has been significantly reduced. The visual narrative fixes the perceptions we have of being miserable with heartache to that person's version. The vividness of the visual depiction eliminates much of what you might have imagined as experiences to which the song alluded. In fact, you may be reduced now to relative passivity, invited to appreciate a scene played before you, rather than an active participant constructing the experiences the song thematizes. To get yourself back into the scene, you have to struggle beyond the visual narrative, perhaps by abstracting from it significance for your own life. Or you may recoil in disgust, rejecting the video as a misrepresentation of "your" meaning of the song. For you, the video has destroyed the song as music and transformed it into spectacle.

What I have been describing is a process of *meaning making.* Stimulated by symbols, we interpret the song in various ways. Across time, as the symbols changed, the meaning changed. As your life changed, you responded differently because you heard and understood differently. These changes were ones of context, making it possible for some interpretations to flourish and others to wither. Further, these contextual changes suggest the multidimensional dynamics that are relevant to understanding how symbols create meanings for audiences.

Meanings Are Mediated

Formerly, theories of meaning held to the conviction that words had proper meanings and that communication was clearest when words were used precisely with respect to their proper meaning. As work like Malinowski's called proper meaning theories into question, a mediatory model came to the fore. This model depicts meanings as the products of interaction between a thinking human and the stimuli of the environment. Its most recent versions in anthropology, psychology, neurophysiology, philosophy, and communication link meaning directly to the way language and experience are intertwined. This language-experience relationship is important to us because it explains meaning in a fashion that is directly applicable to rhetorical understanding.

Contemporary rhetorical theory generally adopts an experiential theory of meaning. It concentrates on how meanings emerge from utterances. The significance of individual isolated words is minimized, since rhetorical meaning encompasses the larger thought units of propositions, arguments, and appeals intended to induce cooperation. Utterances indicate how people understand and share their experiences. So when we talk of "meaning" in rhetoric, we have in mind how symbols evoke meaning as situated utterances. We are interested in how we act with symbols to construct interpretations of our experiences and forge social bonds through these constructions. For our purposes, let us define *meaning* as "the significance of an utterance as it emerges from a context of usage and the perceptions that it invites." By *perception* we mean "the interpretive awareness of a referent." Perception refers to how our minds grasp or understand something, as in these examples:

> "I know that dioxin is a highly toxic chemical. My perception is that the EPA was lax in regulating its use."
>
> "I know that Susan expressed dissatisfaction with her courses this semester, but I perceive her to be happy with her overall program."
>
> "Presidential candidates want us to perceive them as leaders."
>
> "My perceptions of her basic values were mistaken."

With these thoughts in mind, let us advance our discussion by considering four propositions relative to meaning as it emerges in rhetoric:

1. Language usage is experientially based.
2. Perceptual patterns emerge from contexts of experience.
3. Language usage contains inherent frameworks for conceptualizing what we experience.

4. Meaning emerges from the interaction among symbols within their context of use.

Language Usage Is Experientially Based

The way our utterances present our experience is inextricably bound to the way we actually experience our environment, both physically and culturally.[2] At a very basic level, we experience ourselves directly in *orientation* to our environment. This is essentially an experience of spatial relationships: up—down, in—out, front—back, over—under, near—far, and so forth. We also have direct experience with existing objects in our environment. These are referred to as *ontological* experiences because they are of the *being* or *existence* of something. An ontological experience may be of an entity, like a train, or a substance, like food. When we encounter our environment orientationally or ontologically, we simultaneously encounter the language of those experiences. Take *up—down*. We experience *up* as standing erect, as the position of the body in health, contrasted with *down,* the position assumed when ill. We are *up* when in a conscious state, whereas we are *down* when asleep. A person who is *up* is active, but *down* is the position of passivity. When we make comparisons, the greater quantity will be higher or *up* as contrasted with the lesser amount. The experience of *up* is positive, associated with power, health, activity, and progress toward a goal. The very way in which we experience *up* gives us a basis in our physical encounters with our environment for thinking in terms of *up* as an orienting concept.

The meaning of such basic experiences comes not just from our physical encounters with our environment but also from our cultural orientation. In our culture, we think of *up* as the top of something as seen from above. But this is a matter of perspective. For example, a ball literally has no top or bottom, no up or down. But our culture teaches us to orient to it as if it did. The bottom of the ball is the part closest to the ground, while the top is farthest away. Or take *front—back.* If we say, "Pam is hiding in back of the tree," we mean the tree is between Pam and the person she is hiding from. Trees do not have a front or back. Our culture makes an orientational assumption, however, that is present in the very way that we experience front and back. Other cultures may experience spatial orientation differently.

The ways in which we understand our world are conditioned by the interactions we have with our physical environment. But these interactions are themselves experienced in light of the cultural suppositions we share and the language we use. In other words, conceptual meanings that emerge from this interaction are experientially based. Researchers Lakoff and Johnson say that meanings that emerge this way are concepts we live by.[3]

Perceptual Patterns Emerge from Contexts of Experience

When we say that meanings emerging in experience are concepts we live by, we are not confining this claim to the direct experiences we may have of an entity or an orientation. Indirect associations arise from the contexts in which we use language, and therefore our language acts have consequences. These also are part of language's tie to experience. Any context of usage will contain a variety of salient factors that contribute in some measure to an utterance's meaning. Even more, contexts contribute to the development of perceptual patterns that are larger than the meaning of an utterance considered by itself.

Our usage occurs in contexts where knowledge of what is possible or impossible, fact or fiction, true or false interacts with values, emotions, social forces, and cultural conditions pertinent to the events in which rhetoric transpires. Each of these interactive dimensions is individually meaningful, but their union provides a gestalt of meaning that includes not only the reference of symbols but also a pattern of the whole experience of which the utterance was a part. The Kennedy speech at the Berlin wall or the song "Good Morning Heartache" provides more than the memorable utterance "*Ich bin ein Berliner*" or the song title. The former provides us with an experience of a solemn commitment to defend the freedom of a beleaguered people, the latter an experience of the desolation that accompanies the loss of the love of the other. In both cases, the coherence among their constitutive elements provides a pattern for perceiving the experience.

As these gestalts recur in our culture, we develop culturally unique ways of speaking about and responding to experiences similar in kind. These recurrent patterns are contained in our motive terms and in the attitudes toward the future that they imply. As Lakoff and Johnson observe:

> Cultural assumptions, values, and attitudes are not a conceptual overlay which we may or may not place upon experience as we choose. It would be more correct to say that all experience is cultural through and through, that we experience our "world" in such a way that our culture is already present in the very experience itself.[4]

These patterns, inclusive and holistic, remain with us as acculturated individuals, to be called into play in our future language uses. They provide us with the stock of common assumptions, valuings, expectations, and motivations that make it possible for us to share our perceptions of experience with others of our kind.

Language Usage Contains Inherent Frameworks for Conceptualizing What We Experience

When we learn typical patterns for expressing ourselves, those patterns invariably provide frameworks that conceptualize experience in a particular way. For example, we talk about our election campaigns as "races." "The campaign is a race" expresses the following:

1. Elections are contests.
2. There will be a winner and a loser.
3. Contestants need a sound strategy to race well.

4. Those who are not in the race are observers.
5. Contestants are expected to abide by the rules.
6. Contestants must be in fit condition to race well.
7. Observers who favor one of the contestants show support by partisan rooting and cheering.

This list could be extended, but the essential point is sufficiently illustrated. To talk about election campaigns as "races" invokes a framework that conceptualizes our political activity in terms of contests. We could also talk of campaigns as "trials" or "debates," in which case different conceptual frameworks would be involved. It is significantly different to talk about our politics as "games" where we sit as partisan fans, as "trials" where we sit as judging jurors, or as "referenda" where we sit as evaluators of issues and arguments.

Each of these illustrates how the language we use can organize our perceptions into coherent wholes. By virtue of its capacity to organize *perceptions* along specific lines, our selection of symbols shapes the way we understand our experience. It highlights certain features and, necessarily, hides others. Every use of language is therefore partial in the conceptual schemata it advances. Nonetheless, it is the great power of language that these schemata provide the very ways in which we make sense out of what has occurred in our lives. Moreover, it provides the basis for sharing our experiences with others. Insofar as our utterances are within the cultural framework of our audience, its members may participate actively in reconceptualizing their experiences in terms that we provide. Language brings into harmony ideas, feelings, and values shared among speaker and audience.

Meaning Emerges from the Interaction Among Symbols Within Their Context of Use

We defined the meaning of an utterance as the significance that emerges from its context of usage and the perceptions that it invites. Thus far we have been considering language usage in context as yielding patterns for perceiving and conceptualizing experience. Here we need to emphasize that language is *dynamic* in its interactions with other symbols and with its context. Meanings of utterances grow from the interactions among the language used in the utterance. The noted scholar of language use, I. A. Richards, has referred to this interactive character of words as *interinanimation.*[5] That is, words animate meanings in one another. The specific meanings they animate depend on the context of usage—both the external context of situation and the internal contexts of phrase, sentence, paragraph, page, chapter, book, or of statement, contention, argument, case, address. This process of interinanimation is summarized by Richards in the *context theorem of meaning,* which holds that words are successfully meaningful in their contexts insofar as they animate and are animated.

Richards's context theorem highlights the significance of our individual histories as language users. Throughout our lives, we use words to label and understand the events of experience. This union of words with referents is, from the beginning, contextual. Thus our past experiences of situated usage forms our knowledge of what words mean. Our contextual histories are projected into our every utterance, guiding the specific meanings that emerge from the interinanimation process in each specific context.

Obviously, the baggage of our past is not carried as an object of conscious reflection, to be sorted through every time we speak. Were that the case, nothing would ever get said. Abridgment occurs, fusing the individual parts of our past into a gestaltlike whole. In other words, the meanings of our symbols consist of our gestalt of associations from contexts in which they were previously used. In any coherent utterance, these gestalts interact with one another to influence the specific meaning of the utterance for everyone engaged in the rhetorical transaction.[6]

RHETORICAL APPLICATIONS

Thus far we have been discussing the way meaning is developed in rhetoric. Our considerations have emphasized the link between a rhetorical understanding of meaning and the way people experience communication. We have borrowed two major sets of ideas to explain this linkage. We used Lakoff and Johnson's idea of concepts we live by to explain how our language shapes our experiences. Then we used Richards's idea of interinanimation of words to explain how meanings develop dynamically in context.

These considerations are important to students of rhetoric because they help us make wiser predictions about how our language choices will work in a given case. They also help us listen to and read more critically the choices of others. Finally, they allow us to reflect on and understand better why we and others experience a rhetorical transaction in a particular way. Thus our attention to theoretical concerns with meaning should help us make sounder practical language choices and judgments. We can see how this theory relates to practice in some clearly discernable ways.

Within an Utterance

First, there is the interaction of symbols within a single, meaningful utterance. In speech this consists of articulating a complete idea; in writing it consists of a sentence. Within an utterance, interaction occurs in terms of placement of words and phrases relative to one another. Manipulations of *grammar, vocabulary choice,* and *imagery* can alter meaning in significant ways.

Grammar   With respect to grammatical constructions, we can alter the strength of connection between ideas by moving them closer together or farther apart:

> I taught rhetoric to Nola.
> I taught Nola rhetoric.

In the first sentence, *taught* is separated from *Nola*. It is not clear that Nola actually learned what she was taught. In the second sentence, the closeness of *Nola* to *taught* suggests that she learned her lessons. The placement of *rhetoric* immediately after *Nola* reinforces this suggestion because it implies that knowledge of the subject is something she possesses.

We can increase the emphasis on an idea through suggestions of *volume*. Sometimes we do this by elongating a sound, as in *h-u-u-u-g-e* to suggest something very large or *t-i-i-i-n-y* to suggest something very small. At other times the repetition of terms suggests volume:

1. Dan is a hunka hunka burnin' love!
2. Martha put a teeny tiny dent in Charles's fender.
3. Molly wrote and wrote and wrote until she had completed a 600-page manuscript.

The basic rule is that reduplication increases the essential value of the referent. If the referent is one of magnitude (as in sentence 1), it increases magnitude; if the referent is diminutive (sentence 2), reduplication makes it even more diminutive; if the reduplicated term is a verb (sentence 3), the action is intensified. *Voice* is another significant form for modifying meaning. By using *active voice*, the subject engages in action:

Bill hit the books last night.

Passive voice has the noun receiving the action, suggesting a shift in emphasis from the doer to the receiver of an action:

A lot of studying was going on last night at Bill's place.

In general, we perceive the first sentence to be about Bill and the second to be about studying. By increasing the use of active voice, we increase the sense of activity in our rhetoric, whereas passive constructions do just the opposite.

Word order is also a way to alter meaning. In general, we orient to placing the more important or more desirable item first. It is more common for us to say "front to back" than "back to front," "up and down" than "down and up." Because our culture orders items in this way, we can alter suggestions of importance by the way we order items in a series.

In each case, we manipulate meanings by the way our grammatical constructions place ideas in relationship to one another. In other words, the interaction among ideas is altered by the way in which they are related to one another. These interactional variations influence meaning.

Vocabulary Another obvious way in which meanings arise through interaction is by vocabulary choice. The terms that we select carry with them a baggage train of meaning. In any utterance, nouns, verbs, and modifiers serve to animate one another to highlight selected aspects and hide others, to modify one another, and to create the unique meaning of that particular utterance. Even such mundane variations as

> Merry is reading.
>
> Merry is studying.
>
> Merry is researching.
>
> Merry is doing her homework.
>
> Merry is hitting the books.

convey subtle differences in more than our sense of what Merry is doing. If she is *reading,* she is occupied with a book, but we don't know why. If she is *studying,* we may assume that she is involved in some way with reading for scholarly purposes. She is also trying to understand and retain what she is reading. Her work is not a pastime but a serious pursuit. If she is *researching,* she probably has a specific project to focus her work. The questions she wants to answer are more controlling of her activity than the information on the printed pages she reads. We may see Merry as a person who engages in specific intellectual pursuits if she conducts research. If her reading is *homework,* she is answering someone else's questions or fulfilling an assignment. Here we get a clearer sense of Merry as a student. If she is *hitting the books,* she is engaged in an assault of sorts. This image of violence suggests the need for emergency measures, as when she is behind in her work or cramming for an exam.

In each of these cases, an interactive relationship is established between the gestalt of meaning we ascribe to *Merry* and to the verb that presents her activity. The interaction between these two clusters of meaning brings certain senses of Merry and her reading to the fore and suppresses others. The clusters serve to animate each other in an utterance that has a sense for us, a sense that is unique.

Animation is further achieved in word choice by tending to suggestive dynamics. Consider, for example, the exclamation "You dog!" Its meaning depends on who says it, under what circumstances, and even with what tone of voice and facial expression. It could be uttered as a condemnation for engaging in a reprehensible act. Then again, a friend may say this to tease us for playing a prank or to express surprise at something we've done. When we say, "Them's fightin' words" or "Smile when you say that," we express precisely this understanding of meanings developing from use.

We commonly refer to these distinctions under the generic headings of *denotation* and *connotation*. *Denotation* refers to the specific meaning of a word, its literal sense, while *connotation* refers to the suggestive meaning of a word, its associative sense. Take the term *hospital.* It denotes a building in which comprehensive health care is administered. We use *hospital* to refer to a specific place or type of place:

> "Mother worked for Mercy Hospital."
>
> "Uncle George was in the hospital for bypass surgery."

"Medicare and Medicaid payments have a profound effect on hospital fee structures."

At the same time, *hospital* is a highly suggestive term. People are cured or die there; it is the place where nurses and doctors minister to our health needs. We go there when we are seriously ill. *Hospital* can suggest the joy of restored health, the anguish of pain, the sadness of death.

While connotation obviously depends on context, it is also the case that some uses of language rely more heavily than others on the connotative value of words to convey meaning. We may depict this phenomenon by thinking of denotation and connotation as forming a continuum. Usages that emphasizes most heavily the specific meaning of a term fall at the denotative end, while usages that rely extensively on the associated suggestions of a term are at the connotative end. Consider how the reference to "hospital" changes its connotative value in this exchange:

> JAY: How's your aunt? I read about her accident.
> BARB: She's in Mercy Hospital.
> JAY: Where's that?
> BARB: At Abbott and Casinovia.
> JAY: Oh. I know that place. Mercy does lots of emergency work.
> BARB: I'm afraid my aunt will never escape from there alive.

Jay's initial inquiry of concern is met with a reference to a place. In effect, Barb's answer says, "She's in bad shape," relying on the connotative value to convey the idea of serious illness. The next exchange concerns location. Jay's question may connote a desire to visit Barb's aunt, but the exchange relies primarily on the denotative meaning of Mercy Hospital—a specific building at a specific location. In the third exchange, Jay and Barb both rely primarily on the connotation of hospital to construct their understanding of the situation; he seeing this hospital as competent in handling emergency cases, whereas Barb sees the hospital as a scene for death.

Denotation and connotation are two of the principal dimensions of word choice that contribute to meaning. Obviously the "loading" of any term's connotative or denotative value is relative to the way it is used. The continuum ranging between denotation and connotation illustrates clearly how words interact in context to create meanings and establish identifications. By thoughtful word choices, you can greatly influence whether the listener actually receives the "correct" (intended) meaning. You can do much to control connotation.

Imagery A third way in which the interinanimation within an utterance may be modified and meanings managed is through the use of imagery. Such usage is referred to as figures of diction or speech, sometimes called *tropes*. These figures alter a word or phrase from its proper meaning to another.

When we use language in unusual ways, we attract attention to our thoughts. For this reason, rhetoricians historically have stressed the importance of word choice to enliven ideas. When a politician refers to his opponent as a "pusillanimous pussyfooter" (*alliteration:* repetition of identical sounds in successive words) or a restaurant menu urges us to order "Jumbo Shrimp" (*oxymoron:* a seeming contradiction), they put ideas into unusual and even incongruous relationships. As these expressions wheel across the landscape of our fancy (*metaphor:* application of a term or phrase to something to which it is not literally applicable), they attract attention. In this way they may ornament ideas through conscious expression.

Of course, excessive use of imagery may leave your audience with the impression of overdrawn ornamentation substituted for underdeveloped ideas (*antithesis:* the balancing of two contrastive words, phrases, or clauses against each other). Rhetors who seem more intent on sound effects than sound reasoning (*epanaphora:* repeating the same word to begin successive phrases or clauses) may delight the ear but disappoint the brain (*synecdoche:* the use of a part to express the whole). We use imagery not only to beautify but also to create relationships that give new meaning.

The Belgian philosopher of argument, Chaim Perelman, reminds us that figures can argue. "Choice of terms to express the speaker's thought is rarely without significance in the argumentation."[7] Perelman's observation reinforces the thesis we developed in Chapter 9: There is very little in language use that is neutral. Most contemporary rhetoricians agree that language in use induces attitudes; it is sermonic (*apposition:* restatement of a word or phrase next to another so that the second adds to or explains the first). In his work on the criticism of oral rhetoric, Carroll Arnold has shown that tropes may be grouped according to *how* they argue. He reminds us that imagistic devices are practical means to repeat, compare, enlarge, constrain, and contrast[8] (*cumulation:* listing related items together).

The three preceding paragraphs identified devices of imagery that occurred in my attempt to communicate my understanding to you. These devices were noted after the fact of composition. They were the product of my worrying over word choices and sentence structures to explain the concept of tropes. The frequency of these parenthetical observations indicates that while tropes may have strange-sounding names, they are not esoteric considerations when communicating rhetorically. We cannot help but use them. The issue is never whether you will use imagery. Rhetorical concerns are rather which ones you will use and how well you will use them. As both makers and consumers of rhetoric, we must attend to how the interaction among symbols creates meaning. Figures of speech and of thought suggest an attitudinal disposition that invites and shapes perceptions in and through images used.

Extended Verbal Contexts

Interaction also occurs within larger frameworks of verbal context. Here we focus on the context of related ideas. This may be the unit of a paragraph or an argument, or it may extend to the considerations of an entire work. We experience meanings in larger contexts through the ways in which ideas interact. Expressed ideas illuminate and modify one another, giving each argument a special sense for those who experience it as a whole. For example, when Geraldine Ferraro spoke to the Democratic convention in 1984, her appeal to play by the rules was not mere campaign oratory. In the context of the speech, each rule was linked to a basic American conviction and opposed to an alleged practice condoned by the Reagan administration. The cumulative effect was to define a clear agenda for the Democrats that distinguished them from the Republicans. It also gave the delegates a liberal's definition of what values and policies they should espouse. For those who were moved by the speech, that effect rested on the coherence of Ferraro's ideas as a set of interrelated action proposals expressing a liberal perception of the nation's political agenda.

External Contexts

As powerful as these internal sources of interaction are, they are not without modification by the forces present in the external context. Meanings alter as we take into account how a particular rhetorical transaction is situated in an action event. Concerns like the rhetorical situation, the person of the rhetor, the perceived intentions of the rhetor, the functions the message is thought to serve, and the needs and potencies of the audience act as modifying factors on the meanings that emerge.

Kennedy's speech at the Berlin wall is a clear case. The meaning experienced by his audience was influenced greatly by these significant external factors: The physical proximity of the wall, the distance of a football field from where JFK spoke, served as a grim reminder of the Berliners' desperate straits. The presence of American military leaders familiar to the audience was an inartistic reminder of the American military safeguard against communist coercion. The speaker was the American president, singular in his power to make a pledge that would resolve the Berliners' fears. Finally, the audience of Berliners had a history of tense relations with the East German government. These immediate circumstances called forth the context of Berlin's post–World War II history as a source of experience from which Kennedy might draw and of which he had to remain cognizant in presenting his remarks. Everything he said predictably interacted with what his listeners had lived through. How Kennedy put those experiences into meaningful relationships influenced the measure of hope those Berliners had for their future.

In this section we have considered at some length the dynamic interaction that occurs in an experiential account of meaning. We have seen that our language use is tied in basic ways to our experience, that the context of our experiences shapes our perceptions, and that our language usage contains frameworks that conceptualize what we experience. Finally, we saw that meaning in rhetoric emerges from the interaction among symbols within the context of usage.

This last claim is most important. Through our management of language, we structure our perceptions of reality, preserving the past and creating new possibilities for the future. A rhetorical perspective toward language use considers our intellectual, moral, and emotional lives to be the product of meaning making and meaning sharing. Nowhere is this interactive function more apparent than in our use of metaphor. By examining how metaphors create meanings, we can gain greater insight into the practical dynamics of language in use.

METAPHOR

The concept of metaphor has been a major concern of rhetoricians and other students of language since Aristotle wrote on the subject in his *Rhetoric* and his *Poetics.* Aristotle believed that skill at creating metaphors was the mark of genius because metaphor united ideas in ways that were extraordinary and indiscernible in any other fashion.[9] Unfortunately, Aristotle's views never caught on until this century. In the 1920s and 1930s, the writings of I. A. Richards began to appear. Richards argued that metaphor was more than a stylistic device. It was the cornerstone of meaning and of thought. At first this seemed like a radical contention. How was metaphor "thought"? And why was metaphor the cornerstone of "meaning"? But within the framework we have been developing, Richards's claim makes perfectly good sense.

We have been contending that our language provides us with conceptual systems for understanding our experiences. These systems begin with the basic relationship between language and experience. We saw these to be orientational and ontological in their most basic form. The research of Lakoff and Johnson indicates that ontological and orientational systems can be combined to form structural systems.[10] Structural systems are ones in which we talk about one thing in terms of another. Take learning. We talk about learning as a journey ("You've come a long way in your understanding of physics"), as a building ("He has a solid foundation in organic chemistry"), as an organism ("You've grown in your understanding of calculus"). Each of these structures implies a set of relationships that constitute a conceptual scheme. Journeys are over surfaces ("Let's cover the ground"), there are detours ("Why didn't you go directly to the point?"), and we even get lost ("I don't know where Mike is going with his study"). Similarly, buildings have superstructures, floors, windows, and doors and are prized for interesting design and sturdiness of structure. Organisms, on the other hand, have divisions of plant and animal life, with roots, branches, fruits, and harvest, or heart, limbs, the need for nourishment, and the capacity for motion.

These structures are metaphorical. They provide us with elaborate networks of relationships with which we think and communicate about our experience. In a most apparent way, metaphors like these are basic to our ways of thinking about experience. It is so common for us to think in terms of structures like these that we do not notice how pervasive metaphoric systems are in our everyday lives. In fact, most of the metaphors we encounter are not used as imagery intended for stylistic embellishment. They are patterns of thought that we have adopted through their repeated use in our culture. They are so commonly used that we hardly notice that they are metaphors, let alone how they provide conceptual schemes for understanding and sharing experiences. Yet their operation as a mode of linguistic interinanimation is not substantially different from that found in metaphors that express novel ideas and relationships. Metaphors that catch our attention as interesting expressions of novelty we call *metaphoric statements,* and it is this aspect of metaphor we wish to examine more closely.

When we take up metaphoric statements, our interest is in how a statement receives its essential meaning through its metaphoric expression. We are not considering metaphors as literary devices. A literary device may be discarded as a stylistic flourish. We cannot discard a metaphoric statement in this way because the statement relies on a metaphor in an essential way to constitute its very meaning.

When a metaphor is essential to the meaning of a statement, it has several important characteristics. These characteristics were noted and organized in a most influential study by the American philosopher Max Black.[11] Because Black's terminology is so clear and fits so well with the rhetorical view of language use, we will adopt it here.

First, then, another expression cannot substitute for a metaphor in a metaphoric statement. Take as an example the statement "Our moments together are portraits hung in the gallery of my life." No literal equivalent can be used in its place without destroying the essential meaning of this statement. Nor can it be paraphrased adequately. As a metaphoric statement, it relies exclusively on the conceptual scheme of art introduced by the metaphor. If we change the metaphor, we change the whole conceptual pattern.

Further, we cannot translate this metaphoric statement into a mere comparison where the metaphoric system is considered as an analogy. To illustrate, complete the following: "Shared moments are like portraits in that . . ." "Life is like a gallery in that . . ." If you can complete these statements *without* omitting a host of suggestions contained in the original metaphor, we can conclude that the metaphor was used for stylistic purposes. But comparisons of this sort are impossible with a metaphoric statement because it does not use metaphor for style; it relies on metaphoric usage for its very meaning. Metaphor creates this meaning. For ease of expression in this discussion, let us use *metaphor* as shorthand for "metaphoric statement." Our interest will be to discover how metaphors (metaphoric statements) develop meaning interactively.

Every metaphor has the basic feature of one thing talked about in terms of another. The expression that stands as a metaphor is understood as a metaphor precisely because it does not fit literally in its context of use. We say, "Jeff argues with intelligence and zeal," and understand that to be a literal expression, whereas "Jeff is a tiger in debate" we understand to be a nonliteral statement, since Jeff is not a tiger but a man. "Tiger" refers to some mode of behavior Jeff exhibited, namely, the savage and cunning character of his arguments.

In this metaphor, *tiger* is the salient term and is called the metaphor's

Focus

"Bob's usual way of dealing with an issue is to ⎡snake⎤ around it."
Frame

Focus

"Bob was a ⎡snake⎤ when I needed his support."
Frame

Figure 10.1

focus, while the rest of the sentence is called the *frame.* The frame thus consists of the literal portion of the utterance. Frame and focus interplay to create their unique meaning. If the frame is changed, this will cause some alteration in the frame-focus interplay and may result in separate metaphors.

For example, compare the two statements in Figure 10.1. By changing the frame, we emphasize different characteristics of the focus. In the first utterance, the way a snake moves is highlighted; in the second, our cultural aversion to snakes as sneaky creatures comes to the fore. In both cases, there is an interactive frame-focus relationship. Both serve as sources of thought, and both thoughts (Bob's behavior and a snake's behavior) are now supported by a single phrase whose meaning results from their interaction. "Bob is a snake" is a metaphoric statement, a metaphor that can only be accounted for in an *interactive view of* how metaphoric meaning emerges.

What are the elements of this interaction? As noted earlier, metaphor develops meaning by talking about one thing in terms of another. The thing talked about is called the *principal subject,* and what is applied to the principal subject is called the *subsidiary subject.* Thus in the sentence "Bob is a snake," *Bob* is the principal subject and *snake* the subsidiary subject.

While the metaphor's meaning is a result of the interaction between these elements, readers and listeners who lack the meaning of *snake* and of *Bob* won't find the metaphor illuminating. More important than the dictionary meaning of *snake* or the indication of which *Bob* I mean by pointing him out is the *system of associated commonplaces* that attends each.

Each term that is interactively involved in a metaphor carries with it such a system. A system of associated commonplaces consists of the standard beliefs that are shared by members of the same speech community when they use a term literally. These are the associations that grow from our cultural and historical experiences with these terms. They are the residue of the contexts in which these terms have been used. In metaphors that derive their meanings through interaction between frame and focus, these systems must be evoked freely. For metaphors of this type to work, we rely on the audience to supply relevant associations without special instruction.

These associated commonplaces affect our interpretation of the principal subject. These interpretations are not normally found in the associated commonplaces of the principal subject when used literally. Take the metaphor "*Love is madness*" (*Love* is the principal subject, *madness* the subsidiary subject). For our culture, *madness* and *love* have extensive systems of associated commonplaces. Here are some of the more obvious ones:

Only some of which render the metaphor — implicative complex — function... entailment

Love	Madness
affection	insanity
attachment	mental illness
fondness	psychopathology
worship	paranoia
respect	schizophrenia
generosity	catatonia
frustration	depression
commitment	anger
friendship	derangement
sentiment	caprice
tenderness	uncontrollability
protectiveness	irresponsibility
enchantment	dementia
captivation	foolishness
romance	feeblemindedness
amorousness	idiocy
passion	abnormality
ecstasy	hysteria

The two systems become interactive when supported in a single metaphoric expression. Their interaction serves to highlight some elements of the system and hide others. Usually we don't think of lovers as idiots or feebleminded, although spurned lovers sometimes speak of themselves in precisely such terms. Nor do we think of ourselves as literally suffering from a mental illness that requires institutional treatment. But we do find our moods to be unsettled and to experience abnormal states of mind. Lovers sometimes do appear to act compulsively or irresponsibly. Similarly, not all aspects of love pertain to madness. Normally we don't think of those who are mad as motivated to act out of respect, selflessness, or affection. We do see them occasionally as captivated or enchanted, as given to passion, and as suffering violent fluctuations of moods. Together these systems delimit each other to relevant associated commonplaces that are mutually illuminating and that create unique meanings.

From the expression "Love is madness" we form the general image of lovers as people not totally responsible for what they do. Contrast this with the images in "Love is a work of art" or "Falling in love is a free ride, but staying in love requires effort." These are entirely different ways of organizing our love experiences into a meaningful form. They bring different elements to the fore as most salient for understanding what love is. They shape our perceptions in wholly different ways and encourage different anticipations of the future.

The different anticipations encouraged by each of these love metaphors illustrates once more how our language gives us conceptual frameworks for experience. In this case, our conceptual frameworks for love stem from the dynamic character of symbols interacting in a single expression. Metaphors project on the principal subject a set of associated commonplaces that have implications of attitude, value, and behavior. These projections create a set of implied claims. Researchers like Max Black and Lakoff and Johnson find that the intermixing of common beliefs shared by members of the same speech community introduces novel, substantive implications for our understanding. "Love is mad" implies such claims as

1. Love is disorienting.
2. Love is capricious.
3. Love is an abnormal state.
4. Love has profound effects on our moods.
5. Lovers are out of control.
6. Lovers are not responsible for what they do.

entailments

Together such claims, generated by the interaction between principal and subsidiary subjects, form an *implicative complex.*

Yet meaning is not in the utterance itself, as we saw earlier, but in the interaction that occurs between symbols and symbol users. Meaning is the creative response on the part of listeners who are able to comprehend what is being said and to project the significance of that utterance. In metaphor, listeners and readers play an especially active role because they must find a common understanding with the rhetor for the words used. This common understanding requires a shift from a normal or literal meaning to a nonliteral one. Thus rhetor and audience work together to create the meaning of a metaphor.

The elements of metaphoric interaction we have been considering apply to metaphors in general as they influence our perceptions and provide conceptual schemata. All effective metaphors develop meaning through dynamic interaction. This is true for trivial metaphors like "Richard is a lion" and novel metaphors like John Crowe Ransom's depiction of the human as an "oscillating mechanism."

Novel metaphors do have two features, however, that distinguish them from trivial ones: emphasis and resonance. These features contribute to the degree of interesting meaning evoked by a metaphor.

Emphasis refers to the degree to which the focus is essential for the meaning of the metaphor. An emphatic metaphor will not permit substitution for its focus. By changing the word, we change the meaning. Emphatic metaphors require our thought. When metaphors create new meanings, they must be dwelt upon for the sake of their unstated implications. There is no novel meaning without audience cooperation in perceiving what lies behind the producer's words.

Resonance refers to the number of implications we can draw from the interplay between the principal subject and the subsidiary subject. Metaphors that are rich in implications are resonant; those that are not are nonresonant.

When a metaphor creates meaning, it generates new information. This information is the body of implications—the implicative complex—that restructures reality for us. Metaphors that are highly emphatic and resonant have this trait. These are *strong metaphors,* ones with the power to generate novel thought through the implicative weight of their frame-focus interaction.

What is the interplay of such a metaphor? It is the interplay between sameness and difference. It is the tension that exists by violating the normal semantic sense of a term. It is a tension that forces us actively to consider the old in a new light, to displace one conceptual pattern with another, apparently incongruous with the frame in which it is set.

Importantly, this power to present sameness in difference does *not* exist in the lexicon of a language. Metaphors are *not* found in dictionaries. They exist only in discourse. They exist only in the interaction experienced during language use. The meanings that emerge are not ones that can be had in any other terms or in any other way. We began this chapter by indicating that rhetoric's concerns with meaning focused on how our use of language shaped our perception and understanding of our world. The power of metaphor to give birth to new meaning only through utterance demonstrates how thoroughly the human world is the product of the interpretations we develop in and through discourse.

SUMMARY

The concept of metaphor brings the considerations of this unit full circle: the use of language to establish identification. We have investigated how it is that symbols induce attitudes from a dramatistic perspective.

Dramatism holds that humans act with symbols. Our uses of symbols serve to structure our realities because they structure our perceptions. Further, as symbols work in harmony with one another, they provide conceptual patterns that organize experience and how it is understood. When these patterns are shared, we *identify* with one another. The basic way in which these symbolic actions induce identification is through shared motives. In a sense, we speak the same language when we share the same vocabulary of motives.

The motivational dynamics of any message constitute the meaning of that message for listeners. If we know what a message is likely to mean to receivers, we can understand better why they respond as they do. A rhetorician's concern with how people use language requires a theory of meaning suited to rhetorical action. We saw that from a rhetorical perspective, meanings are not in the words themselves but evolve from the contexts in which symbols appear or are used. These contexts are historical, situational, sometimes personal, and linguistic.

The relationship between language or symbol usage and the shaping of perceptions is captured by Kenneth Burke's claim that rhetoric is "the use of language as a symbolic means of inducing cooperation in beings that by nature respond to symbols." His basic idea, and the idea generally adhered to in contemporary rhetorical theory, is that rhetoric *persuades* through establishing *identification.* Simply put, people identify in terms of shared *motives,* which are present in *words, tones, gestures, actions,* whatever has meaning for a rhetor and a listener or reader.

This set of relationships among identification, motives, and symbolic action raises a set of questions that guide our thinking about *rhetorical* actions:

1. What motives are present in a given symbolic exchange, a given instance of language usage?
2. What perceptions do these motives invite?

3. How do these motives work harmoniously to form an appeal to an audience?

4. What do our findings on the patterns of perceiving and thinking induced by motive appeals tell us about why listeners responded as they did, why they identified, misidentified, divided, and so forth?

One way to answer such questions is through inspection of how people actually use language. This requires hands-on conceptual tools we can use to dig into the dynamic interactions of language as it is used. Extensive development of such tools is beyond the scope of our present inquiry. Still, we have shown how the concerns of Chapters 9 and 10 work in actual practice by exploring several basic ways in which meanings are created through the interaction of words in contexts. Next we will pursue this concern further as we explore rhetorical strategies.

NOTES

1. Bronislaw Malinowski, "The Problem of Meaning in Primitive Language," in C. K. Ogden and I. A. Richards, *The Meaning of Meaning* (Orlando, Fla.: Harcourt Brace Jovanovich, 1923), pp. 296–336.
2. The most far-ranging yet accessible discussion of this point can be found in George Lakoff and Mark Johnson, *Metaphors We Live By* (Chicago: University of Chicago Press, 1980). I have relied on their treatment extensively in this section.
3. Lakoff and Johnson, pp. 3–22.
4. Ibid., p. 57.
5. I. A. Richards, *The Philosophy of Rhetoric* (New York: Oxford University Press, 1936), pp. 47–66.
6. Ibid., pp. 23–43.
7. Chaim Perelman and L. Olbrechts-Tyteca, *The New Rhetoric: A Treatise on Argumentation,* trans. John Wilkinson and Purcell Weaver (Notre Dame, Ind.: Notre Dame University Press, 1969), pp. 149ff.
8. Carroll C. Arnold, *Criticism of Oral Rhetoric* (Columbus, Ohio: Charles E. Merrill, 1974), p. 199.
9. Aristotle takes this up in Book III of the *Rhetoric,* especially at 1404*b*–1405*a*.
10. Lakoff and Johnson, pp. 77–105.
11. Max Black, *Models and Metaphors* (Ithaca, N.Y.: Cornell University Press, 1962), pp. 25–47. Black updated his views in "More About Metaphor," *Dialectica,* 31 (1977), 431–457.

chapter 11

Rhetorical Form as Strategy

In the 1970s, television personality Dick Cavett hosted a late-night talk show. One evening Cavett was interviewing Bert Parks, longtime MC of the Miss America Pageant. The gentlemen discussed the pageant in fairly innocuous fashion, recalling the commonplace associations that go with Miss America: beauty contest, pretty women, entertainment, swimsuits, evening gowns, promenading on the ramp, Parks's rendition of the Miss America theme, and so forth. As the commercial break approached, Parks excused himself to catch a plane. Cavett thanked him for his appearance, and a commercial was shown.

After the break, the next guest was introduced: Kathy Hubbie, the former Miss Idaho. It appeared that Hubbie had been stripped of her Miss Idaho title by the Miss America Pageant's directors for behavior unbecoming to the pageant. Hubbie was the editor of an underground newspaper, *The Paper Tiger.* The Miss Idaho people were upset at her political activity, told her to resign from the paper, suggested that she move from her mother's home, where leftist politics were preached, and insisted that her long-haired brother stop riding in her pageant motorcade. Hubbie countered by agreeing that her brother need not ride in parades with her. She allowed that her private residence was her own concern, so she would continue to live with her mom. As for the newspaper, she'd meet them halfway. She would not resign but would edit under a pseudonym. The Miss Idaho people thought this was fair enough and agreed. Two days later the national organization said no deal, resign or be deposed. She was deposed.

To viewers who had not known of Kathy Hubbie's plight these revelations were astonishing. They portrayed the Miss America directors as mean-spirited and left a tarnished impression of the pageant. Cavett did not directly accuse the *or form to show?*

pageant of wrongdoing, yet his interview appeared to indicate such. Why did the pageant appear so low? Why did the contestant seem so victimized? The answers lie in the way viewer sympathies were engaged by the structure of Cavett's back-to-back interviews. Each part fitted with the next in a way that aroused viewer expectations and then confronted those expectations with opposing data. In essence, the form of the two interviews was blatantly strategic. We had to have Parks before Hubbie. The talk with Parks had to be innocuous so that viewers' fantasies would be evoked. We had to have Parks leave, otherwise there would be a debate rather than a persuasive appeal. In this context, Hubbie's appearance confronted viewers with data that denied their fantasy image. The Miss America Pageant appeared to be quashing a contestant's First Amendment rights. What have her political views to do with the contest? Why did the pageant's directors respond in this extreme fashion? Perhaps the contest is not so innocent as it appears. Questions and concerns like these are clearly invited by the way Cavett structured this interview. His interview was a case of strategic action, as rhetorical in its intent and execution as any persuasive speech.

As is apparent by now, the study of rhetoric is centrally concerned with the social uses of symbols to accomplish goals. Whether these goals are mundane or lofty, selfish or altruistic, base or noble makes little difference from the perspective of managing symbols. Regardless of motivation, goal-directed discourse is purposive in its selection of symbols, construction of appeals, engagement of listeners and readers as feeling and valuing as well as thinking beings. Unlike mathematical proofs, which are sound in and of themselves and are available for any and every competent mathematician to inspect, the appeals of rhetoric are adapted appeals. They are devised to suit an audience, an occasion, a presenting persona, a time and place. They are essentially *strategic* acts.

In the concluding chapters of this book we will consider rhetoric as a mode of *strategic action.* We will be concerned with how it "works" in the practices of any person who communicates with purposes to another. We will consider especially how the *form* of a rhetorical message always contains a strategic approach to the problem posed by a rhetorical situation. Moreover, we will see how rhetorical form is not limited to the selection of images. It extends beyond language to any structural feature that shapes a coherent inducement to perceive and respond in a particular way.

In this chapter we will consider the ways in which "structure in the large" functions as a source of identification. We will consider how all rhetorical acts involve form and how forms embody strategies. In well-formed rhetoric, these strategies are invariably geared to move the audience in some way that serves the rhetor's end—even if they be as innocent as understanding information.

STRUCTURE IN THE LARGE

We know from our studies of the sciences that nature is an extremely busy place. Matter percolates with bombardments of energy as atoms and molecules jounce and carom. Through a microscope we see organisms ashimmer with indefinite eddies of cells that seem to jitterbug and bounce. Of course, to the naked eye none of this chaos is visible. We see only the outward forms of tables and cars, of people and trees. We see our world in the discernible patterns of structures.

The claim that we humans perceive our world as structured patterns may seem like an obvious point. Still, it is an important point whose underlying reasons are relevant to understanding how rhetorical communication induces attitudes and actions.

At first glance it may seem that nature's chaos escapes detection because these motions are microscopic. While it is true that atoms and molecules are not perceptible to the naked eye, this does not explain why our perceptions are always of structured wholes. That concern has more to do with the cognitive processes that accompany sensory experience than with what may or may not be beyond our doors of perception.

The topic of human cognitive processing is complex and beyond our concerns with the basic principles of rhetorical action. However, some of the findings on brain functioning are relevant to our undertaking and can be set forth in summary fashion.

Structures Are Basic to Perception

Neurological studies report that the brain does not take in the data from its surroundings as a mass of undifferentiated information. We engage in selective perception. This means that our brains make discriminations among all the elements out there to separate them from one another and to focus more intently on some than on others. This discriminative process is illustrated by our sense of sight. Researchers have found that light rays trigger responses in various parts of the brain. These responses tell us that our ecology has regions of light and darkness. Moreover, our brain tells us about the qualities of light in these regions. For example, light regions may appear more intensely bright or more vibrantly colorful as the surrounding region is made darker or as its color changes. Studies like these reveal a basic principle of perception: The human brain makes discriminations by edging and bordering.

In his study of the relationships among symbolic processes and mental processes, Richard Gregg[1] indicates that without bordering, we could not stabilize the "ecological flux" that surrounds us. In addition, he notes that the bordering process is simultaneously a symbolic activity. In other words, our brains do not copy the external world but perceive the external environment in terms of forms that they are capable of perceiving. Gregg puts it best when he says:

> There is no experiencing but formed experiencing. To say that something is formless is usually only an acknowledgment that we have no handy label for what we are experiencing, but it cannot mean that we are experiencing something unformed, for this is a contradiction and a neurological impossibility.[2]

The basic principles that guide human perception, such as the principle of bordering, constrain our experiences of reality. For example, because our perceptions are bordered, we experience the world holistically. From the most rudimentary level of sensation to the most complex level of ideation, we require borders to perceive distinctions.

Of course, there are limits to what we can and cannot perceive. For example, our species is "wired" to interact with our environment in certain ways. We know that our sense of smell is inferior to a dog's and our sight is less than a bird's. Some sights and sounds and odors that are part of our environment we do not detect because our receptors are insufficiently sensitive. Our "reality" is not the same as Rover's because our neurological capacities are different.

Gregg's investigation of neurological findings uncovered six basic patterns of human perception relevant to our immediate concerns with rhetorical inducements:[3]

1. *The principle of "edging" or formulating "boundaries."* The brain perceives data in terms of wholes. This principle is so important to perception that the brain will construct or fill in borders as necessary to render data meaningful.
2. *Rhythm.* The brain perceives data in terms of motion. Not only are the brain's activities rhythmic, but so too are human perceptions. Rhythm is fundamental to structuring "realities."
3. *Association.* The brain perceives identities. Likeness and difference are basic to discrimination. Comparison and contrast require detection of identical features.
4. *Classification.* The brain perceives groupings. The result of contrast and comparison is clustering of like with like. The brain "groups" likeness at all levels of activity.
5. *Abstraction.* The brain perceives by abstracting data from the ecological flux of their total environment. While abstraction is continuous and helps efficiency of perception, it also distorts because it is always partial.
6. *Hierarchy.* The brain seeks closure on structures of perception. These structures tend to be interrelated as superordinate and subordinate elements and systems. These hierarchical structures influence the meanings of perceptions.

Perception and Structure in the Large

These six basic principles of perception are rife with suggestions for understanding how structures influence us. First, they suggest that all human perception is selective perception. We do not take in *all* of the sensory data "out there," only what we are equipped to detect. The data we do take in are abstracted, grouped, bounded, and in other ways shaped as our brains are equipped to do. Other data are left behind. So while we form an intelligible perception of "reality," it is a partial perception and necessarily distorted perception.

Second, our perceptions of reality require structure. There can be no perception without structure of some sort. Consequently, the "realities" that we know and their meanings for us are welded to the structures we perceive.

Third, the structures we perceive have a variety of forms. They have shape, movement, likeness and difference, and grouping, among other things, as defining traits. In other words, structures are not just material forms but any *pattern* that can be perceived by the brain.

Fourth, all of our experiences have structure or form. In every episode of motion and action, there are patterns of sense, feeling, and thought. Unless and until their patterns are grasped, these episodes remain unintelligible aspects of reality.

Finally, because all experience is tied to structure, it is apparent that changes of structure lead to changes of experience. As changing the speed on a ͏ter͏ ͏ turntable or rotating the eyepiece of a kaleidoscope alters what we hear or see, manipulating the structure of events changes the way they are perceived and experienced.

Significantly, these five points indicate the extent to which we play an active role in structuring our realities. From top to bottom, the only realities we have are the realities we perceive. But the brain that perceives the external world does not record exact images like a camera. The camera frames entities, but the brain creates events. The brain is selective in what it perceives and adroit in forming perceptions. Our experiences are not of what is "out there" but ͏of the symbolic presentations of our mental structurings. Our experience grows from the variety of forms in which our senses, feelings, and thoughts are engaged. It grows from structure in the large.

STRUCTURE AND STRATEGY

The neurophysiological patterns of perception we have just described suggest that all structures are symbolic inducements to some extent. All structures invite a particular expectation of patterned development and completion. Why is this important to rhetoric? Because all our choices of argument, organization, language, action, occasion, setting, medium, and the like are actually choices of structures. In rhetoric, these structures are referred to as *forms.* The unique feature of rhetorical forms is that *they encourage an anticipation of an outcome.* If developed properly, they also *satisfy this anticipation.* [4]

In a sense we have been examining rhetorical forms throughout this book. Enthymemes, the passions, and resources of language are but a few we have considered. Each of these forms shares this quality of involving a listener or a reader in a participatory way: They are ways for getting our audience to anticipate where we're going. Because they arouse anticipations, forms also establish relationships between us and our listeners. Consequently, our selection of forms bears directly on the type of relationship we want and the one we actually get. Considerations like these are strategic; they concern how best to achieve a goal.

Structure and Strategic Choice

When we examine carefully the ancient rhetorical texts, we find important clues to thinking about structure, clues that are most helpful to a basic understanding of structure's function in rhetoric. The earliest known Roman textbook on rhetoric, the *Ad Herennium* ("to Herennius"), is a good example. After advising the reader on how to arrange arguments so that they will have a strong and lasting impression, the unknown author offers this assessment:

> This arrangement of topics in speaking, like the arraying of soldiers in battle, can readily bring victory.[5]

The choice of a military metaphor is both dramatic and informative. Our writer is conceptualizing the structure of a message—its introduction, body of proofs and refutations, and conclusion—as a design with strategic intent. Just as a general arrays troops to exploit terrain, weaknesses of enemy position and numbers, conditions of weather, and the like, so too the rhetor deploys the available means of persuasion with an eye toward gaining the advantage. As Dick Cavett's interview of Kathy Hubbie illustrates, what was true for ancient speeches remains true for contemporary rhetorical events. We still must structure our messages. We still select a specific structure because it arrays our points in the desired light.

The ancient suggestion that dispositional thinking is strategic thinking opens a broad range of possibilities for our consideration. Once we focus on the strategic value of structures, literally any and every symbolic structure can have a rhetorical function. The world may bombard us with a montage of sensory data—sights and sounds in all sorts of juxtapositions—but we perceive it in terms of structures, and we respond to holistic patterns that give coherent form to elements bebopping about chaotically in our environment.

Humans emit sounds strung together, but we hear a coherent utterance. Humans express utterances serially, but we recognize a reasoning pattern. Humans converse by communicative turn taking, but we grasp each turn as a move that opens some possibilities and closes others for coherent response. Humans inhabit physical spaces containing physical objects, but we respond to these as environments that encourage some modes of communication and discourage others. Humans are confronted at any given moment by the utter novelty of a world in flux, but our inherent disposition is to focus on the structural unities amid chaos. Amid novelty we find the familiar elements that permit anticipating the future of unfolding events. We perceive and conceptualize every aspect of physical and human environment as structured in some way. These structures, whatever their stripe, function strategically to shape our attitudes, beliefs, and actions as responses to our world. For this reason, whenever a communicator provides verbal and nonverbal structures to an audience, these can be examined and understood for their strategic value.

Strategizing with Form

The strategic character of rhetorical thinking has been evident throughout our discussion. The point I want to underscore here is that our strategies are present in all the structural features of rhetoric—even those we don't tend to consciously. These structures influence profoundly audience perceptions and outcomes.

To illustrate the way in which structures are strategic, consider these examples of prose and how their *form* encourages different responses. Here's a passage from the beginning of a book:

> We usually use the term *literature* to refer either to (1) imaginative, enduring works or (2) bodies of writing that deal with particular topics of study (e.g., the "literature" on nuclear fission). The second is a fairly specialized usage; "literature" more often carries the first meaning. The phrase "literary criticism" refers almost invariably to the analysis and judgment of imaginative, linguistic works. But the question of where one applies or does not apply the principles of "literary criticism" has never had an obvious answer.[6]

Here's another, quite different beginning:

> To have a reason to get up in the morning, it is necessary to possess a guiding principle. A belief of some kind. A bumper sticker, if you will. People in cars on busy freeways call to each other *Boycott Grapes,* comfort each other *Honk if You Love Jesus,* joke with each other *Be Kind to Animals—Kiss a Beaver.* They identify, they summarize, they antagonize with statements of faith: *I Have a Dream, Too—Law and Order; Jesus Saves at Chicago Fed; Rod McKuen for President.*[7]

And here's rhetoric of still another order:

> Tonight at 8:30 come to a "fraternity party" on the terrace of the Beta Theta Pi house, 220 N. Burrowes Street (on campus). The food and drinks are on the house, the setting is perfect for fraternizing, and the location is convenient to the Arts Festival and downtown, in case you want to keep partying after the party.

As we read these passages, we form three different sets of expectations as to what we have in store. The first passage is written in the style of scholarly prose. Not only is the subject technical, but the writer expresses himself in the manner of a scholar. We have the marks of "either . . . or," "(1), (2)," and "e.g.," and the passage sets forth a definition and raises a question. All of these are the trappings of conceptual treatment, and we, literate in the ways of scholarly prose, can project from these signs the type of treatment to follow. The passage also establishes a relationship between us and the voice speaking through the text. It is a didactic relationship, and the lessons to be taught will be the conceptual lessons relevant to mastering abstractions about criticism.

The second passage takes a different tone. More conversational, it deals with a subject of everyday life in terms and images that have concrete referents for most readers. We have seen bumper stickers, each speaking advocacy, even though we may not have thought of them in that way before. As we read the bumper sticker metaphor, we recognize a more familiar relationship between the voice of the text and us as readers. At the same time, we are led to wonder what the author is getting at. But we are not confused since, as sensitive readers of fictive prose, we frame an expectation that the author will soon clarify why she related bumper stickers to getting out of bed in the morning. Like the previous passage, this one also establishes a relationship between us and the voice speaking through the text. Not only is it the familiar relationship of friends conversing, but there is a teaching function here as well. Unlike the abstract, technical lessons to be taught by the author expounding on criticism, the lessons here will be about our concrete experiences. It comes as no surprise to read in the next paragraph:

> Lying on his back in bed, he gazes around the walls of his room, musing about what has happened to his collection of statements. They had been discreetly mounted on cardboard, and fastened up with push pins so as not to deface the walls. Gone now. Probably tossed out with the rest of the junk—all those eight-by-ten colorprints of the Cubs, White Sox, and Bears, junior-high mementos. Too bad. It would be comforting to have something to look up to. Instead, the walls are bare. They have been freshly painted. Pale blue. An anxious color. Anxiety is blue; failure, gray. He knows those shades.[8]

We have the answer to our question. Those aren't random bumper stickers; they are *the character's*. They aren't on cars; they are on his walls. And we are in his room with him, looking at bare walls and now led to wonder why they are bare—anticipating that the author soon will tell us.

And what of the third passage, informing us of the fraternity party? Clearly the invitation sets an expectation of a good time. This invitation is itself even in the partying mood, for its author is given to whimsy with "fraternizing" at a fraternity house and "partying after the party." Again, because we are literate in the structure of invitations, we understand the jokes and blandishments to be a sign that our host sincerely desires our presence at this affair. Moreover, the informal structure of this invitation creates a relationship quite different than if its authorial voice had adopted the impersonal formality of something like "The Head and Faculty of the English Department request the honor of your presence for buffet and cocktails." There's no denying that the language of the first leads us to anticipate a casual affair. It is all right to wear jeans, T-shirts, and deck shoes. Few of us would be caught dead attending the second in that attire. We would anticipate the polite and decorous behavior that accompanies a sedate reception and would dress accordingly.

Each of these examples presents us with remarkably different situations. They ask us to think of ourselves in vastly different ways. They arouse uniquely distinct expectations of the future. They establish relationships completely unlike one another and call on us to respond in dissimilar fashions for these relationships to be sustained. Finally, and importantly, we are able to decipher these forms and respond in an appropriate fashion. As Burke says, we are uniquely able to respond to symbols. Because we are hereditarily equipped to do so, the management of symbolic structures can induce attitudes, motives, and social cooperation.

STRUCTURES REVEAL MOTIVES

In an important sense, all rhetorical situations may be thought of as posing a question. We are asked, "What shall we believe or feel or do about this problem or concern?" In the same vein, rhetoric is an answer to the question posed by the situation in which it arises. Rhetorical responses are not merely answers but *strategic* answers and *stylized* answers. Their differences in strategy and style can be as marked as those between Lee Iacocca hawking Chrysler products and the ads for Mercedes-Benz or as subtle as those between saying the word *yes* in tonalities that imply "Thank God!" or "Alas!"

When we say that rhetoric is an answer to the questions posed by the situation in which it arises, we imply that rhetorical acts adopt certain strategies for encompassing these situations. When we seek social cooperation, we calculate the ways likely to achieve it. We make these determinations best when we can answer such questions as, What kind of problem is this? What do we want our audience to do? How are we potentially united in a common bond of sentiment and action toward a common world? As Kenneth Burke says, "These strategies size up the situations, name their structure and outstanding ingredients, and name them in a way that contains an attitude towards them."[9]

In Chapter 9 we discussed the concept of motives. We saw that motive terms are cultural shorthand for situations that recur regularly for our group. They provide a definition for our situation and point us toward appropriate action. There we were interested in how language encourages identification. Now our concern is with how specific structures function strategically to answer the demands of a situation. Thus turned around, we may say that the motivation out of which we communicate is synonymous with the structural way in which we put events and values together when we communicate. Whether or not we are consciously aware of it, implicit in our structuring and patterning of symbols are strategies for dealing with the situations in which we find ourselves. These strategies, in turn, are the ongoing constructions of ourselves as symbol-using (or misusing) creatures with individual identities. They construct our world and our place in it and invite others to share it with us.

Looked at from the analyst's perspective, we can represent this process as a circle (Figure 11.1). This circle indicates the considerable information we

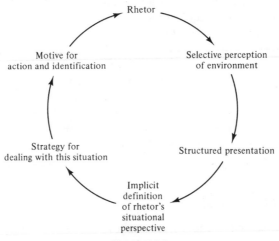

Figure 11.1

divulge about ourselves through the structures present in our rhetorical acts. In every case of rhetorical action, we adopt strategies that can be observed and deciphered. As rhetors, we perceive selected elements of our environment. When these elements create tensions of unresolved conflict, communication is a likely response. We issue messages to rectify these tensions. Our messages are necessarily constructed with structures of some sort, such as language, arguments, and idea development. These message structures reflect our implicit definitions of our respective situations. Further, they function as our strategies for coping with these situations. Our strategies, in turn, contain our motives for action. But our motives are likewise a basis for identification between us and our audience. Insofar as we achieve identification, our audience shares in our perceptions of the environment and our ways of dealing with it.

It is important to note that these structures are not hidden persuaders in any sinister sense. We can detect them in all sorts of messages if we look for them. Whether we have before us the transcript of a speech, an interpersonal dialogue, a movie script, a literary text, or some other symbolic form with persuasive potential, like a film or photograph, we will notice that it has patterns uniquely its own. A message will have structure because, as we just saw, all data that is perceived is perceived as structured in some way. Moreover, perceived structures are coherent to us in terms of the relationships among their parts. The same is true for language structures. Wherever there is purposeful, situated use of language relevant to the question posed by its situation we will find relationships among the rhetor's ideas.

Among the most basic of these structures are *associational clusters*. Associational clusters are terms and ideas that congregate together. They modify one another, delimit the view of the world advanced by the speech or the text, articulate values, and establish intellectual, emotional, and value relationships as a basis for identification. For example, consider the way Salvatore Gentile clusters competing images of a gym:

> It sure isn't the same anymore at the old gym. It used to reek of liniment and sweat, and the stairs echoed with grunts all the way down to the street. You kept your gear rolled up in a damp towel tucked under your arm, and you went with an oldtimer until the guy at the front door got to know your face. From then on, you were greeted with a silent nod when you came in. You worked out in a dimly lit room beneath a ceiling of peeling paint, and if you were lucky, there was a place to shower. But it just isn't the same anymore.

> I thought the gym would put up more of a fight, but even the term itself has passed into disuse. Today it's known as a health club or a fitness center. Or worse, a spa. You need a laminated card to get in, and if you bring a friend, he has to sign a waiver and leave a deposit before he can pass the desk. The gym doesn't smell the same because of the air conditioning. And it doesn't sound the same because of the carpeting, which dulls everything. The mirrored walls look funny, too, like something out of a fun house.[10]

The old gym was dingy and dank. It smelled foul and was not given to creature comforts. It was a place for crusty men given to toil. Clearly, the writer wants us to feel its character. All the images of the new health club contrast with this: fancy names, creature comforts, no crusty gent to greet you, only a sign that reminds us that these are litigious times. This isn't a place where men come to toil; the creature comforts of an air-conditioned, carpeted, and mirrored workout center are too indulgent for that. If anything, the writer wants us to feel the antiseptic absence of character in this space. It is laminated, a plastic module interchangeable with thousands of others across the country and thoroughly lacking any unique identity of its own.

Associational clusters like these are the typical ways in which rhetors give development to thoughts and feelings and texture to their appeals. By looking at messages in search of these clusters, we can gain insight into *how* a message orchestrates various elements of thought and expression to shape responses. Associational clusters will tell us *what goes with what* in the speaker's or writer's mind. The interrelationships among them will provide the rhetor's definition of the situation. In effect, these clusters *are* her *situation,* which as we just saw is another way of saying they are her *motives:* They are the capsule definitions of situations that imply the attitudes and actions her group finds appropriate.

To illustrate how the relationship between a message's structure and its strategy is concretely present in our speaking, let us examine a portion of Richard Nixon's speech of April 30, 1970. In this address he announced an American incursion into Cambodia for the purpose of finding and destroying North Vietnamese sanctuaries located there. The speech triggered a violent domestic reaction. The antiwar movement, which had lost its steam in the months immediately preceding the address, had an upsurge of activity. Demonstrations swept across college campuses, and the conflict between the government and opponents to the war climaxed in the shooting of four students at Kent State University.[11]

If you examined statements by students, faculty, concerned citizens, national leaders, and politicians who opposed Mr. Nixon's action, you would find them harping on a remarkably unified theme. They complained that Nixon cast the nation's worth in terms of its power. His critics thought this was a false issue; the world did not question our might but our wisdom. Yet Nixon himself stated, "It is not our power but our will and character that [are] being tested tonight." In light of this disclaimer, why did so many Americans see the president as acting in an opposite way?

The answer can be found in several important structures of his speech. In a message of approximately 2400 words, Nixon devoted about one-quarter of his remarks to reflections on the nation's character. Quite apart from announcing a military action and the rationale for it, he digressed into an area that went to the core of the nation's self-identity. These remarks were not called for by the situation itself and in fact transformed it from a military crisis into a crisis of integrity. Nixon invited the citizenry to reflect on how our willingness or lack thereof to use military force was a comment on our national values. This digression—a speech within the speech—itself highlighted his comments on character.

In addition to the structure of idea placement, the president's speech contains revealing clusters. After characterizing the Hanoi government as intransigent, belligerent, aggressive attackers and killers, he decries their attitude as intolerable. The United States cannot be "plaintive" in response or its "credibility" will be destroyed "in every area of the world where only the *power* of the United States deters aggression." We try to be conciliatory; the enemy tries to "humiliate and defeat us." Thus we are a nation under attack and must defend ourselves. Here is a prelude that trumpets the centrality of power to our survival and the survival of the rest of the free world. But there is more to it than that. In the next several paragraphs, we find the following remarks. Notice how the clustering of ideas around *power* gives it a special role in defining Americans as a people:

Nixon's comments	What goes with what
1. "If, when the chips are down, the world's most powerful nation, the United States of America, acts like a pitiful, helpless giant, the forces of totalitarianism and anarchy will threaten the free institutions throughout the world."	1. Not using power now makes us helpless. Power must be used to be validated.
2. "It is not our power but our will and character that [are] being tested tonight."	2. Power, in turn, validates our national will and character.
3. "If we fail to meet this challenge, all other nations will be on notice that despite its overwhelming power, the United States, when a real crisis comes, will be found wanting."	3. Power's use is an index of our worth.

In a few brief moments, Nixon established a set of relationships that made power the very sign of national character and that required power be used to validate character. The cluster of ideas about *power* reveal how Nixon defined this situation and simultaneously invited Americans to share in his definition. Those who decried the speech as misguided in its sense of America were not criticizing a mere digression in the address. The way the digression is set off and the structure of its appeal are strategies that call attention to this as a very crucial topic indeed. It informed the nation about some of its president's fundamental views about the United States, confronting them with the choice of identification or division.

SHAPING LISTENER PERCEPTIONS

So far we have considered that rhetorical form presents a structured message, that structures have identifiable features, that these features encourage relationships among speakers and listeners, and that structural patterns such as placement and associational clusters provide an index to a speaker's motives. Now we can extend these ideas to consider how various structural components function to shape a listener's perceptions.

Perhaps it is well to remind ourselves that upon grasping a pattern, we anticipate its completion. For example, patterns like "L, M, N, O, . . ." or "2, 4, 6, . . ." are easy to complete once we learn the alphabet or counting by 2s. In fact, we probably complete such patterns eagerly without consciously trying. Similarly, the patterns of common circumstances repeatedly experienced become ingrained in our thinking. Once they are initiated, we respond deftly to complete them. Patterns of weather lead farmers, sailors, and others whose livelihood depends on atmospheric conditions to set plans for the future. Patterns of the economy lead investors, bankers, and the business community to forecast the financial climate. Patterns of events allow us to predict, in our everyday lives, what will follow and to foresee the likely consequences of our actions.

Our capacity to respond to patterns makes it possible for rhetors to use the form of an appeal as a persuasive strategy. Uses of language, patterns of argument, and methods of appeal guide our reasoning and responses in ways that lead to and reinforce a selected conclusion. Recall the passages cited earlier concerning criticism, rising in the morning, and the party. Each of them selected and arranged ideas and expression with a goal in mind. Each sought to establish a thinking or feeling relationship with the reader. More than this, each channeled thoughts and feelings toward specific goals: It isn't clear where literary criticism does or does not apply; this character is depressed, has lost his purpose in life; we're going to have fun tonight.

In short, when we recognize a pattern, we expect its completion. This expectation of the future allows us to listen with intelligence and to act with propriety. Once we know where a thought, argument, or theme is headed, we can anticipate what will come next, be alert for evidence and reasoning necessary to make a case, listen with increased critical sensitivity, and evaluate how the thought, argument, or theme fits with the overall pattern of the whole speech.

For example, if our speaker tells us that the costs of college education are outstripping the ability of Middle Americans to borrow and to pay, you anticipate that she will develop this observation as a problem and then propose a solution. A variety of themes are available for development, such as *magnitude* ("Fully one-third of those who now attend soon will no longer be able to afford college"), *expediency* ("It is contrary to the nation's economic well-being to reduce its numbers of technically trained and higher-educated citizens"), and *morale* ("Placing college beyond the hopes of these youths will deny them the American dream of opportunity for social and economic advancement"). Magnitude, expediency, and morale as patterns of problem development encourage us to listen for different types of evidence, underlying assumptions, and even language. Because these are familiar patterns in American culture, each also allows us to participate at some level in its development as we experience it in the overall pattern of the speech.

The rhetorical uses of form need not be artistically managed for them to influence us. Because all uses of language are necessarily structured, their strategies are implicitly present and waiting to be uncovered. Whenever we communicate seriously with another person, in some way our language serves to induce an attitude, even if it is the counterattitude of rejection.

Kenneth Burke suggests five major patterns by which audience expectations are aroused: syllogistic progression, qualitative progression, repetitive form, conventional form, and minor or incidental form.[12] Each of these patterns can guide reasoning and responses that lead toward selective conclusions.

Syllogistic progression is the form of an argument that is perfectly conducted, with each premise leading to the next. We find this form in literary examples like mysteries, where each step leads to the next. It can take the form of historical progression in a lecturer's exposition of a topic. We would find it also in an attorney's tightly knit reasoning from facts to conclusions to prove a point in court. The important element to look for in this form is the logical progression from one element to the next. Given certain premises, others must follow. The audience participates in the framing of such an appeal. Their familiarity with the premises conditions them to know and feel the rightness of a conclusion. Thus when Richard Nixon presented his famous "Checkers" speech, he revealed his financial earnings and expenditures, what he owned and what he owed. Having done so, he prepared his audience for his later call that the other candidates for president and vice president make similar financial disclosures.

Qualitative progression is a form in which the presence of one quality prepares us for another. We do not have the pronounced anticipatory response to qualitative progression that we do to syllogistic. Rather, we recognize the rightness of the progression after the event. We do not demand that a premise follow so much as we are encouraged to adopt a frame of mind that inclines us to accept a pattern of development. For instance, when Geraldine Ferraro, the first female candidate for the vice presidency, attacked Ronald Reagan as an incompetent old man who catered to the military and the wealthy, the public was prepared to hear that her politics were more egalitarian and served the common interest. The negative state of mind associated with the opposition prepares us to adopt a positive state of mind toward the rhetor's position.

Repetitive form occurs when we consistently maintain a principle by presenting it in different ways. It is restatement of the same idea in a new guise. Lecturers do this when they state a principle and then provide an example. The example repeats the principle, in the guise of a particular case. A trial attorney uses this form when she parades a host of witnesses to testify that her client is a person of sound character. An orator uses this form by advising conduct that agrees with basic premises established throughout the speech. By the consistency of repeating, the audience comes to expect that the principle reasserted will be adhered to in other aspects of the appeal. For example, when Alan Alda addressed the 210th graduating class of New York's Columbia College of Physicians and Surgeons, he wanted to impress on the doctors in his audience their need to determine their values and how to live by them. To reinforce his point, he provided a series of typical situations physicians face and used humor to express the role of values in each case. Each illustration repeats in specific fashion his general point on values.

Conventional form is the appeal of a form that stems from our recognition of it as a form. This recognition requires audience familiarity with the form itself. The "Once upon a time" and "They lived happily ever after" of children's fairy tales are conventions. We expect them to be there. Unlike other forms, in which anticipation is developed during the actual listening or reading, conventional forms have anticipations that exist prior to performance because we are familiar with the form. For example, a homily is based on Scripture. We expect the preacher to cite a biblical passage, explain it, and apply it to our lives. In an acceptance speech, we expect a presidential nominee to speak of the general themes to be developed in the campaign. We do not expect a detailed exposition of specific proposals but broad and inclusive principles that will define the candidate's overall position. In genres of oratory, as in genres of literature, adhering to conventions provides a means for statisfying one set of audience demands, regardless of what we intend to say.

Minor forms, finally, are devices of expression, each of which can be regarded as a formal event in and of itself. Indirect question, metaphor, reduplication, antithesis, apostrophe, and other figures of speech and thought can be examined as though they were episodes within a discourse. Each form contains its own mode of appeal. All involve listeners in anticipating how an expression will be completed or how one thought will lead to or amplify another. At the same time, taken together, they can enhance our anticipation of the whole. For example, John Kennedy's speeches were marked by the use of antithesis, a figure that sets one idea off against the other. ("We should never negotiate out of fear, but never fear to negotiate.") Each figure served as a vehicle for clarifying points JFK thought important. They also contributed to an overall perception of America as in transition from the postwar consolidation of the Eisenhower administration to the expansionist vision of the New Frontier that Kennedy espoused.

In these basic ways, the management of symbols prepares an audience to receive ideas and participate in their development. By structuring ideas, they also structure the orientation we bring to a rhetorical situation, the perceptions we frame of ourselves and our social realities, and our anticipations of feelings and actions that will be appropriate to our felt needs. Our ability to respond to form makes it possible for us to participate actively with the rhetor in the coconstruction of our social worlds.

SUMMARY

Our discussion of strategy has focused on the fact that the human world is the one we perceive—a world of structures and patterns. These are prerequisites for human understanding and response, it appears, due to the way our brain and nervous system are "wired." Our mind finds shape, boundaries, size, and so forth in objects of its environment. It simplifies details by finding connections in them or imposing connections on them. These patterns eventually shape our cognitions of reality. Structures provide the order necessary to the elements of our experience for them to have meaning and for us to act.

But as soon as we recognize that structures impose meaning and are necessary to frame appropriate action, we also recognize that structures argue for a particular vision of the world. Structures have a rhetorical quality to them; they make appeals. For this reason, they have psychological consequences. When we notice, for example, that events proceed in a chronological order, we find *time* a meaningful structure to organize them. But perceiving the temporal quality of events also invites us to anticipate a future and events then to transpire. In other words, *time* not only relates the elements of our experience, but it also has the psychological consequence of inducing us to frame an anticipation. This same relationship between structure and form can be found throughout discourse, making all symbolic acts in some sense rhetorical.

In sum, the structural components of discourse—elements of language, argument, organization, setting, and the like that are available for all to notice—compose a data base of persuasive features. As we saw, these structures significantly reveal *associational clusters* among the rhetor's ideas. Clusters tell us what goes with what in the conceptual patterns that guide a message. As such, they are the rhetor's *strategic* answer and *stylized* answer to the questions posed by the rhetorical situation. At the same time, we noted that structures function strategically with respect to establishing identification with audiences because they arouse audience *anticipations.* Specifically, we noted five general patterns of such arousal: syllogistic progression, qualitative progression, repetitive expression of the same essential idea in different ways, conventional expression, and minor or incidental forms as devices of expression.

Noting these aspects of structure, the questions we must address in any rhetorical transaction are whether and why a given use of symbols is geared to the audience's readiness to respond. Rhetorical concerns with symbol-using behavior focus on how symbolic constructions arouse and satisfy an appetite and on how they enhance identification. We will address these matters in Chapter 12.

NOTES

1. Richard B. Gregg, *Symbolic Inducement and Knowing: A Study in the Foundations of Rhetoric* (Columbia: University of South Carolina Press, 1984), pp. 40ff.
2. Ibid., p. 41.
3. Ibid., p. 50.
4. Kenneth Burke, *Counter-statement,* 2d ed. (Los Altos, Calif.: Hermes, 1953), p. 31.
5. Harry Caplan, trans., *Ad Herennium,* (Cambridge, Mass.: Harvard University Press, 1954), p. 189.
6. Carroll C. Arnold, *Criticism of Oral Rhetoric* (Columbus, Ohio: Charles E. Merrill, 1974), p. 4.
7. Judith Guest, *Ordinary People* (New York: Viking, 1976), p. 1.
8. Ibid.
9. Kenneth Burke, *The Philosophy of Literary Form,* 3d ed., rev. (Berkeley: University of California Press, 1974), p. 1.
10. Salvatore Gentile, "Perspective," *Sports Illustrated* (December 19, 1983), 85.
11. For an account of these events, see James Michener, *Kent State: What Happened and Why* (New York: Random House, 1971).
12. Burke, *Counter-statement,* pp. 124–128.

chapter 12

Strategic Forms of Argument Structures

The way we make arguments and the way we respond to arguments depend on how we think of arguments.[1] If you think of arguments as "journeys," you will doubtless see their value in terms of the "ground covered" and their power to "explore" new dimensions of ideas. If arguments are journeys, they will have a "destination." Since "pitfalls" are inevitable, your interlocutor may "guide" you around them onto safer "routes." Viewed in this way, arguments are positive and cooperative enterprises.

Then again, you may be of the school that views argument as "war." For you, each argument is an intellectual "battle" in which you "fight" for your ideas. The objective in this case is to "defend" your contentions against the "force" of "attacks." This requires that you set a "strategy" to "defeat" your "opponent" and "carry the day." Viewed in this way, arguments are combative affairs with clear winners and losers.

The metaphors of journeys or wars are not the only ways in which we think of arguments. They illustrate, however, that the way in which we conceptualize arguments can have a radical effect on how we approach and behave in situations that call for arguments. These metaphors reflect our *implicit* theories of argument, our personal conceptions of what an argument is, of what takes place when people are called on to participate in arguments, and of standards we use in our everyday lives to evaluate arguments. We reveal these theories by the way we talk.

This does not mean that all arguments are idiosyncratic, however. These implicit theories are shared by others who use our language. Many people conceptualize arguments as journeys. Many more think of them as wars. Our shared conceptual frameworks make it possible for us to use arguments instead of force to change people's minds.

Since antiquity, philosophers and rhetoricians have studied how people make arguments. They have tried to capture these implicit theories and make them explicit. Their objective has been twofold: to make us better arguers and to make us better critics of arguments.

In this chapter we will concern ourselves with arguments as strategic forms. We will consider arguments first in terms of several major perspectives on argument structures. Then we will consider how other dimensions of rhetorical form function as arguments. Throughout this chapter our controlling interest will be to determine whether and why a given use of symbols functions as an argument structure and whether and why an argument structure is suited to the audience's readiness to respond.

ARISTOTLE'S SYLLOGISTIC STRUCTURE

For centuries Western thinkers understood arguments in terms of Aristotle's syllogistic logic. Aristotle's syllogistic theory maintains that we can test the value of an argument by examining the relationships among its premises. Depending on the type of premises and how they are related, we either can or cannot deduce a conclusion. When we genuinely deduce a conclusion, the argument is called valid. For example, we know that summer winds are erratic and violent when a cold front passes through, and we know that sailboats handle best in a steady breeze. So when we hear that a cold front is predicted for later in the day, we may validly deduce that sailing will be treacherous. On the other hand, if we only pretend to deduce a conclusion, the argument is called invalid. For example, if we know that Joe is in the coast guard and that the coast guard patrols the navigable waters of the United States, it may appear to follow that Joe patrols the navigable waters of the United States. But this is not necessarily so. He may be a clerk or a mechanic who is always on shore. At best we only pretend to deduce a conclusion.

To test the validity of an argument, its premises are set forth in the form known as a *syllogism:* an argument consisting of two premises and a conclusion; for example:

All members of the New York Yankees earn over $100,000 a year.
Fritz is a member of the New York Yankees.
Therefore, Fritz earns over $100,000 a year.

By examining the types of premises used and the relationships between their terms, Aristotle maintains that we can determine whether any conclusion genuinely follows.

Aristotle sets forth his theory of the syllogism in his *Prior Analytics.* There he discusses both valid and invalid syllogisms and the rules for testing each. For our purposes, the technical aspects of syllogism are not of concern. Rather, we need to be mindful that Aristotle thought that the syllogism applied to all reasoning regardless of subject matter. Consequently, his logic is called a *field-invariant logic.* This means that the rules for testing the validity of an argument are the same for all people and for all arguments. History, biology, mathematics, politics, and all other fields are subject to the same rules for valid inference.

Because Aristotle thought all arguments could be reduced to the same pattern of reasoning, he used this theory to describe rhetorical arguments. His rhetorical application of syllogism provides an intelligent form for speakers to use when they make arguments. As we saw in Chapter 6, the rhetorical uses of this form, called the enthymeme, provide the reasoned basis for rhetorical appeals.

In addition to providing a reasoned basis for persuasion, enthymemes also serve strategic ends. As the basic unit of popular appeals, Aristotle discusses them as arguments geared to the psychology of the audience. Successful enthymemes use premises that connect with the audience's assumptions. They relate these assumptions to the speaker's desired conclusions. Because they draw on audience beliefs, the form of enthymematic arguments makes active partners of the listeners in the persuasive process.

TOULMIN'S WARRANTED STRUCTURE

Aristotle's views were not rigorously challenged until the twentieth century, when a number of thinkers took exception to the idea that reasoning in all fields was the same. Aristotle's most notable critic was the British philosopher and physicist Stephen Toulmin.[2]

Toulmin's objection to Aristotle's syllogistic logic was twofold. First, it did not reflect the way people actually argue. In real life, people don't talk in syllogisms. Consequently, the analyst has to rearrange the parts of talk into the form of the syllogism to examine their logical relationships. Second, the syllogistic form was insensitive to different patterns of reasoning as they develop in arguments. Syllogisms are closed systems, like proofs in algebra or geometry. Relations are evaluated by logical necessity. But Toulmin believed arguments are actually open systems that develop more like legal reasoning. Their validity depends on the case in hand, varying from field to field. Consequently, Toulmin held that arguments are *field-dependent.* What counts as a valid inference in theology, say, might be completely unacceptable in chemistry, and vice versa.

To clarify the open-ended character of the way people actually argue and the ways in which people argue in different contexts (or fields), Toulmin developed a new system for laying out an argument (Figure 12.1).[3]

The system consists of two triads of elements that show how evidence and assumptions combine to support conclusions. The first triad describes the main line of the argument and consists of *data, warrant,* and *claim. Data* answers the question, "What have you got to go on?" Under *data* you find evidence of fact and opinion made available by the arguer ("56 percent of entering freshmen at State University indicate a preference for a professional curriculum, compared to 40 percent five years ago"). *Claim* is the inference drawn as a conclusion from the data. It is where we are going with the argument ("State University must shift

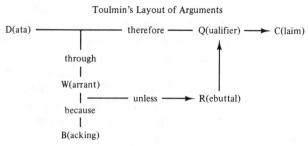

Figure 12.1

faculty lines from less popular curricula to professional programs"). *Warrant* answers the question, "How did you get there?" It provides the rationale for drawing an inference from data to claim ("Faculty distribution should reflect student demand"). Importantly, the warrant does not have to be explicit.

Toulmin's second triad consists of elements that pertain to the force of the argument. Its elements are *backing, rebuttal,* and *qualifier. Backing* contains evidence and argument to support a warrant. It guarantees our confidence in the warrant as legitimate ("Our land-grant charter establishes the mission of State University as educating the sons and daughters of the working class"). *Rebuttal* is the part of an argument that states exceptions or reasons why the warrant shouldn't hold ("Student demand fluctuates too often to shift faculty; the general education requirements of State University cannot be met if faculty numbers are reduced in Arts or in Sciences; the costs outweigh the benefits"). Finally, *qualifier* indicates the strength with which we hold the claim. In other words, the force of the claim depends on the strength of the rebuttal ("State University *must* shift lines" or "*probably* should shift lines" or "*perhaps* should shift lines" or "should *do nothing* at the present time—should send the matter to a committee for further study").

Toulmin's analysis of arguments was not originally intended to describe rhetorical features. He was interested in the logical aspects of reasoning embedded in the ways people actually speak their arguments. But rhetoricians soon grasped the utility of his model for describing rhetorical structures as well. For example, Wayne Brockriede and Douglas Ehninger[4] noticed that the claims speakers make correspond with the ends of arguments: establishing facts, defining problems, advancing values, establishing policies. These ends are traditional ones not unlike the questions formalized in the ancient doctrine on stasis: fact, definition, quality, and procedure.

Brockriede and Ehninger also noticed that Toulmin's notion of warrant governed the mode of reasoning in an argument. These modes were traditional concerns of rhetoricians since Aristotle first classified arguments under logos, pathos, and ethos. Modernized, they suggested that warrants could be grouped as substantive (logos), motivational (pathos), and authoritative (ethos) rules that permitted the inference from data to claim. In this respect, warrants provide a line of reasoning much like topoi, as we saw in Chapter 5. Thus, for example, review topics such as Wilson and Arnold described or material topics like those in Aristotle's *Rhetoric* may provide bridges between events and how we respond to them. Whether stated explicitly or implied, like unstated premises in an enthymeme, warrants provide authorization for judgments and actions.

Rhetorical arguments succeed only to the degree that they satisfy listeners' requirements for acceptable evidence and relevant warrants. These vary with topic, audience, and rhetorical aim. The value of Toulmin's discussion to rhetoricians is that he provides a means to analyze how arguments are actually made. His model is sensitive to how the actual elements of the argument interrelate to authorize an inference. In short, by thinking of arguments in terms of data, warrant, and claim, backing, rebuttal, and qualifier we are better able to grasp the whole structure of an argued appeal as a rhetorical form, a strategy for shaping perceptions.

Consider, for example, this argument advanced by Alan Alda. Speaking to graduating physicians at Columbia University, he wished the males in his audience to consider their values with respect to female medical students. He asked, "And if the day comes when you are teaching, what can young women medical students expect from you?"

> Questionnaires filled out by women at forty-one medical schools around the country have revealed a distressing pattern. The women were often either ignored in class or simply not taken seriously as students. They were told that they were only there to find a husband and that they were taking the places of men who would then have to go out and become chiropractors. (Logic is not the strong point of sexism.) [1]

> They were often told that women just didn't belong in medicine. And at times they were told this by the very professors who were grading them. They would be shown slides of *Playboy* nudes during anatomy lectures—to the accompaniment of catcalls and wisecracks from male students. And in place of discussions about their work, they would often hear a discussion of their appearance. These are reports from forty-one different medical schools. [2]

> I'm dwelling on this because it seems to me that the male-female relationship is still the most personal and intense test of humane behavior. It is a crucible for decency. [3]

> I hope you men will work to grant the same dignity to your female colleagues that you yourselves enjoy.[5] [4]

Most of the materials in paragraphs 1 and 2 are presented as data, reports from questionnaires administered at 41 different medical schools. Alda begins paragraph 1 with the claim that these questionnaires "revealed a distressing pattern." How does he get from these results to his conclusion? In paragraph 4 he makes his warrant explicit: These results violate his sense of equality; he calls on the male doctors in his audience to treat their female colleagues with "the same dignity" they enjoy. Notice also how paragraph 3 reinforces Alda's point. By claiming that the male-female relationship is "a crucible of decency," he adds considerable force to his claim of distress. Without verbal fireworks or resorting to superlatives or exaggeration, his qualifying reference to "a crucible of decency" encourages the conclusion that these women have been treated in a shameful and intolerable fashion.

As this illustration indicates, Toulmin's approach reveals the structure of the argument *as made*. By clarifying its form, we are better able to see how the structures of arguments are strategies for shaping listeners' perceptions of the rhetorical situation, the speaker, and themselves.

PERELMAN'S ASSOCIATIVE AND DISSOCIATIVE STRUCTURES

Although students of rhetoric have adapted Toulmin's treatment of argument to their interests, the fact remains that his discussion focuses mostly on the logical requirements of validity important in law, science, philosophy, and other fields of technical discourse. Accordingly, the bulk of his discussion explores whether and how inferences are authorized. It does not attempt to elucidate the argumentative function of rhetorical devices or the rhetorical potential of argument structures to induce attitudes. The scholar who has made the most impressive contribution in these areas is Chaim Perelman. This Belgian philosopher of argument and law has maintained that all argumentation is a rhetorical process and that rhetoric provides a logic for making rational appeals.

For Perelman, the test of whether an argument is rational or irrational rests with the audience. He contends that audiences judge an argued case in terms of how they process and remake the appeals they hear. Argument structures are important to their remaking process because they supply patterns of theme and information that listeners regard as valid. Argument structures guide thought.[6]

This guiding function is important. Perelman reminds us that rhetorical arguments are different from proofs. Proofs lead to certainty. They are demonstrations that occur in isolated systems. For instance, geometry is such a system. Given its axioms and postulates, we learn to deduce correct conclusions about lines, planes, and angles. Arguments do not occur in isolated systems. They occur in contexts that are complex, dynamic, evolving, and open-ended. Consequently, the conclusions to arguments are not certainties in the absolute sense of geometric proofs. They are "characterized by a constant interaction among all [their] elements."[7]

Perelman identifies a number of these schemes as structures of association and dissociation. These are structures commonly used and accepted to show the presence or absence of relationships. As accepted common practices of reasoning, they lend authority to an argument, since "only agreement on their validity can justify their application to particular cases."[8] Perelman shows how these argument structures themselves function as topoi, or places for arguments.

Processes of *association* are "schemes which bring separate elements together and allow us to establish a unity among them, which aims at organizing them or at evaluating them, positively or negatively, by means of one another."[9] These processes are similar to the associative clusters discussed in Chapter 11. They function, much along Burkean lines of determining what goes with what, to produce identification. The counterpart processes of *dissociation* are "techniques of separation which have the purpose of dissociating, separating, disuniting elements which are regarded as forming a whole or at least a unified group within some system of thought: dissociation modifies such a system by modifying certain concepts which make up its essential parts."[10] Dissociations are schemes that highlight division; they are the correlative opposing process to identification. Perelman makes this joining-dividing pattern concrete in terms of associative processes related to structures of logic and of reality and in terms of dissociative processes separating the apparent from the real. We need to consider these schemes more carefully to see how argument structures are used to shape perceptions.

Quasi-logical Arguments

Sometimes we argue in ways that seem to partake either of formal reasoning or of mathematical reasoning. These patterns are called *quasi-logical* because they are nonformal reasonings about everyday affairs. The first pattern is based on its similarity to formal reasoning. It suggests that there are formal relationships among data that compel a conclusion or are violated and require rejection. Most commonly we employ these patterns whenever we criticize another person's arguments. Our criticism suggests that this person's reasoning is faulty. Our objection is intended to straighten out an error of logic. For example, when we say, "You contradicted yourself" or "You made an emotional appeal," our suggestion is that this person needs to work on the logic of his argument.

Arguments like contradiction, identity, and transitivity (Table 12.1) get their persuasiveness from the appearance of being rigorous, formal reasoning. They borrow the prestige of logic through their form. These schemes encourage a perception of their maker as a clear thinker and of their contents as being thought through.

Let's consider the example of point 1 in the table, argument from contradiction. Contradiction attempts to indicate glaring inconsistencies in a person's position. These flaws undermine the rational basis for what she claims. Bette Ann Stead, a marketing professor at the University of Houston, illustrates how this argument structure works with her comments concerning President Reagan's position on affirmative action:

> On March 14, a *Houston Post* article noted that President Reagan's chief civil rights enforcer told a labor group that the administration abandoned affirmative action because it created resentment and tensions that threatened thirty years of progress. We will not use our time wisely this morning to dwell on the fact that anyone who truly knew what affirmative action was knew it was equally good for women and men and that much of that progress he referred to was the result of affirmative action.[11]

Professor Stead's argument illustrates attacking another person's position as contradictory. Note that she attacks this unnamed civil rights enforcer's expressed views by suggesting an inconsistency in his position: One cannot claim

Table 12.1 QUASI-LOGICAL ARGUMENTS

Logical relations

1. *Contradiction:* attempts to indicate glaring inconsistencies in a person's position ("You claim to be for equal rights, yet you oppose an equal rights amendment.")

2. *Identity or difference:* reduction of elements to points they share in common or that divide them ("All men are created equal.")

3. *Reciprocity:* gives equal treatment to two elements that are counterparts of one another ("If it is no disgrace to allow the accused his day in court, it is no disgrace to provide for his defense.")

4. *Transitivity:* states that because one set of relationships holds (between A and B and between B and C), another relationship follows (between A and C) ("Any friend of Dianne's is a friend of mine.")

Mathematical relations

5. *Inclusion of the part in the whole:* the whole includes the part and therefore is more important ("We are a government of justice for all, not privilege for a few.")

6. *Division of the whole into its parts:* the constituent parts of the whole are enumerable and can be recombined to give a different whole ("Because Carole killed her husband to put him out of his misery and not with malice, you should not convict her of murder.")

7. *Comparison:* consideration of several objects in order to evaluate them through their relations to each other ("Jay is handsomer than Adonis.")

8. *Sacrifice:* consideration of what one is willing to surrender to achieve a certain result ("I'd rather lose the next election than sacrifice our nation's honor.")

9. *Probabilities:* calculation of a likelihood based on the reduction of the real to series or collections of beings or events, similar in some ways and different in others ("If Anne were not serious about her work, she would not spend so much time away from her family and in the library.")

Source: Based on Chaim Perelman and L. Olbrechts-Tyteca, *The New Rhetoric: A Treatise on Argumentation,* trans. John Wilkenson and Purcell Weaver (Notre Dame, Ind.: University of Notre Dame Press, 1969), pp. 193–260.

to be for advancing equal opportunity and against affirmative action; these are incompatible positions. Then note how Professor Stead's argument structure forces a dilemma on the administration. She says she won't waste time instructing her audience on affirmative action, implying that this is so obvious that she need not dwell on it. She then states the virtue of affirmative action in a way that suggests this enforcer either does not know the intent of affirmative action (that is, you are an ignoramus) or said something foolish (you are ridiculous). Either way, this person's opinion is not one we can take seriously. Perelman thinks that the ridicule that results from exposing an inconsistency is the source of contradiction's persuasive force.[12]

A second group of quasi-logical schemes depends on mathematical relations. These include whole-part relationships, relative quantities of larger and smaller or more and less, and the frequency of occurrences or probabilities (Table 12.1). These argument structures have "the general effect of imparting an empirical character to [their] problems."[13] They suggest that values and likelihoods attached to data can partake of the logic of measurement, although this is seldom, if ever, the case.

For instance, here is an excerpt from an editorial that appeared in the *Cape Times* of Cape Town, South Africa. The editorial carried a London dateline. The writer, Stanley Uys, was commenting on the vociferous objections white South Africans raised to Senator Edward Kennedy's outspoken criticisms of apartheid during his January 1985 visit to their country.

> But much as Senator Kennedy's visit sticks in the gullet of some South Africans, wait until the Rev Jesse Jackson gets there.
>
> If the [Afrikaans newspaper] Burger thinks Senator Kennedy's bearing reminds it of the "white paternalism of the arch capitalist" what is it going to say about Mr Jackson, the epitome of the cheeky black man, with his thin moustache and sharp clothes?[14]

Uys's argument rests on *comparison,* "where several objects are considered in order to evaluate them through their relations to each other."[15] The attitudes of the *Burger,* the Afrikaans morning paper in Cape Town, is "measured," so to speak, by the structure of this argument: With so much objection to this rich foreign white man criticizing our system, it will find much more objectionable the criticisms of a foreign black man—especially one it will perceive in racist stereotypes of demeanor and dress.

Reality-Structure Arguments

Arguments that rest on various reality structures form a second major group of associative schemes. Some of these arguments influence perceptions and judgments by arguing from reality structures we already accept (Tables 12.2 and 12.3). Others are schemes whose persuasion stems from new reality structures that the arguments themselves construct (Table 12.4).

Table 12.2   REALITY-STRUCTURE ARGUMENTS: SEQUENTIAL RELATIONS

1. *Causal link:* attributes a causal connection between events, objects, processes, etc. ("The past forty years of deficit spending have caused our present economic woes.")

2. *Pragmatic argument:* permits the evaluation of an act or event in terms of its favorable or unfavorable consequences ("Although allowing students on work-study programs more hours of employment relives their financial needs, it also reduces their time for course work and jeopardizes their grades.")

3. *Waste:* the loss of previous effort if an activity is stopped ("All our programs for improving life in Central America will be to no avail if we do not support their struggles against communism.")

4. *Direction:* criticizes acts or events on the basis of tendencies that fill us with alarm ("By continuing to run federal deficits of one hundred billion and more, we are mortgaging our children's future.")

5. *Unlimited development:* the absence of foreseeable limits permits optimistic projections for continuing unimpeded on a course ("Their relationship is well on its way to recovery; each day they draw closer and closer.")

Source: Based on Chaim Perelman and L. Olbrechts-Tyteca, *The New Rhetoric: A Treatise on Argumentation,* trans. John Wilkenson and Purcell Weaver (Notre Dame, Ind.: University of Notre Dame Press, 1969), pp. 261–292.

Table 12.3   REALITY-STRUCTURE ARGUMENTS: RELATIONS OF COEXISTENCE

6. *Person and act:* evaluates an individual in terms of relationships that stress the essence of the individual and the character of that person's deeds ("It is one thing not to love and confess it; it is another not to love but pretend to. One party can earn our eventual respect, the other only our contempt.")

7. *Group and its members:* evaluates the relationships of an organization as they influence and are influenced by the characteristics of its membership ("I do not rest easy knowing that academic priorities are being set by accountants and politicians but not by scholars.")

8. *Act and essence:* evaluates relationships between deeds and their defining characteristics ("Patty's harsh comment was more a sign of frustration than meanness of spirit.")

9. *Symbolic relation:* the integration of symbol and referent into a common reality ("Uncle Sam is losing patience with terrorist acts.")

10. *Double hierarchy:* correlates an accepted set of criteria with a second, sometimes contested set ("Extremism in the pursuit of freedom is no vice.")

11. *Degree and order:* assesses acts and events in terms of differences of quantity and quality ("Mother Theresa, frail of body, moves the earth with her compassion and love.")

Source: Based on Chaim Perelman and L. Olbrechts-Tyteca, *The New Rhetoric: A Treatise on Argumentation,* trans. John Wilkenson and Purcell Weaver (Notre Dame, Ind.: University of Notre Dame Press, 1969), pp. 293–349.

Arguments based on the structure of reality encourage associative patterns quite different from quasi-logical arguments. Quasi-logical arguments seek the appearance of validity through the logical or mathematical form they build into the appeal. Arguments based on the structure of reality make use of what people accept as real to build a bridge to a new assertion that we wish to promote. The essential characteristic of reality-structure arguments is that their basis in reality be sufficiently secure that it goes without challenge. Once our listener accepts that reality is actually as we have presented it, we may draw out further, previously unnoticed implications.

This basic structure is illustrated by Thomas J. Peters and Robert H.

Table 12.4   REALITY-STRUCTURE ARGUMENTS: ESTABLISHING REALITY STRUCTURES

12. *Example:* the use of particular cases to make a generalization possible ("We lowered taxes in 1962 and the economy improved; we lowered them in 1968 and 1981 with similar results. Now is no time to raise taxes.")

13. *Illustration:* the use of a particular case to provide support for an already established regularity ("It isn't what happens to you but what you do with it that matters. So in times of difficulty, remember that your fate, like that of a person cast overboard, can be reversed only if you exert the effort.")

14. *Model:* the use of a particular case to encourage imitation ("Christian charity can best be practiced by following the pope's lead when he forgave his would-be assassin.")

15. *Analogy:* the use of relationships placed in juxtaposition to establish a new understanding ("The effects of these policies on the poor will be as deadly as a viper's bite.")

Source: Based on Chaim Perelman and L. Olbrechts-Tyteca, *The New Rhetoric: A Treatise on Argumentation,* trans. John Wilkenson and Purcell Weaver (Notre Dame, Ind.: University of Notre Dame Press, 1969), pp. 350–410.

Waterman in their much publicized study of successful corporations, *In Search of Excellence.* Here they are making a point about how actions and words get divorced:

> Probably few of us would disagree that actions speak louder than words, but we behave as if we don't believe it. We behave as if the proclamation of policy and its execution were synonymous. "But I made quality our number one goal years ago," goes the lament. Managers can't drive forklifts anymore. Yet they do still act. They do *something.* In short, they pay attention to some things and not to others. Their action expresses their priorities, and it speaks much louder than words. In the quality case alluded to above, a president's subordinate clarified the message. "Of course, he's for quality. That is, he's never said, 'I don't care about quality.' It's just that he's for everything. He says, 'I'm for quality,' twice a year and he acts, 'I'm for shipping products,' twice a day."[16]

Their account of the relation between actions and words reminds us of the many times we have experienced such inconsistencies. It encourages us to focus on these inconsistencies and to agree that actions speak louder than words, that reality frequently does reveal a split between words and deeds. Agreeing to this, we are less likely to resist their major claim several paragraphs later concerning employee motivation: "Only if you get people *acting,* even in small ways, the way you want them to, will they come to believe in what they're doing."[17]

Typical arguments based on the structure of reality include sequential relations (Table 12.2), where emphasis is placed on the order of events' leading to some significant conclusion. These schemes depend on the pattern of ordered series as an argument strategy. These reality structures are of coequal parts. However, not all reality structures are equal. This fact accounts for a second pattern of schemes that depend on relations of coexistence in which items on different levels are united (Table 12.3). The result of their union is a reconstruction of reality.

A third group of reality-structure arguments uses schemes of relationships especially suited to *establishing* the structure of reality (Table 12.4). Typically, these arguments are invoked when we have an implied disagreement over the rules that describe our world. Arguments are effective in these cases because people who are willing to talk seriously must accept the possibility that their differences may be resolved.

Perelman outlines two general patterns that these arguments follow. The first establishes reality structures by pointing to particular cases. A particular case may be used in a variety of roles: "As an example, it makes generalization possible; as an illustration, it provides support for an already established regularity; as a model, it encourages imitation."[18] The second pattern for the use of particulars establishes reality structures through analogy. By careful choice of terms, ratios are set in proportion (A:B::C:D). As we saw in Chapter 10, terms in proximity interact to create meaning by, in Perelman's words, "increasing or decreasing the value of the terms."[19]

Dissociation of Concepts

The patterns we just discussed establish connecting links. They are associative patterns. Dissociation does the opposite; it breaks links. Dissociative patterns object to associative links that are accepted, assumed, or hoped for on the grounds that these connections do not exist. If the links don't exist, the arguments resting on them may be discounted as irrelevant. On the constructive side, dissociation encourages us to perceive divided elements as independent. In other words, it resolves problems of incompatibility by remodeling our conceptions of reality.

That probably sounds terribly abstract, but if you reflect for a moment, you will recognize that this remodeling function has been our major concern throughout our study of rhetoric. Every time we persuade or are persuaded, our outlook on reality is altered in some way.

Perelman helps us to recognize the application of dissociation to concrete problems of speaking and writing by indicating that this argument structure frequently signals differences between *appearance* and *reality*. This is the difference between things as they seem and things as they actually are. We can imagine such instances as lawyers arguing over the letter and the spirit of the law, legislators deliberating the social and individual impacts of a bill, and nutritionists distinguishing between the natural and artificial properties on the foods we eat as relying on this difference between appearance and reality. The consequence of driving these appearance-versus-reality wedges is that acts and ideas may be freed from old relationships and considered anew in fresh relationships, and our understanding of our world may be modified as a result.

Consider, for example, how Woody Allen uses dissociation to state the "predicament" of the modern era:

> Put in its simplest form, the problem is: How is it possible to find meaning in a finite world given my waist and shirt size? This is a very difficult question when we realize that science has failed us. True, it has conquered many diseases, broken the genetic code, and even placed human beings on the moon, and yet when a man of eighty is left in a room with two eighteen-year-old cocktail waitresses nothing happens. Because the real problems never change. After all, can the human soul be glimpsed through a microscope? Maybe—but you'd definitely need one of those very good ones with two eyepieces. We know that the most advanced computer in the world does not have a brain as sophisticated as that of an ant. True, we could say that of many of our relatives but we only have to put up with them at weddings or special occasions. Science is something we depend on all the time. If I develop a pain in the chest I must take an X-ray. But what if the radiation from the X-ray causes me deeper problems? Before I know it, I'm going in for surgery. Naturally, while they're giving me oxygen an intern decides to light up a cigarette. The next thing you know I'm rocketing over the World Trade Center in bed clothes. Is this science? True, science has taught us how to pasteurize cheese. And true, this can be fun in mixed company—but what of the H-bomb? Have you ever seen what happens when one of those things falls off a desk accidentally?[20]

Allen's comments use humor to raise a serious question about the place of science in our lives. The various combinations of science with mundane or exaggerated situations serve to separate science from its normal lofty association with truth. In this way, he depicts science as dependent on humans, as sometimes providing solutions that wreak havoc or as confronting puzzlements it cannot resolve. Allen's dissociative argument structure invites us to remodel our conception of reality and the role of science in it.

In these illustrations we see how argument schemes can encourage a perception of reality. Perelman's account reveals the persuasive dynamics of argument structures. Through the structures of their reasoning patterns, arguments build a sense of validity, of empirical foundation, or of remodeled understanding into the very way in which ideas are related. Argument forms not only control the types of inferences we are encouraged to draw, but they also anchor these inferences in *patterns* of thought and experience that we already accept as valid.

RHETORICAL STRUCTURES OF DRAMATIC ENACTMENT

The approaches of Aristotle, Toulmin, and Perelman tell us a great deal about argument structures as forms that shape perceptions. Each provides major insights, especially into arguments as forms of reasoning. In this respect, Aristotle, Toulmin, and Perelman concern themselves with certifying the validity of claims. They emphasize the logical scaffolding from which rhetorical premises are hung. But what may we say apart from its "logic" about how the structure of a message contends for the rightness of a view? We can get a clue if we step back for a moment to consider how form in the large, as represented by genres of discourse, argues.

Dramatic Form Shapes Arguments

When we consider a genre of symbolic acts, such as painting, dance, literature, or oratory, from a rhetorical point of view, we invariably focus on how audiences respond to these performances. To rhetoricians, audience responses of applause are not the major concern. We are more interested in responses of thought, emotion, and value that lead to the acceptance or rejection of an attitude, proposition, belief, or action. Consequently, genres become important when their very structures, quite apart from matters of logic, urge audiences to think and respond in certain ways. Dramatic *form,* for example, urges us to look for revelation of motives, for a clash among competing motives, for resolution of the clash, for intimation of this resolution's implications in the lives of the characters.

Drama focuses our attention on motivations because it is a genre of action. It portrays the encounters of life and the motivations for resolving them. Moreover, dramatic portrayal is unique. In a film, we see the action through the eye of the camera. It necessarily focuses on one character at a time. We see that character's experience of the action. Film is selective in this respect. But in drama all the characters are before us, and we witness simultaneously their diverse experiences. In addition, in drama we typically know more than the characters portrayed. We know that A hates B for loving C and seeks revenge, while B trusts A but is insecure about C's love and could be moved to kill out of jealousy, and C thinks A and B are bosom buddies though she distrusts A and is totally devoted to B. And while *we* know all of this, *they* know only a few of these things. Thus the form of a drama brings us into a relationship with the characters in which we see them before us as in life and weigh the consequences that will follow from what each character does, but we are helpless to intercede. That is why we are fascinated and moved by drama. We experience the heightened tension and emotion of knowing all this while the characters are sitting about the parlor engaged in conversation and not fully aware of what will result from their words and deeds.

The very form of a drama thus influences what will count as "reality" and how we will respond to it. Considered rhetorically, drama establishes a relationship with its audience. It asks us to think, feel, and value in certain ways while we are in this relationship. In fact, we must do so to sustain the relationship between ourselves and the dramatic performance. But in accepting the playwright's terms, we actually create a world with its own matrix of thoughts, emotions, and values as a proper motivational basis for action.

What counts as an argument for or against such action is conditioned by the terms of this symbolically constructed world. The form brings words and deeds before us. The form creates a need for A to respond to B. Something will happen. The form requires that the characters have a motivation for what they do. Their motivations will elicit our sympathies or evoke our resistances toward the characters. In all of this, we will not give primacy to the formal codes of legal rules or to the theoretical laws of nature. The form urges us to judge the rightness or wrongness of what transpires on the basis of how the characters acted. In sum, arguments in drama are products of dramatic form and the way symbols are used in it.

Dramatic Patterns of Argument

Having said that dramatic form shapes the way arguments develop, we still face the question of patterns that specific arguments take in dramatic development. Considering a play with a romantic theme, we might expect to find courtship. Courtship is itself a symbolic form with discernible elements and a pattern of development: Boy meets girl, boy courts girl, girl falls for boy, they marry and live happily ever after. Even in this oversimplified version, there is more to be said. All along the path from first encounter to the blessed nuptuals, we witness a myriad of partisan blandishments designed to secure the girl's affections: praising her virtues, bestowing gifts, showing himself as intelligent, sensitive, and humorous. Each enactment of the courtship is an argument for his sincerity and worth.

Now take the same pattern as it is developed in *Evita*. On balance, we are encouraged to reject Eva Perón; she is not a sympathetic character. There is pathos in her humble origins, but she is not unique in this respect. She is victimized by men early on when she arrives in Buenos Aires, but she accepts this as necessary to achieving her ambitions. Soon she appears consumed with power lust. We reject her primarily because her life is a corruption of courtship. She is equally insincere whether teasing men or the people of Buenos Aires. We do not need the conscience of Che to tell us this; her own actions belie the sincerity of her words. How do we know this? Because the playwright develops his play through a montage of public and private scenes. The form of juxtaposing her public words with her private deeds has a doubling effect. We see her arguments as deceitful, and we see the play itself arguing against her vision of reality.

Drama reveals most clearly how a form of life unfolds in a way that argues. From a rhetorical perspective, this dramatic unfolding is not unique to the stage. On the stage we see in capsule form the highlights of events marked by tension and emotion marching toward their resolution. But the same is true, though in tones more generally muted, of all discursive forms. As we noted earlier, all symbolic acts are dramatic in character; they unfold in a pattern of action. We have enactments whose impacts as symbolic forms are profoundly influenced by their patterns of development and of audience involvement. This occurs quite apart from their specific subjects and yet may reinforce or undermine their specific premises.

Abraham Lincoln at Cooper Union illustrates the way rhetoric argues through dramatic enactment. There he made a speech addressed to the question of slavery. But his address was also an enactment of leadership in which a local politician from Illinois thrust himself into a position to claim the Republican nomination for the presidency. Lincoln reasoned a case against the expansion of slavery based on the criteria of his opponents. He addressed southerners to refute their objections against the Republicans and to confound them with the self-contradictions of their words and deeds. He spoke to his fellow Republicans, urging them to be true to their principles in the face of criticism. As the speech unfolded, its form reinforced his specific contentions. He said things that could only have infuriated the South. But to a northern audience looking for an articulate spokesman, he displayed himself as a qualified candidate. The structure of his arguments and their order in the speech themselves were a means of enticement. They encouraged identification with Lincoln as a leader capable of influencing the fate of his party and of his nation.

Some 120 years later, Edward Kennedy addressed the Democratic national convention with similar hopes. In a different era, with economic issues to the fore, he attempted to wrest the leadership of his party from Jimmy Carter. Kennedy did not gain the nomination; the party rules made Carter's renomination a foregone conclusion. But he won sufficient support to force significant changes in the Democratic platform.

Kennedy's major contention held that his campaign was a "cause." Consider the implicative complex of his metaphor. If we have a *cause,* we have a *goal.* Such a goal is pursued *over time.* Achieving it requires *sustained effort.* Causes tend to have a *moral impulse* and *justification.* Therefore, they require *fervent,* even *zealous commitment.* Causes run into *obstacles* that must be *overcome.* Usually, the more *formidable* the obstacle, the more *worthy* the goal. Here we have a whole shelf of implications that defined and gave value to Kennedy's quest. In advancing his case, he meticulously provided appeals that played on this implicative complex. The very way in which he discussed the cause—the form of his address—encouraged the people in the convention hall and those viewing him on television to identify with him as a patrician warrior— the slayer of Ronald Reagan, the heir of Franklin D. Roosevelt, the champion of the common and the needy American. His manner of arguing was itself an enticement to share his vision of reality.

Every symbolic act considered as a whole has patterns that serve strategic ends. Each form in the large involves us in a creative relationship with the rhetor: we cocreate a world. This world unfolds through the patterns of evidence and reasoning presented much as a drama on stage. We are enticed to see our world as this symbolic form presents it because the very structure of rhetoric considered holistically enacts its realities, replete with the unifying links of associations and values. In addition to argument types, the ways in which rhetorical forms argue serve as powerful strategies suited to our readinesses to respond and capable of remodeling the truths we live by.

SCENIC STRUCTURES AS ARGUMENTS

The final form we will examine as a mode of inducement is the structure of scene. We know from experience that a setting can have meaning or symbolic value. Further, we can respond to a scene in terms of its symbolic value. Take the middle of your hometown. If you come from a New England village, chances are that there is a village green with trees and benches that is surrounded by shops. It's a good place to gather and meet with your neighbors. The space is designed to encourage social congregation. But if you come from a large city, the center of your town probably has a square that is purely monumental. It may have a circle designed to handle traffic flow, and there may be offices and department stores around it. But it is not a place that encourages congregating. One scene invites meeting with neighbors and strangers; the other invites continued movement. One encourages conversation; the other discourages it.

The floor plan of an office has a similar effect. Office planners have found that if there are private places, such as individual offices or partitioned areas, workers will use them as places to congregate. Here they will interact with greater ease than if there were no partitions. In an open space, workers lose their sense of privacy. For self-protection, they retreat into themselves; socialization declines, and work output increases. By manipulating the space, managers can influence workers' behaviors.

Consider also the way your communication is influenced by your instructor's office arrangement. If your instructor's desk allows her to sit behind it, the desk acts as a barrier between you and lends her an air of authority. But if your instructor moved her desk so that she sat facing the wall, the barrier would be removed, and the openness of your body positions to each other would suggest greater equality.

Physical surroundings are significant in public address as well. Hitler, for example, was given to exploiting the suasive potential of scene by holding his mass meetings outdoors at twilight in monumental settings. The scene of a *mass* of

enthusiasts lent the reinforcement of collective emotional energy to his exhortations. The scene of *twilight* had special significance for the Germans, since this
was the bewitching hour when the mythical Nibelungs were alleged to be about.
It was a magical time. Holding meetings *outdoors* opened the very heavens to his
oratory, suggesting that no barriers existed between his pleas and the throne of
God. Finally, the *monumental* backdrop of statues, pillars, arches, and massive
buildings lent the reinforcements of solidity and visual grandeur. Here was scaffolding worthy of great causes! For Hitler, all these features conspired to form
a whole that lent righteousness to his harangues and encouraged a perception of
this deranged madman that was quite the opposite. In this setting, Hitler seemed
inspired on a scale larger than life.

Presenting Scenes Rhetorically

Quite apart from these nonverbal aspects, scenes encourage and thwart audience
responses through the ways in which they are presented rhetorically. One way
in which scenic inducements are enacted is by *structuring scenarios.* As we saw
in Chapter 3, when we succeed at imposing our definition on a scene, we set
expectations of what should occur in that scene. A classic case of structuring
scenarios occurred during the Nixon administration following student protests in
the wake of the Kent State shootings. The president indicated that students would
be invited to Washington to discuss matters of mutual concern regarding the war
in Vietnam and student protests against it. By labeling the purpose of the meetings
as *discussion,* Nixon set expectations of what should transpire. Discussion assumes open exchange, give-and-take, willingness to compromise, seeking of common ground on which to build agreement. In our culture, we typically understand
discussion in these terms. We also expect norms of civility and decorum to
prevail. Chanting antiwar slogans, singing protest songs, shouting obscenities,
delivering ad hominem invectives, and the like are inappropriate modes of communication while engaging in discussion. For many of the students, the rhetoric
that they had perfected to radicalize their peers was ruled out of bounds. An
expectation was set for communication of the type at which administrators were
especially skilled.

The president invited the students to come to Washington. Here was a place
where officials met and weighty decisions were made. It also meant that the
students would meet on the government's turf. The meeting rooms were paneled,
carpeted, had plush chairs, and invited the moderate tones of reasoned talk. The
scene even denied the students their familiar garb, for these were places where
suits and dresses were in order.

When President Nixon invited the students, he also labeled the nature of
the problem as a communication breakdown. This was a scene in which agreement was possible only if the participants were reasonable. But the strategic
advantage of structuring the communication event in scenic terms meant that the
only information available to an observing public were summary reports of discussions that they never got to witness. If discussion stopped, the purpose went
unfulfilled, and someone had to be at fault for that. We assume, after all, that a

communication breakdown can be repaired if both parties try hard enough. The structure of the scene as a whole functioned as a rhetorical strategy. By orchestrating the setting (Washington), by defining the scenario of what was to transpire there (discussion), and by labeling the problem that motivated the participants' efforts (communication breakdown), the president exerted enormous control over public perceptions. These elements structured events in a manner that argued for a particular interpretation of reality. Together they set expectations for what would transpire. Consequently, when students finally broke off discussion in frustration, the administration got to point its finger in dismay and bemoan the fact that the students obviously were not serious or they would have continued talking. By labeling the scenario as one for discussion and by reducing the differences to a communication breakdown, Nixon exploited the form of these meetings to shape public perceptions more favorably toward his administration.[21]

Another way in which we argue with scenic elements is through the location of the scene. Where we picture events occurring greatly influences what we perceive as the event and the nature of its concerns. For example, recall the way in which American television located the scene of the Iranian hostage event. Where was the story, in the embassy or in the streets? If we go by what appeared on American television each evening, we would have to say that it was in the streets. Viewers hardly saw the hostages during their 444 days of captivity. But they saw mobs of shouting Iranians burning effigies of the president and Uncle Sam, destroying the flag, and hurling invectives that vilified the United States. What was the story about? Was it about the plight of the hostages? They remained unseen, their story barely told. Was it about the Iranian grievances? That was not articulated; their street speakers were given to shouting slogans, not offering rationales.

How were Americans to respond to such a sight? The serious and extreme nature of the hostage situation notwithstanding, the point remains that the setting in which this story was told worked as an argument structure; it argued for a response. The grievances of Iranian militants were not set in a deliberative assembly but in the streets. For Americans watching this event unfold on television, judgments were not invited through reasoned appeals but through actions. Televised behaviors were the focus of attention; they were also premises in the Iranian case. Because they so violated the Western cultural norms of an American viewing audience, is it any wonder that the argument of this scene solidified a nationalistic prejudice against Iran? Largely ignorant of Muslims, lacking in historical perspective on their country's 35-year involvement in Iranian affairs, Americans had only the vivid elements of scene to respond to. Off camera were Americans held hostage; on camera were mobs of aliens acting hatefully toward the United States. This crisis was presented as street theater; its scenic structure made an insane though dramatic argument. The setting for these episodes controlled the story in a way guaranteed to arouse domestic anger and frustration at seemingly irrational behavior.

The important feature in each of these scenic cases is summarized in the commonly used expression "Don't lose sight of the forest for the trees." This admonition warns against the danger of getting lost in details. The fact is that details, in and of themselves, are not terribly meaningful. As raw data, they are what they are, isolated and lacking connection to anything else. We need some way to relate individual bits and pieces of data to one another so that we can understand their meaning in terms of a unit or whole. We require patterns. Structural features such as those we have examined simplify details by finding among them or imposing on them patterns that relate ideas to audiences in meaningful ways, that provide arguments of some sort for an interpretation of reality, and that shape perceptions and encourage specific responses.

SUMMARY

We have considered how patterning a message plays an important role in inducing social cooperation. We have seen how structural patterns shape perceptions that in turn encourage audiences to see a subject in a similar light. This led us to inquire into why audiences respond as they do. Analysis of structures proved helpful as a source of explanation.

Rhetorical works composed with an eye toward the audience go beyond the informational level to consider how each element of the work establishes a relationship of thought and feeling that involves the audience in the composition. They argue, through their structures of thought and composition, for a view of reality. We recognize in a Shakespearean play, for example, how a protagonist's speech sucks us into the play and shapes our desires for what is to follow. We don't just observe Othello's anguish; we share in the horror of his jealous rage. We don't just see the Roman mob turned against Brutus by Antony's speech; we are moved ourselves to desire revenge against his crime. In reading the Gettysburg Address, we don't just witness the dedication of the cemetery; we are pulled into a sympathetic relationship with basic American values. In each case, the composition affects us because its form is attuned to our capacities to feel and think and value, our capacities to respond. It is not the facts but the pattern of development or form that shapes our perceptions and gives us an active role as participants who identify with the rhetor.

Audience-involving rhetoric of this sort is artful. Its artfulness isn't in the truth of its facts but in the rightness of its structure to express something in a way that pulls us into sympathy with the rhetor's cause. We are in a sense stuck with the facts. Art consists in how the facts are presented, related, juxtaposed to create arguments. In short, art resides in the form. This, after all, is the source of true eloquence: appeals attuned to our inherent appetites for meaning, life, community, and happiness.

NOTES

1. This discussion is drawn from George Lakoff and Mark Johnson, *Metaphors We Live By* (Chicago: University of Chicago Press, 1980). See especially pp. 3–6 and 97–105 for ways in which we talk of argument.
2. Stephen Toulmin, *The Uses of Argument* (Cambridge: Cambridge University Press, 1958).

3. This diagram is based on Toulmin, pp. 94–146.
4. Wayne Brockriede and Douglas Ehninger, "Toulmin on Argument: An Interpretation and Application," *Quarterly Journal of Speech,* 46 (February 1960), 44–53.
5. Alan Alda, "A Reel Doctor's Advice to Some Real Doctors," cited in Stephen E. Lucas, *The Art of Public Speaking* (New York: Random House, 1983), p. 366.
6. Chaim Perelman and L. Olbrechts-Tyteca, *The New Rhetoric: A Treatise on Argumentation,* trans. John Wilkenson and Purcell Weaver (Notre Dame, Ind.: University of Notre Dame Press, 1969), p. 189.
7. Ibid., p. 190.
8. Ibid.
9. Ibid.
10. Ibid.
11. Bette Ann Stead, "Why Does the Secretary Hate Me?" *Vital Speeches of the Day,* 48 (May 1, 1982), p. 439.
12. Perelman and Olbrechts-Tyteca, p. 205.
13. Ibid., p. 260.
14. Stanley Uys, *Cape Times* (January 11, 1985), 8.
15. Perelman and Olbrechts-Tyteca, p. 242.
16. Thomas J. Peters and Robert H. Waterman, Jr., *In Search of Excellence* (New York: Warner Books, 1982), pp. 73–74.
17. Ibid.
18. Perelman and Olbrechts-Tyteca, p. 350.
19. Ibid., p. 378.
20. Woody Allen, "My Speech to the Graduates," in *Side Effects* (New York: Random House, 1980), pp. 57–58.
21. This discussion is drawn from Peter M. Hall and John P. Hewitt, "The Quasi-theory of Communication and the Management of Dissent," *Social Problems* (Summer 1970), 17–27.

chapter 13

Rhetoric in an Age of Change

Be a craftsman in speech, for the tongue is a sword to a man, and speech is more valorous than fighting.

AKHTOY III

It is difficult to imagine a modern father advising his child that skill in speaking is among the highest of public virtues. Mastering a technology and knowing the right people come readily to mind as more likely candidates for Dad's esteem. But for most of Western history, King Akhtoy's counsel to his son King Merikau was sensible. In every age until our own, orators inspired the people to mobilize against oppression, to repel invaders, to right injustice, to fight for holy causes. Only recently have orators been conspicuous by their absence.

Since Franklin Roosevelt's presidency, the United States has had few public figures whose powers of speech might earn them the label "orator." This scarcity is not for absence of speakers. A legion of men and women daily address audiences in the churches, conference rooms, auditoriums, legislative assemblies, and classrooms of America. But few are able to captivate and mobilize their listeners consistently and on a grand scale.

Most critics lay the blame for oratory's decline at television's door. There is no denying that television provides new and powerful means for presenting ideas, that it reaches masses, that it comes into our homes to be experienced in relative privacy, and that it lacks the emotional connection of proximity that a live audience provides and on which oratory thrives. Moreover, Americans turn to television not only for information but for the analysis and opinion formerly provided by public speakers. These are selected facts, however, not the entire picture of contemporary communication. They indicate merely that patterns of communication are altering, not that oratory is a thing of the past. After all, decline is not the same as death.

Still, oratory is not as eminent as it once was. We may profit from puzzling over this because its present state tells us something about communication in our age. Surely to say that television—or any single factor, for that matter—caused the decline of oratory is simplistic. And to conclude that expanded communication technologies render this older mode obsolete is premature. The public is still capable of responding to stirring oratory, as the successes of Mario Cuomo, Jesse Jackson, and Geraldine Ferraro at the 1984 Democratic convention testify. More to the point for us is how conditions of the late twentieth century have shifted the arena for rhetoric from the podium to the TV screen, from the soapbox to the conference room. Oratory may be receding as an authoritative form, but rhetoric remains a vital force in our lives. People still talk and write; they use symbols with intent to effect beliefs and actions. They cannot avoid practicing rhetoric. Significantly for most of us, however, the conditions under which we practice rhetoric are vastly different from those confronting our grandparents or even our parents at a similar age. We need to reflect on these differences so as not to lose sight of how rhetorical communication fits with the circumstances of our lives.

TECHNOLOGY AND COMMUNICATION DEMANDS

Since the end of World War II, technologies that harness energy, invent matter, and transport information and objects have quickened and complicated our lives. As early as May 1962, John Kennedy expressed the profound effects of technological innovation on problems of governance:

> Most of us are conditioned for many years to have a political viewpoint—Republican or Democratic, liberal, conservative, or moderate. The fact of the matter is that most of the problems . . . that we now face are technical problems, are administrative problems. They are very sophisticated judgments, which do not lend themselves to the great sort of passionate movements which have stirred this country so often in the past. [They] deal with questions which are now beyond the comprehension of most men.[1]

Kennedy's remark has much in it that rings even more true today, much in it that frightens as well.

Management science has combined with computer technology to develop managerial models that rely extensively on quantifiable data. These models, in which numbers are frequently decisive, guide decisions of enormous consequence to the public and private sectors. Questions concerning the economic impact of pollution regulations, the profitability of increasing production demands, the consequences of budget adjustments, or the quality of worker performance are reduced to the "bottom line." Contemporary managers likely decide questions such as these on the basis of computer-analyzed data. They rely on the logic of statistical inference to predict the odds for alternative consequences. Such models have greatly increased precise determination of profitability, input-output ratios, and environmental consequences, to name just a few examples.

At the same time, the technology of a computer model may well ignore humans, who are on the other side of these numbers and whose life-worlds are altered, sometimes radically, by each of these system-based decisions. When a decision to expand a marketing territory ignores the fact that the company's truck drivers now have to endure the monotony of longer, uninterrupted delivery routes, profit ratios based on the dollars and cents of cost per unit may not tell the whole story. Those drivers may have increased sick days or accidents or poor job performance because their assigned task is alienating.

This is the reality that the student preparing to become a manager will face. The fact is that technological breakthroughs in a number of areas have radically altered the shape of our life-world and the rate at which it continues to change. For most of us, life in the late twentieth century presents challenges that did not exist as recently as 1960. For most of us, these changes are unsettling even beyond the effects to which Kennedy referred in 1962. As Alvin Toffler tells us, the rate at which change occurs and the pervasiveness of change in our lives induces a state best described as *future shock*. [2] There are at least three areas where the consequences of technologically induced change bear special significance for rhetorical communication: increased newness, increased complexity, and increased speed.

Increased Newness

We are told repeatedly that scientific knowledge has advanced more in the last half century than in the entire preceding history of the human race. These advances may seem theoretical and remote from the lives of the average person, but the technologies they have spawned certainly are not. They are tangible, affecting every aspect of life from the farming of abalone to the marketing of zircons.

Consider the following short list of technological innovations commonly available in the average American household: telephone, television, video recorder, audio cassette recorder, radio, personal computer. Each of these makes it possible for information to be transported from any place to any place at any time. With the network of satellites that exists today, we can receive this information the moment it is transmitted, the moment it occurs.

The consequences of this battery of communication technologies are enormous. For one thing, we are vulnerable. At any moment we may receive information that is important to us but that we are ill-equipped to handle. We live with the increasing stress of coping with novelty because our environment bombards us with an overwhelming volume of information. For another thing, our sense of continuity is undermined. These personal information receivers bring us into contact with problems and people that are distant but related to our concerns in important ways. These media expand the boundaries of events that touch our lives, but they do so in a way that makes plain that our point of view is not held by everyone. Consequently, we have a heightened awareness of change but very little sense of what binds us with the people with whom we are changing.

Still another consequence is the way our communication technologies encourage us to remodel our conceptual schemes. For example, the VCR was originally thought to have slim prospects as a mass consumer item. That prediction was wrong. Consumers are so taken by this innovation that owning one is fast becoming commonplace. The VCR permits us to preserve a live event and play it back at any time. It makes video images portable. Consumers relish this portable feature because it gives them power over time. Instead of being "locked in" to the schedule of the networks, we can record an aired program or event automatically and then view it later when convenient.

While time management may be the initial attraction for this technology, it has side effects that remold other significant aspects of experience. The VCR has a dramatic effect on our sense of *space.* For instance, we don't have to go to a movie theater to see a film; we can rent a cassette and watch it at home. It has a significant effect on *social gathering,* since we don't have to view the film at a public place or mingle with strangers assembled to enjoy a special performance. In a way, the VCR destroys the eventfulness of cinema as part of the viewing experience. Finally, the VCR has a profound effect on *imagination* through the content of its images. For instance, music video transforms an aural form inviting a high level of imaginative participation into a visual form inviting passive reception.

Each of these media common to our homes provides us with new information, new patterns for processing information, even new definitions for what counts as information. Each alters our communication relationship, making the very act of communicating an adventure in novelty. Unlike our parents, we require presentational skills that are sensitive to this broad band of electronic media, to new ways of processing information, and to new types of relationships between communicating partners.

Increased Complexity

Life in the latter part of the twentieth century is more complex than it was for our parents. We are a mobile and increasingly urban society; we are often forced to live amid strangers. We are a technologically advanced society, requiring new skills and knowledge from our young people if they are to enjoy the same benefits of occupation and income as their parents. We are an interdependent society locked in an enormous grid of specialized providers of goods and services necessary for our survival. At the same time, we are a pluralistic society, composed of different religions, races, creeds, and interests. These factors make it very difficult for us to find common ground with our interlocutors.

Obviously, people who lack technical knowledge are more likely to feel alienated by a technologically based society than those with technical skills. For the person who has put in 25 years on the job, the demand to retrain or be reassigned to some lesser task is demeaning. Denied meaningful work, it is difficult to make positive contributions in other aspects of life. But is the technological demand any less alienating for the student pressured to enroll in a professional curriculum though it is not his natural choice for a discipline of study? The complexity of technology seems to force decisions on us. Either we make the right choices or we may be discarded as occupationally dysfunctional.

Our dependence on technology also makes it difficult to communicate to a general public about important technical matters that affect their lives. The problems encountered by the Nuclear Regulatory Agency, Metropolitan Edison, Governor Thornburg of Pennsylvania, and the major television networks in communicating important information about the accident at the Three Mile Island reactor illustrate our limitations in presenting technical matters to non-technically trained audiences. At the same time, this incident illustrates the importance of such communication.

More and more, today's college graduates will face precisely this communication problem of presenting technical materials to nontechnically trained audiences. When a staff economist briefs the boss or a lawyer advises a client or a consulting firm outlines its data processing recommendations, the audience is not likely to be a specialist in the area under discussion. Number crunching or jargon won't do. At these times we face a special need to overcome the fog of complex data so that those who must make decisions can do so with understanding.

Just as basic but seldom fully appreciated is the complexity created by increased diversity among people. In the United States, recent evidence suggests that individuals are relying less and less on dominant groups for their self-image.[3] As a result, we don't see ourselves in similar terms. When there is little homogeneity in self-perception, it is frequently easy to overlook the fact that our problems are shared by others and that our acts affect them.

For the person who markets designer jeans in Atlanta, trades stock in Dallas, or administers a railroad in Chicago, the sale of Conrail may have significantly different meanings. One sees it in terms of cost and speed in moving merchandise, another sees it in terms of quotes on the financial page, and for the third it represents a new source of pressure when competing for shipping accounts. Further, none f these orientations is even remotely in touch with the impact this sale may have on the guy who fixes brakes in the Altoona train yard. The Conrail sale is one act, but it has different personal and professional consequences for individuals scattered across the nation—each wanting not to be a victim, each searching for effective means to influence the future, each having the capacity to act in some way that will have an impact on these unknown others.

When the criteria and values we bring to a common situation are so varied, rhetoric becomes our most important means for ensuring social cooperation. Only by talking about our problems can we share an appreciation for the interconnections in our lives. Only by listening and responding to the concerns and hopes of others who share our problems can we find sensible solutions with which all concerned can live. The complexity of our age makes us especially vulnerable to domination by elites of knowledge, power, or wealth. We render our experiences mutually intelligible only by speaking a commonsense language that sets our shared problems in a tangible context.

Increased Speed

While growth in novelty and complexity places strains on our lives, it does not outstrip our ability to adapt. However, when this growth is combined with the sheer speed at which we experience change, we find ourselves suffering various forms of disorientation.

Today everyone is on the move. We are a mobile society, frequently lacking in roots from infancy to the grave. People change jobs on the average of every five years. This means that we are constantly adapting to new workers, new surroundings, new organizational structures, and often new communities. In our careers we find that organizations are in flux. Their structures change to meet new demands, often making it difficult for workers to understand where or how they belong. Outside our careers we find ourselves moving to new cities, going through the painful process of leaving an existing social network of neighbors and friends and the counterpart process of creating a new one. Neighbors who are transients find it difficult to grow close, knowing that shortly they or the person next door will leave. In our personal lives, matters aren't much better. The sad fact is that each of us has a 50 percent chance of *not* having a relationship that lasts. One-half of all first-time marriages end in divorce. Unlike our grandparents, we seem fated for a life of transience. Not surprisingly, psychologists tell us that loneliness is common across our society.

The speed at which we use up the people in our lives—our coworkers, our neighbors, our friends, and our lovers—is on a par with the rate at which we consume things. The result is decision stress: problems determining where and with whom to invest our energies. So we find young Americans turning to sex, drugs, or vandalism as forms of escape. And we find their parents unable to make commitments—to their spouses, to their children, to their employers, and ultimately to themselves. For both, the transience of the late twentieth century is so unsettling because it lacks permanent benchmarks that set problems and feelings in perspective.

For students facing change as the defining condition of their future, their communication needs are different from their grandparents' and their parents'. They will confront new situations with relative strangers to whom they are uncommitted and with whom they share few attachments. Their efforts to persuade will not be blessed with a large stock of common experiences to which they can allude with confidence of being understood. They will be called on to adapt to a context in flux, and their ability to adapt will depend on the communication skills they develop.

AN AGE FOR RHETORIC

Though the influence of oratory may have decreased, rhetoric remains essential to the well-being of our age—an age of diversity, of interdependence, of complexity, and of rapid change. This may seem like an odd claim, especially since we typically think that rhetorical communication requires common ground and we have just considered factors that erode any large-scale consensus on values, principles, interests, or ends. However true, this litany overlooks the fact that rhetoric also involves us in a relationship and that this relationship has constructive possibilities.

Whenever two people communicate sincerely, each must assume that the other can speak his mind and support what he says. When we don't take the other person seriously, how can we genuinely communicate? Only a fool takes to heart the statements of someone he thinks is a liar or an ass. Nor can we listen soberly to someone whose opinions we've already decided are wrong. So whenever two or more of us communicate in any serious sense, we must assume that each of us is competent to say what we mean and have reasons for the things we say. From the outset, genuine communication establishes a bond that enables us to exchange ideas and feelings and to achieve mutual understanding.

We need the cooperation of others for our physical survival. We need their cooperation just as much to make our personal relationships thrive, to accomplish group goals, to prosper as a community, to act in union as a nation, to live in harmony as brothers and sisters in the family of humankind. From the couple trying to make their relationship work to world leaders seeking peace, the common thread that binds us to one another is our openness to communication and the possibilities it can create. So long as we are talking and listening, our communication relationship already has us cooperating in a way that can lead to a happier world.

The relationship of communication doesn't require that we share the same dogma. It does require that we use the same procedure: that of having open discussion with an audience we take seriously in order to advance our understanding of what is true and to act in ways that are just and right.

Rhetorical communication is the procedure that enables a Lee Iacocca to persuade the government to bail out a failing Chrysler Corporation and to persuade his employees to settle for lower wages than other United Auto Workers members. Rhetorical communication is also the procedure so frequently forgotten in relationships that disintegrate. Couples stop sharing their hopes and fears, ironing out their problems, growing together. Is it any wonder that partners who don't discuss their problems eventually look upon each other as strangers?

In simpler times, people shared unifying visions, such as a shared religion or common set of values, to help them find meaning in their lives. Today we don't have beliefs or values or goals that everyone shares. Some people react to this by trying to force their views on others. Others go to the opposite extreme, talking and acting as if truth is whatever they believe it to be. But these views of privilege for one ism over another or of the relativity of everything are ill-suited for our problems. When people don't share strong bonds of common ground but are enmeshed in common problems, it isn't very realistic to think they'll be happy swallowing foreign values or that our problems will be eliminated if everyone marches to the beat of a different drummer. Such approaches are more likely to intensify problems than resolve them. What is needed in these circumstances is the mediating influence of communication. That is why rhetoric is so important to our age. Rightly practiced, rhetorical communication fosters cooperation. We become partners in the shared procedure of giving reasons and making appeals that take one another into account. A rhetoric of this sort gives us a procedure for working out agreements on *our truths.* It requires that we be tolerant of others, open to their criticisms, and willing to consider that change may be for the better.

From the earliest times, the objection to rhetoric has been that it presents a distorted picture of the truth. Plato complained that it makes the better appear the worse and the worse appear the better. This assumes there is an objective truth, uniform, absolute, and available for mortals to know. A rhetorical perspective toward existence and experience rejects that assumption. Throughout this book we have considered the many and profound ways in which our human world is a created world—the product of symbol and argument, subject to interpretation and change.

We know that there have been, are, and will continue to be people who use rhetorical means to lie and to cheat. That is a fact of life. But their false and corrupt practices do not diminish this essential point: The human world is one we make through countless acts of social cooperation that are symbolically induced. It is a product of rhetoric. Every time we speak and write, we give voice to what we would like to transpire, to a world we would prefer. Amid our many differences, rhetoric provides the means to forge an expression of the future that all concerned can abide. Rhetoric is our last best alternative to a world run by power or privilege; it offers a world run by the people. In the final analysis, it may also be our last best hope for avoiding mutual obliteration, for a world of political, social, and personal amity.

NOTES

1. Quoted in Christopher Lasch, *The Culture of Narcissism* (New York: Norton, 1978), p. 77.
2. Alvin Toffler, *Future Shock* (New York: Bantam Books, 1970).
3. Stephan P. Spitzer and Jerry Parker, "Perceived Validity and Assessment of Self: A Decade Later," *Sociological Quarterly,* 17 (Spring 1976), 236-246.

Index